The Body of Stars

The Body of Stars by Kate Hubert

First published by Three Awens Press in 2021

Text © Kate Hubert 2021

ISBN: 978-1-913642-79-2

Kate Hubert

The Body of Stars

ASTROLOGY &
THE WISDOM OF THE BODY

Three Awens Press

Contents

*For his considerable assistance on this project,
my thanks to Marcus Williamson.*

*I wish to express my appreciation also to the folks
who allowed me to use their charts and
stories as case studies.*

Prologue

She Who Holds a Thousand Stars

The Ancient Egyptian sky-goddess, Nut, arches her starry body over the whole of the earthly creation, balanced on the tips of her toes and fingers in something like an everlasting downward dog pose! Her hands and feet mark the four cardinal directions, which in the birth chart are marked by the the major axes: ascendant (east), descendant (west), midheaven (south) and nadir (north). Nut gives birth to the Sun every dawn and it travels along her deep blue, star-filled sky-body until dusk, when it disappears into her open mouth, creating night. The fertility of her darkness is such that Nut gives birth to the rejuvenated Sun again after a few hours, and thus a new day begins.

The arch of Nut's body suggests the Milky Way and the *zodiac*,[1] equally she can be seen as the celestial sphere itself. Nut is *the* Heavenly Body, scintillating with consciousness (the sparkling stars), sheltering the order of our earthly realm from the forces of chaos beyond. Known as *She Who Protects*, and *She Who Holds a Thousand Souls*, she has a vessel on her head that represents the womb, and it is within her body that we all originate and to whom, upon death, that we all, like the setting Sun, hope to return. An inscription on the lid of an

---

[1] The belt of stars eight degrees to either side of the *ecliptic*, the apparent path of the Sun.

Egyptian coffin reads, 'O Mother Nut, stretch yourself over me, that I may be placed among the imperishable stars which are in you, and that I may not die.'

The continual lovemaking between Heaven (Nut) and Earth (Geb) is the source of earthly creation. And it is in this realm of fertile creativity and erotic embrace that we live our lives as the effects of divine, loving celebration. Nut's body is the *Body of Stars*, sometimes in esoteric thought referred to as the *Heavenly Man*. The word 'man' has been considered to represent human beings, but for some of us it really does not. It *does* represent a time during which the *feminine*, especially the divine variety, has for many centuries been excised from discourse, and demeaned and denigrated in all aspects of life. The masculinisation of thought and expression really misses a trick, for however marvellous a man may be, he cannot give birth. The myth of Nut is powerful because it presents the starry realm as a womb-like vessel that is protective, fecund and creative: the sheltering sky as Mother of all that is.

Nut is the over-arching firmament, the fertiliser and mirror of earthy reality, the cosmic one. Her *Body of Stars* is the macrocosm of the microcosmic human body. It is fairly standard in astrology to see the human body as an iteration on a tiny scale of grand cosmic forces. Medieval and Renaissance images of the human form show Aries the Ram at the head, Taurus the Bull round the neck, Gemini the Twins on the arms, etc. [2] It is worth remembering that science, medicine, magic and occultism have only been considered separate pursuits since the mid-eighteenth century when, as a result of the Enlightenment, the elevation of rational empiricism as the only valid path to knowledge began to be established. I have found many people incredulous to learn that Newton – at the forefront of creating our contemporary (pre-quantum) scientific worldview – was, himself, an astrologer. When challenged by a detractor he famously retorted (with words that have soothed the ruffled feathers of many an astrologer since): 'I, Sir, have studied it. You have not.'

I offer this as a reminder of how very recently it is that we have lost our understanding of the Unseen from systems of knowledge in western thought. Prior to this the view that the human being was a cosmos in miniature (and therefore interfused by, fully connected with, and a functioning part of the Whole) was generally accepted. The hermetic principle, 'As above, so below,' was once the key to knowledge (the Caduceus of Hermes – or Mercury – is still a symbol associated with the medical profession) and has always been valid for astrologers.

For us, the macrocosm and the microcosm belong to each other and interact, and therefore the idea of Nut and her *Body of Stars* is particularly relevant because it reflects that

---

[2] A famous example is the early fifteenth-century *L'homme Zodiacal* in *Les Très Riches Heures du Duc de Berry*, in the Musée Condé, Chantilly (featured on the back cover of this volume).

we each have a *body of stars*. The project of astrology from ancient times has been to seek to establish *principles* by which to interpret cosmic Unseen forces as they work through our embodied lives in the earthly realm. Cosmic energies form the medium in which we live, move and have our being; they have interpretable forms, directions and patterns, and also relate, distinctly, to our body parts and physiological processes. The following essays focus on the human body as the reflector of cosmic energies, and seek to reclaim for us a sense of our belonging to Life through our own amazing *body of stars*.

> In order to interpret anything, we need a frame of reference which lies beyond the level at which whatever we are trying to interpret is manifesting itself. Consequently the events and initiatives of the material world – the world of forms – can be interpreted only by bringing in some metaphysical reference-system.[3]

---

[3] Dethlefsen and Dahlke (1990), p. 5.

Introduction

Towards the Body of Stars

In the early '90s I spent five years writing a PhD thesis about the idea of the self in European modernity, at the turn of the nineteenth century. My investigations showed me that the body is always necessarily at the centre of the mysterious thing we call 'self'. Technologies of the time, like photography, sound-recording, typewriting and telephony were having a significant impact on human beings' sensory experiences and therefore disturbing notions of embodiment and selfhood. I was examining this theme through the lens of vampire-themed literature of the time, including Bram Stoker's *Dracula*. I became fascinated with the human body as the medium of consciousness. After my viva exam I was asked to make some changes to my thesis and re-submit, something I had no appetite to do. My postgraduate experience of academia was extremely strained; I felt embattled and had no idea why. Eventually, in a state of crisis, I took the path of last resort and in 1998 consulted an astrologer, Suzanne Rough (who went on to form the D. K. Foundation), and it all began to make sense.

This consultation began a three-year association as Suzanne shared with me her developmental perspective, drawn from the Alice Bailey writings. I shelved my thesis and became an astrologer. At the same time, adding to the intensity of this moment of crisis, my father had been diagnosed with cancer. The shock of this led me to start exploring vibrational healing modalities. These are entirely consistent with astrology (as a language for describing the timing and effects of vibrational energy). Astrology as it is practised in the West is preoccupied with selfhood: personal experiences and individual identity. The themes of body, vibration, self, healing and the human task of finding meaning were constellating in my imagination. For over twenty years now they have been at the heart of my enquiry both as an astrologer, and as a member of the Order of Bards, Ovates and Druids. My path is one that runs through the house of the flesh: being and becoming through the body, as a part of the natural world.

Synchronistically, as I was working with Suzanne, I was also in therapy with a Jungian analyst, Nicole Reilly, absorbing the humane, life-affirming wisdom of that perspective, which has fed so positively into astrological literature. Astrology, healing, the Jungian perspective and druidry: these are the streams of endeavour to which I am indebted, and to Suzanne Rough and Nicole Reilly, in particular.

What Is the Body?

My body – not just my mind – is also conscious. How does one truly open to something like this?[4]

---

[4] Sanford (2006), p. 184.

A friend of mine used to attend court in a professional capacity as a social worker. One case she attended dealt with a child who had what we used to call Multiple Personality Disorder.[5] A testifying doctor referred to the child having one personality that presented with a dislocated shoulder. When the child moved into that personality his shoulder would become freshly dislocated. When he moved out of that personality, the shoulder would bear no evidence of the injury.

This confounds our normally accepted sense of what the body is and how it works, suggesting that it is not as fixed as we suppose. Perhaps also, that it is not only more fluid but also more influenced by our thoughts, feelings and beliefs than we realise. There is an unacknowledged potential for consciousness to affect the condition of the body, as well as for the body to affect consciousness.

So, what is the body?

The human body is the vehicle for the entirety of our experience: it is our very mode of consciousness. Our experiences, circumstances, health and wellbeing are outward expressions of inner conditions. All of these things are mediated and known only through the body. Nothing changes with us to any meaningful degree, unless adjustments are made on the inside, at the level of perception and consciousness, of which the body is the storehouse.

---

[5] Now known as Dissociative Identity Disorder.

The body is an interface between the worlds. It is here that the Seen and the Unseen realms meet; where past, present and future collide; where ancestors and descendants meet and mingle; and a place for the confluence of the personal and transpersonal worlds. The body is a physical manifestation of subtle energies – thoughts, emotions, feelings and impulses – animated by intangible, invisible life forces. This body is a vehicle for thinking, feeling and willing. It is the house of that ineffable thing, *the soul.*

This collection of essays and case studies about the body and somatic experience through the lens of astrology is intended to stimulate enquiry about lived experience that might help people find real significance and guidance in bodily symptoms and in life more generally. When the patterns and principles behind our experience are glimpsed we begin to discern meaning in our lives. Having a context of significance in a life that can otherwise feel fairly random and strange is not only healing, it is redemptive. The possibility of guidance arises when we catch glints of meaning shining in the darkness. This guidance is available to us fairly consistently through the medium of our bodily experience. It is this somatic experience that these essays explore in the attempt to share precious jewels of meaning in what the body shows us. I am not here dealing with medical diagnostics but with elucidating the elegant, even poetic, ways the body communicates with us through its symptoms and processes. Illness – the arising of symptoms in the body or the mind – is not something going wrong. It is an attempt to rebalance and regain wellness: to put us back into alignment with the energy of life and of our full potential. The body is eloquent; its information, soulful.

I hope also to be able to share the wonderful usefulness of astrology as a language that describes the Unseen, the energetic aspect of life, and help the reader gain a real appreciation for what this under-used and widely misunderstood discipline has to offer. Ultimately it restores to us a sense of our place in the cosmos, as part of a much greater being and becoming.

> All disease is the result of inhibited soul life, and that is true of all forms in all kingdoms. The art of the healer consists in releasing the soul, so that its life can flow through the aggregate of organisms which constitute any particular form.[6]

How to Use This Book

If you are not astrologically-minded, and I have attempted not to assume prior knowledge on the whole, there should be plenty of material that prompts reflection and enquiry into the nature and meanings held in our bodies and on how the physical realm supports and communicates with us.

---

[6] Bailey (1953), p. 5.

I suggest you read the sections pertaining to body parts and processes that are challenging (see pages 38-39) , to see if the astrological themes help deepen an enquiry into your experience.

It would be useful to have your birth chart to hand and to be familiar enough with it to know which signs, planets and houses are emphasised; the essays dealing with those signs (and the planets and houses corresponding to them) will be especially relevant to read. The sign and house in which the Moon resides will be of particular significance; the ascendant or rising sign, and the sign and house of the Sun will also provide guidance. There is more information on assessing emphases in the birth chart in the chapter, The Grammar of Astrology.

The Body as an Index of Consciousness

Illness is always a crisis, and the purpose of every crisis is development.[7]

As above, so below; as within, so without; as the Universe, so the Soul. This is the hermetic principle of correspondence, fundamental to occultism. It proposes linkage between cosmic and mundane arrangements; between cosmic patterns and processes, and our lived experience. Ultimately it

---

[7] Dethlefsen and Dahlke (1990), p. 82.

suggests that all things are connected as aspects of the unfolding of the One Life in which we all participate.

The principle of correspondence is not easy for our minds to accept. We might be attracted by it as a notion, but accepting it as a reality is challenging because we are so strongly conditioned by rationalism, which claims that the Unseen can only exist in our imaginations, and is therefore fanciful. If we cling to the rationalist view, we find ourselves severed from the immense world of broader significance that enfolds us, oblivious to our connectedness with the Whole and incapable of discerning the meaning of our existence. This is a terrible situation that renders ineffable qualities such as love, wisdom and humanity to be passing fancies of little consequence to real-world concerns. It cannot be proven in scientific terms, but it *resonates* with intuitional intelligence to say that to live well in the visible world we need the wisdom and the context of the invisible world. *Resonance* could, indeed, be deemed the only mode of 'proof' that we have for matters beyond the material realm that are not subject to scientific proof.

Everything is vibration, from the dense (visible, material, physical) to the highly refined (invisible, occult, spiritual), hence the travesty of failing to recognise the existence of refined 'content'. It is helpful to our understanding if we can take the point of view that all of life is an energetic happening. Perhaps it is rather like a 'murmuration' of starlings, where we see birds coalesce and disperse, folding towards each other and then fraying away, creating patterns of density and thinness. Where energy is tightly compacted it will take *form* and be visible on the physical plane; where it is more refined, it will not.

Our physical bodies are the most dense points of expression for our energy systems. The physical vehicle manifests the energetic pattern in which our subtle energies (thought, feeling, will, etc.) participate. The body is the storehouse of consciousness, a visible index of our condition at the Unseen level. Its particularities and peculiarities, whether deemed sick or healthy, testify to the quality and characteristics of our consciousness. Sensations and symptoms arise within the body as informants from the invisible world. Consciousness and sensation (within the tangible body) are continuous. They are in a continuum: neither separate nor alienated from each other.

Therefore, a challenge arising in the body expresses something that is happening correspondingly at a higher level – in consciousness, perhaps at the level of thought, emotion or impulse – that needs to be addressed.[8] Symptoms of illness, if we choose to observe and listen to them, are uncannily informative about the issues that need to be looked at. However, it is our way to regard symptoms of illness with intolerance and even anxiety and fear: we suppress them rather than take an interest in them. Symptoms of illness are, at bottom, unwanted or disliked sensations arising in the body

---

[8] By 'higher' and 'lower' levels of consciousness I do not mean to imply greater or lesser; there is no hierarchy here. I simply indicate energy more or less refined on a continuum of density from the coarse material to the spiritual.

or mind (which we might usefully refer to as the body–mind). When sick, we busily apply ourselves to eliminating symptoms, getting ourselves back to normal and our habitual show back on its weary road, rather than recognising that our symptoms are expressing a need – perhaps a readiness – for change, growth and development. Challenge of any kind, illness included, offers us the possibility of needed change. Nobody would suggest that change through crisis is an easy way to learn, but ultimately the need to learn is far more important than whether or not we, as individuals, find it packaged in an acceptable form.

Life forces or cosmic energies, whatever we want to call them, are not random but follow patterns and principles. These principles collectively are known in other traditions as the *tao*, *dharma*, etc. Lacking a word in my English vocabulary, I refer to *the way it is*. When we do not conform to the *way it is* we go against the grain of Being, pitting ourselves against the *tao*. This is neither right nor wrong, but it will have consequences at the level of health and wellbeing. For example, Saturn's planetary principle is contraction: all matter becomes denser over time. Failing to recognise this can lead to strain in the joints or broken bones. Not aligning with life forces, especially chronically, leads to disturbances and impediments in our energy systems that will eventually manifest in the physical body as symptoms of unwellness. The symptom will be a wonderful clue to the way in which we have departed from *the way it is*. Symptoms are always elegant expressions of where and how we have pulled ourselves out of shape;

hence, they are valuable triggers to developing consciousness and cultivating deep change.

We readily theorise that life on earth is a great school for learning and development. We less readily accept that the only things that prompt most of us to consider change in our lives are challenges like sickness and misfortune – the 'blows of fate'. We need to be able to learn from our symptoms rather than silence them. Allopathic medication is often aimed at the management or eradication of symptoms (which is very sensible from a limited perspective), which often serves to drive them deeper into the organism, where they become more pernicious (like any chronic needs left unmet). An example of this might be the chronic suppression of the symptoms of eczema leading to athsma. The authors of *The Healing Power of Illness*, Thorwald Dethlefsen and Rüdiger Dahlke, use the analogy of a warning-light flashing on the instrument panel of a car to describe symptoms. When this happens you don't remove the bulb to stop it flashing; you pull over and check the oil, or whatever.

It is the precept of this work that illness is the physical manifestation of a problem in consciousness, a problem in consciousness being the going against the grain of *the way it is*. Therefore, the first step towards healing can be made by bringing interest and creative engagement to symptoms and trying to understand, consciously, what life is trying to teach us, what our own bodies are expressing. The intention of these essays is to help people use the principles of astrology to interrogate and understand the role of challenge, generally, and health challenges, in particular, however large or small, in their lives. I will address each of the signs of the zodiac and its relationship to health and healing issues from the standpoint that symptoms of illness present an attempt to come to consciousness and bring change into lived experience. From this perspective symptoms of ill health are not flaws or obstructions to an otherwise good life; they are steps along the path of self-actualisation: the healing path. They express the urge towards a more inclusive and, crucially, a more authentic consciousness. Symptoms in the body represent an attempt to make a change in our hearts, minds and spirits, at the level of consciousness.

The horoscope, as a map of the psyche, can be used to describe physical, emotional or mental difficulties and present them within the context of an individual's developmental journey. The astrologer that understands how to use the birth chart to interpret challenges that manifest in the body is extremely well placed to help a person understand their problem and find ways of responding to it creatively, usefully and meaningfully. The result of this is the personal growth awarded by having a *context of significance* that is sourced from the Unseen world.

Healing is the process of becoming more whole: more truly ourselves, responsive to our opportunities and more aware of our purpose in life. It is not just for the sick in body; the healing path is that which leads us towards a fuller expression of self, vitality and consciousness. Healing is about understanding our unique challenges and our unique life forces and learning from them.

> Healing occurs through the incorporation of that which is missing, and thus is not possible without an expansion of consciousness. Illness and healing are twin concepts which have relevance only to consciousness and are not applicable to the body, since a body itself can be neither ill nor healthy. All that it can do is reflect the corresponding states and conditions of consciousness itself.[9]

---

[9] Dethlefsen and Dahlke (1990), p. 12.

Fixing the Spirit

*Don't turn your head, keep looking
at the bandaged place. That's where
the light enters you.* [10]

Physical Life and Consciousness

There is a curious medical condition, hypoaesthesia, which is
the loss of sensation in the skin: the nerves of the skin are
unreceptive to stimuli. Interestingly, this results in a condition
that we tend, in our mental, emotional and bodily lives, to
strive towards: painlessness. We often consider comfort and
painlessness to be the markers of wellbeing. They could well
be the markers of closure, stagnation and imminent danger.
A person suffering from loss of sensation in the skin is in
danger of serious physical damage; the warnings, experienced
as pain, are not registered, so such a person can get into

---

[10] Rumi, 'Childhood Friends' (1998), p. 39.

threatening situations very readily. Pain is not the problem in our lives; suffering is not the problem. The problem is the *disconnection* between pain and understanding, sensations and awareness, which results in unconsciousness.

Pain is the signal that we are going against the grain, against the *way it is*; that something is going on that threatens wellbeing. We often mistake the signal (or symptom) for the threat, and this approach to sickness arising at any level of our beings (i.e. thinking that the symptom is the source of the problem) is tantamount to shooting the messenger. Suffering at any level requires us to question what is manifesting, what is going on with us. It is a natural, knee-jerk reaction to go into fear, anxiety, intolerance or impatience when we experience pain. If only we could override fear and hostility and get interested in the process that is trying to work out through our beings. Pain, suffering and symptoms are not the source of the problem; they are the guides that will illuminate healing paths, paths towards greater consciousness. They are the signals that something is ready for change and healing, and if we work with them with rigorous honesty they will direct us on a journey towards greater authenticity and fullness of being.

It is the way of mainstream medicine and our cultural disposition to see disease as the enemy. We talk about being the victims of illness; we even describe illnesses in moral terms, as cruel or vindictive. Illness is seen as something that invades us from the outside and disrupts our otherwise healthy lives: random misfortune. Medicine accepts that our mental–emotional states make us more or less susceptible to the agents of illness, but it does not accept that illness arises within us as a direct expression of mental–emotional states. When our bodies become ill, we need fixing at the level of consciousness.

We are physical beings, sure enough. Physical life is a vehicle for non-physical aspects of ourselves: thoughts, feelings, will and soul forces. An actor takes on a role in a similar way to the soul taking on a personality.[11] In the birth chart the Sun represents the authentic current identity; its condition, by sign, house and aspect, indicates how and where the soul is seeking to break new ground for consciousness in this lifetime. It is the source of vitality, organisation and, crucially, of purpose. It 'focalises' the personality so that it may act on behalf of the soul. By 'personality' I am indicating character, disposition, constitution, a set of life circumstances and a body. Personality is animated by spiritual forces, which at an individual level we can call 'soul'. Soul, in turn, is a vehicle for spirit, which connects us to all of life. Spirit incarnates. Soul forces infuse the body, just as an *idea* precedes, inspires and infuses something we might create.

We forget that we are soul-actors playing the roles of our personalities. We usually become totally identified with our personalities and their conditions. It is part of human life to feel alone at times, and oblivious to the truth of our connection with greater forces. It is part of human life to

---

[11] This analogy was offered by David Matthews, convenor of Totnes Astrology Group.

suffer and to seek. The gift of this situation is that it puts the personality into communication with its informing spirit, soul, and this interaction is productive of consciousness, development and, potentially, of remembering the truth of spiritual identity.

 A rudimentary image for expressing the purpose of human life is that of the transmitter/receiver. Occupying our space between heaven and earth we receive star energies from heaven and transmit them into the planetary body; we receive earth energy from below and transmit it out towards the stars. We are agents of the interchange between the Above and the Below. All energy is consciousness; it is information. At its most dense level the energy of consciousness coheres into manifest physical expression: the physical plane. Just because the energy is dense and physical does not mean that it has ceased to be consciousness, simply that it is vibrating at a lower (and lower is not lesser) level. Consciousness operates at different vibratory rates. It can have a very high vibration, which makes it refined and extremely subtle; or it can have a low vibration, which results in coarseness and density. The physical plane is where consciousness is so dense that it manifests in form.

'Consciousness,' as Dethlefsen and Dahlke remark, 'is to the body as a radio programme is to the receiver.'[12] The experience we get to have on Planet Earth is one of manifesting idea, thought and emotion in the world of form.

---

[12] Dethlefsen and Dahlke (1990), p. 6.

The invisible realms of consciousness are translated into visibility at the level of the physical plane. The visible mediates the invisible (form mediates idea). When something arises in the body it will always have its correspondences, or counterparts, in thought and emotion. A block in the flow of energy (i.e. information/consciousness) at a higher level will manifest in the body. The body is the agent through which the unknown (or disregarded) is made known to us. To seek to eliminate symptoms without hearing their messages, though entirely understandable, is to close our eyes to what is manifesting, to persist in the somnolence we associate with being OK.

Why do we do this? There are two layers of explanation. One is personal, the other cultural. The personal layer of explanation is that disease (at whatever level) challenges us to change. Pain is scary; being ill feels like being out of control. Physical challenges are the manifestation of challenges that are occurring in consciousness, because, as we have established, consciousness is continuous with the body. The challenge arises because our energy is not flowing; it is getting stuck and stagnant. The flow of energy has to be reinstated if we are to keep on doing our human job of transforming energy between heaven and earth. Reinstating the flow will also move us towards greater wholeness and authenticity. Fear and habit are the enemies of change and we cannot over-estimate what a tight grip they have on us.

Astrologically they are represented by Saturn and the Moon, which together construct the conditioning and limitation of consciousness that we are seeking to develop beyond. The Moon and Saturn are descriptors of the past; we have to break through the habits and preconceptions of our conditioning in order to avoid simply repeating the past, which is a pointless exercise. Do what you have always done, as they say, and get what you have always got.

In *A New Earth*, Eckhart Tolle introduces the useful concept of the *pain-body*. The mental conditioning of thought processes (Saturn, in astrological terms), and the emotional conditioning expressed in our reactions to our thoughts (the Moon) – give rise to the experience of the pain-body:

> Although the body is very intelligent, it cannot tell the difference between an actual situation and a thought. It reacts to every thought as if it were a reality. It doesn't know it is just a thought. To the body, a worrisome, fearful thought means 'I am in danger,' and it responds accordingly, even though you may be lying in a warm and comfortable bed at night. The heart beats faster, muscles contract, breathing becomes rapid. There is a buildup of energy, but since the danger is only a mental fiction, the energy has no outlet. Part of it is fed back to the mind and generates even more anxious thought. The rest of the energy turns toxic and interferes with the harmonious functioning of the body. ...
> Unconscious assumptions create emotions in the body which in turn generate mind activity and/or

instant reactions. In this way you create your personal reality.[13]

Our thinking, feeling and willing take hold of our bodies.[14] Reflect on how it makes you feel *in your body* if you allow the feeling of anger or outrage or sadness to take hold of you. An angry outburst can leave you, for example, with a sore throat and a stiff back – at some level the outburst has been registered as an offence against the self. The nervous system, after all, cannot distinguish between anger towards the self and anger towards another, or between trauma experienced in the past and the memory of trauma in the present. When we experience feelings of upliftment, tensions are released, our holding patterns are 'gentled', flow begins to be restored. Negative emotions or thoughts will lock us back down in the conditioned patterns associated with security and invulnerability.

Our thoughts and emotions, our beliefs and even our opinions, *live* in our bodies. Where else, after all, might they dwell? They grip our bodies in patterns of holding as we defend ourselves against our perceived realities, and push forward that which we wish to show and obscure those things we prefer to keep hidden. Potentially our bodies can be lit up with vitality and purpose. They are always changing and

---

[13] Tolle (2006), pp. 134-135.

[14] By 'will' and 'willing' I am referring to the energy of impulse, when we determine or decide (consciously or not) upon action and reaction. We could also call will the 'power of decision'. It is conditioned by our thoughts and feelings, or lack thereof.

growing, susceptible to healing in every moment; revelatory in every moment. These ideas are common in some other cultures. For example, the *I Ching* refers to the way in which false ideas depress health and vitality: 'Disruptions in the flow of chi occur when we harbour ideas which are foreign to the Higher Truth.'[15] Higher Truth is inner truth and higher self, but also 'cosmos' – the place of wholeness. To restore health, the *I Ching* suggests, we need to bring false ideas to the surface to free ourselves from their depressing effects.

Development and growth involve us in challenging our fears and habits: resisting the conditioning of Saturn and the Moon. This is difficult and painful; the more we resist, the more difficult and painful it can become. When we are confronting illness in ourselves or in those close to us, fear and habit really start kicking in. They make us want to give up responsibility, to give ourselves over to the hands of experts, to turn our heads away from our wounds. Saturn and the Moon also represent the Father and the Mother, respectively (the agents of conditioning in early life); resistance to responsibility is perhaps an infantile response. This is entirely natural, but ultimately it is where the challenge lies: in assuming responsibility and looking at what ails us, our woundedness, and taking care of ourselves. We may well need to enlist the help of doctors, therapists, etc. but we can do this as well as, rather than instead of, attending to our own predicament.

---

[15] Anthony (1988), p. 214.

There is a danger in this approach to illness/challenge that people may feel that assuming responsibility means saying 'I have made myself ill,' the inference being that in some way one has failed. This is not the assumption of responsibility but the futile placing of blame. It leads people into judgement of self and others, which only deepens the sense of shame and separation that often accompanies illness. Illness is a necessary component of health and a totally valid experience for consciousness.

There is no judgement of illness or of people experiencing illness in my approach. Assuming responsibility means accepting that our experiences belong in particular and unique ways to us; we are in a process of calling ourselves into being, and our life stories (our experiences) are in our bodies. Caroline Myss, in *Anatomy of the Spirit*, makes the point that biography becomes biology.[16] Illness merely indicates that there is work to do, something that needs fixing, a story that is creating a distortion and a current impulse to address the issue. Judith Blackstone refers to the same idea in *The Subtle Self*:

> Our bodies are a record of our psychological history, of both our pain and our happiness. They show the economy of our survival from all the pressures and frustrations of our childhood. They reveal the pattern of openness and defence which makes up our

---

[16] Myss (1997), p. 40.

perspective on the world. This pattern is as unique to each of us as the pattern of our thumb print.[17]

While we may make use of the wonderful help that mainstream medicine and natural healing methods can provide, if we wish to find healing we have ultimately to rely upon a process of coming to consciousness for ourselves. Fear and habit (Saturn and the Moon) catch us in patterns of resisting in some way the *tao* of life, *the way it is*. Resisting the *tao* creates the blockage that will eventually, if ignored, manifest in the body. Here, fear and habit involve us in ignoring or suppressing and further resisting the message of life; so it is that we close ourselves off from life and give even greater potency to our fear. The possibility that we have through illness is of re-establishing an honest and open dialogue with life and with the *tao* of our beings by hearing the message of the body and opening to its teaching. This is what is meant by assuming responsibility.

The second layer of explanation as to why we ignore or resist what is manifesting in our bodies (and in our lives more generally) pertains to our cultural experience. Culturally, we have tended to denigrate the physical realm of experience. Religious attitudes have regarded the physical realm as the place of sin and separation from God. We have polarised spirit and matter, idealising one and demonising the other. We see them as discontinuous, alienated from each other, utterly separate. The sacred is immaterial; the material is

---

[17] Blackstone (1991), p. 41.

profane. In these deep-seated attitudes we neglect the value of the physical level's role in the development of consciousness; we forget that sensation (at the physical level) is continuous with awareness (at the spiritual level). It seems absurd to the point of tragedy that we incarnate on earth, where the *principle* of experience is manifestation on the physical plane, and seek either to identify only with the ideal and immaterial, or else just give ourselves wholesale to the animal, physical life without any sense of purpose or meaning. When we reject the physical or resist engaging with it, we miss the point and the opportunity of life on Planet Earth: consciousness is manifesting here; spirit is here made flesh.

In a real sense, this denigration of the physical realm and its artificial severance from the higher realms of being constitute our sickness. We have polarised heaven and earth; we have severed our heads from our bodies, and our bodies from our souls. These polarities are false. Heaven participates in earth. Heaven and earth do not exist without each other. Likewise, sickness and health do not exist without each other: they are in a dynamic, continuous relationship of interchange. Our minds are distributed throughout our bodies; soul quickens and gains experience through the body. Our healing, as individuals and as cultures, will rely upon our ability to integrate spirit and matter in our understanding and in our experience of the body.

This work will involve us in patient listening as we cultivate a relationship with our bodies and with the body of the earth, the planetary consciousness. We need to develop intuitional understanding of the physical plane. Blackstone makes the simple point that sensation never arises in the body without counterparts in thought and emotion. Where there is an emotion there is also a thought and a sensation in the body; when there is a thought, it will be accompanied by emotion and sensation. It is through interrogating the emotional and mental content of our physical sensations that we will be able to begin to develop a dialogue with the physical realm and to infuse physical experience with consciousness and intelligence:

> Polarities are actually contractions of continuums [sic]. For example, the body–mind dichotomy is a contraction of the underlying body–mind continuum, or spectrum. We experience the mind as separate from the body because we have defensively withdrawn our consciousness from our body. As we release our defences, we realise that there is nowhere we can definitively draw the line between physical and mental experience. Because polarity is conflict and contraction, resolution is experienced as expansion. In this example of the body–mind dichotomy, both our physical and mental experience become richer as the dichotomy is resolved.[18]

The great usefulness of the physical plane is that it is totally undeceptive. We can be very unrealistic about how things are in the invisible realms of being. We can lie, cheat and steal at

---

[18] Blackstone (1991), p. 72.

the levels of thought and emotion without it even occurring to us that we are handling things falsely. The body, however, does not lie. It tells us (and others) what we are longing and needing to be made known. The body expresses our truths with total honesty and unerring appropriateness. Therefore, it can teach us truthfulness and self-acceptance in such a way as to reconnect us with a wider sense of meaning, through making our suffering conscious and understandable. From this point real progress in development can be made. Such progress serves not only the individual, but all of Life.

Conditioning: the Moon and Saturn

'We don't see things as they are, we see things as we are.'[19]

The placement of the Moon creates a weakness in the body as it is the fastest moving 'planet' and so receives the impact of all the other planets. Because it pertains to the emotional conditioning set in early life (a reflection, we can theorise, of conditions carried over from the soul's past lives,[20] impressed upon the memory), the Moon creates a strong default pattern that a person needs to outgrow in order to orient towards the current identity and the opportunity for development it

---

[19] In *number9dream*, novelist David Mitchell has one of his characters wear a t-shirt with this phrase written on it. It was also written by Anaïs Nin in 'Seduction of the Minatour', 1961.

[20] Tom Jacobs makes the point that the soul exists outside time, that we are multi-dimensional beings. So when I speak of past-life experience, I am referring to the soul's other lives. Tom Jacobs (2010), pp. 62-63.

represents. Each of us has a struggle to overcome the pull of the past as shown by the Moon. If we remain oriented towards the Moon and lunar consciousness we fall into a habitual pattern that is insusceptible to evolution; this will be devitalising. If we persist in this state, illness ensues. The Moon, it should be remembered, has no light of its own. It is the reflector of the light of the Sun, which represents the authentic identity of the current lifetime. The Moon shows where we have experience and, thus, resources; it is a translator of the light of the Sun. This is its usefulness, which can be claimed increasingly if we learn to override its default settings and scripts in our emotional bodies: our conditioned emotional reactions.

The placement of Saturn is also a challenge in health terms. It represents past-life conditioning at the mental level of perception (that we can describe as the mindset), such that it is mistaken for *reality* and is therefore unconscious. We are largely unaware that our perception of reality is highly conditioned. Saturn is the planet of karmic redress and, in the birth chart, it describes a dilemma that may well come into the body as, being unconscious it cannot be readily addressed. Suffering consists in persisting in habitual patterns of thought and emotional reaction that stifle enquiry and growth. What Eckhart Tolle refers to as 'the pain-body', I would regard as the negative influence of Saturn and the Moon.

In psychological parlance we can see the Moon and Saturn as 'protectors': defence mechanisms against perceived threat.

These patterns of defence are laid down in the neurological conditions of the body, as habits, waiting to be triggered by new threats. But they are operating in terms of a former reality, which no longer pertains, and therefore stymie attempts to move into the legitimate identity of the current lifetime as signified by the Sun. This process readily manifests through the body as illness.

Saturn and the Moon, when we are not in thrall to our conditioning, provide us with highly positive influences: Saturn enables and empowers, and the Moon nourishes and sustains us, opening us intelligently to the feeling level of experience. Saturn exemplifies the 'power of decision': the realisation that how we perceive, feel and think gives birth to our reality and that we have a *choice* about that. We can be reactive and fearful, or grounded and loving. Positive Saturn is less the *teacher through pain* and more the *bringer of opportunity.* The Moon warms and humanises our thinking, and also gives rise to a sense of continuity and containment that actually allow a coherent experience of identity to arise. A present with no memory of the past is a definition of dementia.

Making Meaning

Astrology is a language that describes the Unseen. As a system of knowledge and a mode of understanding and explanation it has the capacity to describe the interchange of consciousness that is occurring between heaven and earth via humanity. It suggests that each of us participates uniquely in this interchange, as we are all designed to channel different aspects of the energetic exchange: the birth chart represents the energy matrix with which the individual is impressed. This matrix conditions the quality of consciousness and predisposes us to certain experiences in the personality, or *form life* (at the level of physical manifestation in the world of bodies and events), depending on our rate of vibration.

Astrology offers us a frame of reference through which to interpret and understand the world of form as we experience it, thereby gaining meaningfulness and the faith bestowed by having a context of significance that makes sense of life. Such a context can be redemptive – and there is a real need to redeem the massive cost of our unconscious suffering. We need to find divinity in our flesh and in the rubble of our personal, cultural and political experiences. We need to re-member (put back together) our connections to heaven and earth and to each other, and recover the deep significance of our lives: 'Our existence is deeper and vaster than both our suffering and our memory of suffering.'[21]

Illness is always the expression of a desire to reconnect to meaning, wholeness and authenticity, and the possibility of any illness is nothing less than initiation. If consciousness is to become more inclusive, then life requires that we locate the stagnant areas within our energetic beings, where energy is not flowing fully; it asks that we restore the flow of

---

[21] Blackstone (1991), p. 64.

information and awareness to these areas. Life requires we draw ourselves into alignment with *it*, rather than insisting that *it* gets into line with how *we* think it should be. Life includes everything; it rejects or excludes nothing. As our undertaking is the development of consciousness, nothing (however unpleasant, frightening or painful) can be excluded or rejected. What is the point of accepting this, but not that; of liking this and disliking that? All forms of challenge are grist to the mill of consciousness and can be engaged with as such. Life requires nothing less than everything.

> Lowering his voice to almost a whisper, he said that if I really felt that my spirit was distorted I should simply fix it – purge it, make it perfect – because there was no other task in our entire lives more worthwhile. Not to fix the spirit was to seek death, and that was the same as to seek nothing, since death was going to overtake us regardless of anything.
>
> He paused for a long time and then he said with a tone of profound conviction, 'To seek the perfection of the warrior's spirit is the only task worthy of our manhood.'[22]

---

[22] Castaneda (1974), p. 124.

The Grammar of Astrology

Signs, Planets and Houses

The essays that follow this chapter are organised around the signs of the zodiac, and the planet and house with which they correspond. The energy of a particular sign is also carried by its planetary ruler and by the 'natural' and 'accidental' houses with which it is associated in a chart. For example, Aries energy will express in the area of life denoted by the condition of Mars (Aries' ruler), by the first house of the chart (which is under the 'natural' rulership of Aries) and by the house placement of Aries within the chart (under the 'accidental' rulership of Aries).

Planets, signs and houses form the basic grammar of astrology and signify, respectively, *what* is happening, *how* it is happening and *where* it is happening (i.e. in what area of life). Signs and houses are connected with parts of the anatomy; planets refer to physiological processes. An emphasis in any sign will bring that energy forcefully into the life. Using the birth chart to describe problems arising in the body–mind is a somewhat subtle and nuanced business, as shown in the case studies contained in this volume; but any illumination we can gain, however incompetent we are with the astrology, will always be valuable. However, getting to grips with the nuts and bolts by understanding the *principles* of astrology's grammar considerably deepens comprehension.

I am offering some key words here for the planets and the houses, while the signs are dealt with more fully in following chapters.

Defining an Emphasis in a Sign

An emphasis, for example, in Aries, would be constituted by any of the following features:-

- Sun or Moon in Aries or the first house;
- focal planet of an aspect configuration being in Aries or the first house;
- Aries ruling one of the angles (ascendant, descendant, midheaven or nadir);
- a stellium in Aries or the first house;
- Mars (Aries' ruler) conjunct Sun, Moon or angle (especially ascendant);
- Mars as the focal planet of an aspect configuration;
- Mars on 29th degree of any sign.

Planetary Principles

Sun　　　　　*Consciousness.* The force of integration presented by the current identity, authenticity, personal power, purpose. *Vitality, vision, heart function.*

Moon　　　　*Continuity.* Emotional conditioning, emotions, mother, women, home, sanctuary. *Limbic* *system, menstruation, fertility, pregnancy, lactation.*

Mercury   ***Communication.*** Rationality, mentality, schooling, learning, sibling. *Nervous system, respiration, digestion, sensory processes, mental faculties.*

Venus   ***Attraction.*** Love, the lover, relationship, values. *Homoeostasis, venereal diseases, kidney function.*

Mars   ***Assertion.*** Motivation, desire-nature, drive, energy, effectiveness. *Inflammation, infection, fever, adrenal function, acute illness.*

Jupiter   ***Expansion.*** Faith in life, quest for meaning and expansion, wisdom-knowledge. *Blood, arterial system, liver function.*

Saturn   ***Contraction.*** Mental conditioning (mindset), authority, father, establishment, responsibility. *Ossification, sclerosis, skeletal function, chronic illness.*

Uranus   ***Liberation.*** Autonomy, eccentricity, freedom, disruption, innovation. *Rhythmic processes, spasm, 'electrical' impulses in nervous function.*

Neptune	***Unification.*** Mysticism, artistic inspiration, spiritual service, illusion. *Immunity, lymphatic system, psychosis, dementia, misdiagnoses.*
Pluto	***Transformation.*** Power, penetration, depth-awareness, sexuality, death. *Elimination, reproduction, destruction.*
Chiron	Scar on the soul, woundedness, the Wounded Healer, compassion, wisdom, the bridge between personal and transpersonal planets.

The Houses[23]

First   Assertiveness, autonomy, self-image, personality. *Awareness through self-projection and personal effectiveness.* Head, face, upper jaw. (Aries)

Second   Values, resources (including body), possessions, security. *Awareness through material responsibility.* Throat, neck, lower jaw. (Taurus)

Third   Rational mind, mental attitude, communication, learning, education, siblings, surroundings. *Awareness through communication.* Hands, arms, shoulders, lungs. (Gemini)

Fourth   Roots, heritage, home, women, nurturing parent, psychology, history. *Awareness through experience of belonging and dependency.* Breasts, stomach, womb. (Cancer)

Fifth   Creative individuality, joy of uniqueness, pleasure, children, Inner Child, romance, play. *Awareness through creative energy.* Heart, spine, eyes. (Leo)

Sixth   Self-purification, work, rituals, habits, health, vocation, service. *Awareness through use of functional energy.* Small intestine. (Virgo)

---

[23] The body areas associated with each house are governed by the ruling sign of that house, given here in brackets.

Seventh Committed relationships, one-to-one relating, advocacy, sense of justice, aesthetics. *Awareness through relating.* Kidneys, bladder, skin. (Libra.)

Eighth Crisis, death, regeneration, emotional/sexual relating, occult, shared resources. *Awareness through emotional/sexual experience.* Large intestine, sex organs. (Scorpio.)

Ninth Search for meaning, faith in life, higher knowledge, religions, the law, tertiary education, foreign cultures, travel. *Awareness through quest for meaning.* Hips, thighs, sciatic nerve, liver. (Sagittarius.)

Tenth Authority, career, status, life-path, social values, disciplining parent. *Awareness through achieving recognition and authority.* Skeleton, knees, joints, hair, nails. (Capricorn.)

Eleventh Friendship, ideals, conscience, the future, groups, community. *Awareness through communal endeavour.* Ankles, shins. (Aquarius.)

Twelfth Universal consciousness, self-transcendence, sacrifice, background of the life, places of withdrawal and seclusion: hospitals, prisons, retreat centres. *Awareness through experience of non-separation.* Feet, lymphatic system. (Pisces.)

ARIES
Birthplace of Ideas

Spring equinox is marked by the Sun's alignment with the *celestial equator*[24], its entry into the very first degree of the zodiac, in the dynamic, assertive sign of Aries: the will to be. The dawn of the year: this is the energy of beginnings and becoming. Growth is coming, change is coming. Things cannot remain as they are: 'For staying is nowhere'.[25] Ready or not, here I come. The Sun in Aries leads the lifeforce out into the open and urges us to act. Therefore, we need to know what it is we are doing, what are our intentions. The unstoppable drive of Aries can be unnerving, exhausting too, for the parts of ourselves that are sleepy or hiding. But life cannot stop and wait until we are ready for it to happen! We are called to enter into creation by the wilful energy of Mars-ruled Aries.

Behind all the experiences and perceptions of our little, separated personalities there is soul force, a higher self: 'the

---

[24] The celestial equator is the circle of the Earth's equator extended out into space, in our imaginations.
[25] Rilke (1964), 'The First Elegy', p. 61.

Self, that mysterious process within each of us which summons us to ourselves'.[26] We are called by Mars and Aries to know what we are doing and to respond to the summons of the Self. That is the challenge!

After experiencing the great *merge* in the collective waters of Pisces, we *emerge* into individuality in Aries: 'The first impulse is awakened in Aries, for Aries is the place where the initial idea to institute activity takes form. It is the birthplace of ideas, and a true idea is in reality a spiritual impulse taking form – subjective and objective.'[27] This is reminiscent of what has been said about the impulse of the soul to find form and incarnate in a body; the soul then is the informing *idea* that manifests in the vehicle of the body and the personality. Aries governs this stage, the initiating idea, of the process of incarnation.

Aries energy is the will to be and to do that is fundamental to the process of *becoming*. Impulse. The divine spark of life. Mars is one of the planets of individuality and personality, being within the orbit of Saturn. The principle of Mars is **assertion.** It is the first *superior* planet (its orbit is beyond the orbit of Earth at 687 days) and it brings a restless onward and upward drive. Aries/Mars/first house is about my assertion of myself, my ability to hear my own message and to free my own drives (including the sex drive) in activity. Nietzsche said that 'a living thing desires to vent its strength' and this is true of Aries, which can be forceful, tactless and thuggish when

---

[26] Hollis (1993), p. 25.
[27] Bailey (1951), p. 92.

unconstrained. It is absolutely necessary to conscious identity for a human being to have a sense of self, and this Aries bestows to the extent of knowing what it wants (which indicates at least that it can sense itself as a separate being). However, Aries is in *polarity* with Libra, the sign of self's relationship with other. Appropriate regard for the reality of other and a coherent understanding of *right relationship* between self and other mitigates some of the excesses of Aries energy, which can, of itself, be heedless.

> If I am not for myself, who will be? If I am only for myself, what am I? And if not now, then when?[28]

Remember that we are looking at this energy in isolation; in our lives it is always part of a weave, tempered by all the other energies of signs and planets, even though a time or an individual may be strongly marked by a particular sign or planet.

Aries rules the head and Aries people have a reputation for bashing their heads. The energy of Aries is emergent, energetic, impulsive and very competitive. Reflecting these qualities, the Aries native is often impulsive and headstrong, hence the bumps to the head. A head injury, a scar on the face or a broken nose are good indications that Aries, Mars or first-house energy is not being constructively channelled. Mars provides the qualities of strife, struggle and combativeness associated with the sign. Mars can operate

---

[28] https://www.jewishvirtuallibrary.org/rabbi-hillel-quotes (accessed Aug.'21)

with great belligerence and disregard for others. It can be frankly charmless, and is therefore not much loved by those who consider themselves charming. Aries energy is also fiery and 'masculine'.[29]

All in all, this is difficult energy for those who do not consciously identify with the assertive and desirous aspects of their beings. This is a problem, for it means that Aries and Mars are often suppressed and thwarted within the personalities we present to others and therefore we cut ourselves off from the vital energy they provide, cultivating falseness and a quality of repression in our identities and depriving ourselves of constructive outlets for our Mars energy. Mars gives us fuel in the tank for the journey of becoming, so we really need it. Mars without a constructive outlet manifests as anger, aggression and destructiveness. This can be turned in upon the self or out upon others. Turned upon others it is violence; turned upon the self it can attract aggression or bullying behaviour from others and becomes a potent source of depression, fatigue, headache, irritation, muscular pain and inflammation. To work for us it needs our clear *intent*.

If we are to become effective we need to find a positive outlet for our Mars energy. It must be marshalled. This is the

---

[29] The terms 'masculine' and 'feminine' refer to energies that are found in all beings, sometimes also called *yang* and *yin*, or 'positive' and 'negative' respectively (implying no value judgement). Masculine energy tends to be active, upward, outward and discharging; feminine energy tends to be receptive, downward, inward and charging up.

energy of self-actualisation; through Mars we project ourselves, focus our efforts and desires, and become independent. The qualities of sheer presence and drive are Mars' gifts, giving us fire in the belly and delight in exertion, action and the full expression of strength. So while Mars has a bad press among those of us who see ourselves as refined and civilised (and we are many!), it is actually our source of passion, engagement with life and motivating power. Without Mars, we are bodies without muscles, and brains without ideas. Mars brings courage and unflinching honesty. While it may be ungifted in terms of subtlety and nuance, it is unsentimental and straightforward.

Howard Sasportas describes Mars as the 'henchman of the Sun',[30] inferring that Mars is the energetic principle by which the Sun seeks to enact its purpose (perhaps to the point of ruthlessness). Therefore, we can suggest that when Mars is problematic it is because an individual is not sufficiently engaged with the Sun energy in the chart (which, after all, organises and calibrates the energy of the being and of the lifetime as a whole). Liz Greene writes: 'Whatever the natal relationship between these two planets [the Sun and Mars], they need ultimately to be friends, for Mars must offer the Sun its fighting power and the Sun must provide meaning for Mars' battles.'[31]

---

[30] Sasportas in Greene and Sasportas (1993), pp. 223-259.
[31] Greene in Greene and Sasportas (1993), p. 194.

Mars conditions manifesting in the body (fever, inflammation, fatigue, hyperactivity) or in mental states (aggression, anger, depression) can be examined by interrogating the relationship between the Sun and Mars and the factors within the chart as a whole that might be undermining it. The placement of Mars and Aries in the birth chart will show where and how one needs to galvanise the will and convert energy into activity that *serves the purposes of the Sun*. These placements will similarly show where problems might arise in the being and the body due to Mars not being provided with outlets.

The Sun's entry into Aries at the vernal equinox (around 20th March in the northern hemisphere), brings the balance of day and night forces all around the globe. From this point on until the midsummer solstice (the Sun's entry into the cardinal sign of Cancer) the daylight force waxes. The Sun is the representative in our corner of the universe of a higher order of being (the stellar level); our star is related to purpose and consciousness and confers these qualities upon us through the principle of identity. Likewise Aries, the time when day overcomes night, is related to the *initiation* of consciousness and awareness of being (the signs of the cardinal cross – Aries, Cancer, Libra and Capricorn – are concerned with inaugurating or initiating phases of activity).[32] The vernal equinox is the time marked by the great budding and

---

[32] In *Esoteric Astrology* (Bailey, 1951), Bailey notes that the phases of activity ruled by the cardinal cross are as follows: Aries pertains to Creation, Cancer to Manifestation, Capricorn to Initiation and Libra to Legislation.

blooming of spring, and this creative activity reflects the energy and focus of Aries.

Aries has the capacity to *break through* just as new plants break through the earth, powered by moisture and the growing heat of the Sun. For this reason Aries is a good fighter on the front line. Positively expressed, it focuses courage and willpower and, as Aries is straightforward and not of itself concerned about popularity, it can achieve a great deal. Negatively, as we have seen, this force can be expressed as heedlessness and unremitting self-assertion for the sake of it. It is important to realise that astrological principles operate at different registers: they can have coarse expressions, which we would see as negative or afflicted; or they can be expressed with greater refinement, purpose and awareness, which is likely to be positive and helpful. Each principle, then, has the potential of a whole range of 'registers'; spiritual activity is about transforming and refining our energy fields. Mars can yield aggressive behaviour or highly purposeful, effective activity. It is up to us.

In *Esoteric Astrology,* Alice Bailey associates Aries with the impulse to 'enter into battle for the Lord'. This is a refined expression of Aries, using personal forces to serve the will of life. Spiritual activity is any activity that raises the register of planetary energies, transforming and refining them in our experience and expression. Aries produces the spiritual warrior, in touch with the *idea* of Spirit (the creative force behind all manifest life) and focused within divine will. At a lower level of expression, the spiritual warrior is simply a warrior, and Aries can go into battle whether there is anything to fight for or not.

Aries rules the head, face and upper jaw (the lower jaw belongs to Taurus). The face is the body part with which we meet the world. When we meet another person, we interact face to face, reading and measuring character and what the other person is presenting as self. The face is the part that, in most cultures, shows. 'Facing it', in common parlance, suggests courage and candour. The face announces our presence, displays our alertness and projects our quality of being. The use of the face and head as ways of meeting the world and projecting our presence are functions of Mars and the first house of the natal chart (which describes *how* a person asserts themselves and seeks to become effective). In the book, *Body Signs,* Hilarion ascribes significance to characteristics of the facial features and the head:

> Every soul incarnate upon the earth knows that it is through the *head* that the main connection between the body and the inhabiting soul arises. ... The divine spark from the mind of God dwells in the centre of the head, directly beneath the crown chakra ....
> When one imagines a person without a head, the inner knowledge sees a body with no connection to a higher plane ....

> Moreover, when the head is missing, so are the eyes
> – which are the portals through which the soul literally
> looks out upon the earth plane.[33]

This passage alludes to a much deeper sense of identity than the mere projection of personality or 'persona' that the first house is said to rule in orthodox astrology. This depth of meaning might serve also to deepen our understanding of Aries as the energy that carries the divine spark towards human incarnation.

With Saturn, Aries rules the skull; with Pluto, the sinuses; and with the Moon, the upper brain. Mars rules acute illness and conditions of heat, redness, irritation and inflammation; it should be considered where there are hyperfunctioning and reactive physiological processes. Conditions suffixed by 'itis', characterised by inflammation, are likely to be attributable to Mars. Louise Hay could be referring to Mars problems when she describes the physical manifestations of anger: 'boils and burns, cuts, fevers, sores, "itis" and inflammations are all indications of anger expressing in the body. Anger will find its way to express, no matter *how* much we try to suppress it. Steam that is built up must be released.'[34] Mars needs activity and exercise, otherwise torpor, low mood and low energy begin to inhibit the energy field. Migraine, regular headaches and fatigue are ruled by Mars and are ways of carving out some space for self, which might suggest a struggle to do that in a more straightforward way, perhaps

---

[33] Hilarion (1982), p. 130.
[34] Hay (1984), p. 142.

because there is emotional content of which we need to become aware. Much of what we are is below the threshold of consciousness and it is precisely this information that the sensations and symptoms of the body are so useful in conveying.

As we all know, anger can find some very canny ways of manifesting, and acute illness allows a person to assert themselves in strong, yet seemingly passive, ways. Control and effort are issues for Mars: out of balance, we can be overly controlling, stressed and straining or, conversely, uncontrolled and flopped out. Naturally, we all go in and out of balance. A migraine makes someone withdraw from activity. No one suffering with a migraine headache would react well to being called controlling, yet the need to withdraw is an assertion of sorts; a physical problem is the manifestation of a problem occurring in consciousness. The sufferer is not *wittingly* cultivating a disabling condition; nobody does. However, looking at the difficulty with honesty and cool objectivity allows us to interrogate the patterns and triggers surrounding it, which may give rise to insights.

Greater consciousness might allow for some softening of the patterns, that in turn enables energy to flow better: healing. What is the migraine syndrome making someone do that they would not be doing otherwise? What is it preventing them doing? What effect does it have on the sufferer? What effect does it have on his/her family/partner/friends etc.? Liz Greene notes a connection between Mars and 'manipulative illnesses' (which sounds offensive, but the manipulation is not conscious):

> I have found that manipulative illnesses (and many apparently organic ailments have a manipulative component) are invariably bound up with a badly afflicted Mars in the horoscope, and all the anger and aggression and will are compressed into a form of covert control of others through bodily symptoms. ...
> Mars seems to be a major key to physical as well as psychological health... .[35]

Such conditions express the ways in which we clip our own wings, repressing our natural force, in a desire to preserve harmony or the status quo, perhaps because there is a lack of permission in the family, or in the culture more widely. We should note that the expression of Mars energy by women is generally considered unwelcome (just as the more relational, yielding energy of Venus is not typically encouraged in men). There is massive judgement socially and culturally about women who are strong, direct and know what they want. We are definitely encouraged to tone it down, compromise and be nice – and this impacts upon mental and physical health.

Hay asserts that migraine can be averted by orgasm. This is interesting in the context of Mars, whose energy drives sexuality and the desire nature. She associates headache with self-invalidation, self-criticism and fear; headache attacks may

---

[35] Greene in Greene and Sasportas (1993), pp. 181, 189.

testify to Mars energy turned in upon the self as the inner enemy. When self-assertion is abdicated it is often because we are afraid of showing our anger, or fail to see it as an aspect of our personalities, and it is therefore rejected as irrational. Anger that has not identified its appropriate object, like energy that has not found its appropriate function, is often unleashed upon the self:

> The rage of a blocked Mars can be directed against oneself as well as against the world outside. This is particularly the case with a gentler … temperament… . This may result in self-destructive behaviour, emotionally or physically (difficult Mars aspects are known for being accident-prone); or it may lead to a typical group of illnesses which seem to embody frustrated Martial energy. No other planet turns up so frequently as a trigger by progression or transit, or as a natal 'hot spot', when emotionally linked symptoms (such as migraine headaches and colitis) erupt.[36]

It is important to remember that Mars is a great triggering principle: by transit and by progression it triggers the effects of natal aspects, eclipses and the long-term transits of natal planets by outer planets.

As Mars governs inflammation, a feature of infection, how an individual responds to infection is a barometer of their Mars function. In *The Healing Power of Illness*, Dethlefsen and

---

[36] Greene in Greene and Sasportas (1993), p. 189.

Dahlke discuss the course of infection as indicating how a person deals with conflict more generally. They describe conflict as 'the very engine of development'.[37] Infection is a warlike situation: the body's immune response is compromised and must fight. This is a classic Mars scenario. Dethlefsen and Dahlke refer to the fact that we cannot avoid encountering conflict in our lives: 'all we can do is choose the level on which it occurs.'[38] We can have our battles consciously or fight them out through our bodies. Conflict and the willingness to grapple with our tensions are strengthening and creative. It is the suppression of conflict (through not admitting it to consciousness or through the unnecessary use of suppressive medication) that creates a harmful, threatening situation for the body and mind. Fever, a typical manifestation of Mars activity in the body, is these days often read as a bad development in the course of infection: we have to bring it down. However, fever is the response to infection of a constitutionally strong body, driving out pathogens and toxins. Aries/Mars can purify the being by burning off the dross, just as it can cleanse the body through the expression of a healthy fever:

> For it is not only the fever that is healthy: grappling
> with our conflicts is even healthier. And yet people
> everywhere do their utmost to smother both fevers

[37] Dethlefsen and Dahlke (1990), p. 105.
[38] Dethlefsen and Dahlke (1990), p. 99.

and conflicts at birth, even to the extent of being positively proud of their skills in suppressing them.[39]

Aries energy inaugurates activity, using the willpower and combative energy of Mars, in order to bring ideas (spiritual impulses) into manifestation. Aries can cut to the chase: it is the energy of the activist for spirit, the warrior and the pioneer. Aries and Mars offer the challenge of being clear about our intentions and activity. Mars energy is strongly directional; it needs to be focused and channelled. When we do not know clearly what we are about, then we can get into trouble (impulsive actions can lead to accidents). When we are clear about our *intent* then the drive of Mars facilitates our *becoming*, our self-actualisation. When intent is clear, Aries/Mars give us a sword and shield, making us effective, even audacious, spiritual warriors.

---

[39] Dethlefsen and Dahlke (1990), p. 100.

TAURUS
Refining Desire

The Sun is in Taurus at the time of the great fertility and flowering of early summer in the northern hemisphere. Traditionally it was the time when the herds were driven between the twin fires of Beltane to purify them after their long over-wintering, as they were freed to graze in the pastures once more. This sensual, earthy time of Taurus is marked by abundance. Taurus rules agriculture and our connection to the land, and to the symbiotic relationship between our earthly bodies and the greater body of the earth. It is the sign of embodiment and its drive is to establish conditions in which life can thrive. Astrologically, Taurus rules the throat chakra, which is the energetic counterpart of the thyroid gland. Taurus is ruled by Venus, which represents the principle of *attraction*. As Venus also rules Libra we need to establish a distinction between the planet's activity in the two zodiacal signs respectively.

In orthodox astrology Taurus and the second house of the natal chart describe the values and resources of the individual, whereas Libra and the seventh house describe partnership. Venus in earthy Taurus pertains much more to sensation, sensual appetites and to what (and how) one likes, loves, desires and attributes value; while Venus in airy Libra suggests how these things are embodied in 'other' and encountered in relationship, and in the abstract sense of fairness and aesthetics. Taurus/Venus reveal our appetites and modes of sensuality and how these are expressed physically. It refers to our self-expression as well as to how we engage, sensually and practically, with our environments. Being sensually driven, Taurus is a pleasure-oriented sign; it likes nice stuff and plenty of it. It is highly attuned to and appreciative of the tangible world. Libra (belonging to air) is more social than sensual in character, and shows how we interact with others one to one, and with whom we choose to interact.

Taurus rules the throat, neck, mouth, adenoids, lower jaw and lower brain; with Mercury it rules the larynx, tongue and thyroid; with Pluto, the tonsils. These body parts pertain to speech, self-expression and ingestion. The mouth is the place of nourishment and, in Freudian psychology, the primary site of erotic activity. Babies investigate the world through their mouths: everything is tasted and explored through sensitive oral enquiry. How we feed, how we explore and how we love – our human hungers for nourishment, knowledge and sexual fulfilment – all begin with the mouth. Taurus represents these primary needs and how we go about meeting them.

Problems such as throat afflictions and infections, stiff necks and thyroid imbalances relate to Taurus and the second house, and to difficulties in satisfying those human hungers.

The role of Taurus can be made clearer by thinking about the function of the throat chakra, which is the vortex of force concerned with creative self-expression. It is located at the back of the neck and reaches up towards the base of the brain and the medulla oblongata, and down towards the shoulder blades. All problems emanating from this region pertain to throat chakra imbalance. This chakra is positioned to link the head chakras with those below the throat. In this way it represents what theosophy calls the *antahkarana*, the energetic bridge that links the mind, the brain and the soul, thus allowing higher spiritual forces to flow into the embodied individual:

> Of this connecting 'bridge', the neck itself is the symbol, as it relates the head – alone and isolated – to the dual torso, consisting of that which lies below – the symbol of the soul and the personality united, fused and blended into one.[40]

This symbolism reveals that an aspect of the throat's function is to form a conduit between higher and lower, and between higher, unified forces and the duality experienced in the earth realm.

The throat chakra is in an energetic relationship with the sacral chakra (ruled by Scorpio and the eighth house: the polarity of Taurus and the second), which illuminates the fact that these two chakras are involved in procreativity, creativity

---

[40] Bailey (1953), p. 153.

and the transmutation of sexual desire into spiritual aspiration (the project of tantra). In developmental terms, creative energy is raised from the sacral centre to the throat centre in one who is committed to a spiritual path and practice. This means that sacral chakra energy is not just burnt up in reactive activity, but is refined and expressed through expression (throat). The next step from here would be the raising of creative activity from the throat centre to the brow chakra, the mark of a higher level of refinement, cited here to show the trajectory of the journey. Therefore, the sacral centre is the lower correspondence of the throat centre, which in turn is the lower correspondence of the brow centre.

The throat is the avenue of expression. It is a channel for expressing matters of the head (thought, inspiration) and of the heart (feeling, emotion). Its connection to both head and heart suggests that the throat chakra has a part to play in bringing thought and feeling into right relationship. Thought, unwarmed by feeling, can be calculating and potentially cruel; feeling, untempered by thought, is infantile and reactive. As we represent ourselves in speech or creative activity, we become more aware of the preoccupations of our minds and hearts, and thus create some possibility of building a bridge between them. When we resist self-expression we cultivate (perhaps quite inadvertently) inauthenticity; head and heart are then susceptible to becoming separated and unrelated to each other. The alienation of head and heart is a serious rupture between thinking and feeling; it causes a strain to develop in the throat, which is attempting to bridge the two areas. Strain in the throat is often the result of anxiety, even fear, of unworthiness and inadequacy. Withholding our speech and creative expression is a way of hiding from ourselves and from the world; it signifies that we do not trust the world to accept us as we are.

The more the activity of the throat centre is withheld, the more alienated from each other grow the head and the heart. We get to the point where we are not even sure what we think or feel. Our heads seem to be severed from our bodies. Alice Bailey refers to the resistance of the personality to the influx of soul force, affecting the activity of the throat.[41] If the throat is not kept active, expressive and open, self-expression is starved of true thought and true feeling. The correspondence of this starvation at a more refined level is the personality refusing the nourishment of the soul. We do not readily swallow (accept) what might upset our perceived, cherished stability; we resist accommodating the requirements of our higher selves because we are emotionally attached to our views, reactions and personal identities. In this way, we are prone to becoming exceedingly stuck in obsolete personality conditions.

The loss of relationship between head and heart is an emblem of the general disconnection between the individual and the environment. We have forgotten our relationship to the four directions: north, east, south and west. We exist in a state of chronic forgetfulness, which requires we consciously invoke

---

[41] Bailey (1953), p. 137.

our relationship with the directions and elements (fire, earth, air and water) and the qualities they represent. To join our heads on to our bodies, our feet to the earth, and our whole beings to the cardinal directions is a work of healing that many individuals are interested in undertaking at this time of increasing instability in conditions both external and internal. This healing is an act of intention and imagination working in unity; it requires us to come to consciousness about the fact of our being human and the qualities and responsibilities humanity confers upon us.

It is through human beings in human bodies that the material and the spiritual realms can be brought into alignment; we are bridges that link the worlds; we walk between worlds; similarly, we are the conduit through which planetary and extra-planetary forces can be brought into alignment.

There is a great deal of bridging work going on it seems! It finds its symbolic correspondences in many areas of the body, but very particularly in the neck/throat area, which shows how important the energy of Taurus is in bringing spiritual illumination to shine upon physical conditions:

> For the great task of Taurus is not the simple instruction to 'go forth and multiply' but the far deeper one of ushering in the physical manifestation of the exquisite harmony of the spheres. Into the heart of life on earth, into daily toil, into family life, into spheres practical, mental, emotional and artistic, Taurus must bring down

what his spirit has learned when he pastured in the fiery stars. ...

> Mankind must gain mastery over the powerful, vigorous bull of its animal nature, and make of it a sacrificial offering so that the vitality of its blood might be poured upon the germinating seed of the spirit, the Light Within.[42]

Taurus is the birth sign of the Buddha and the sign in which the Wesak festival occurs, celebrating Buddha's enlightenment. The Buddha is the exemplar of enlightened human life. It is through bodily experience that consciousness arises; this is, in a basic sense, the foundation of Buddhist teaching. Through mindful observation of the arising and ceasing of physical, emotional and mental phenomena we come gradually to awareness of the true nature of mind and of experience. Our physicality is continuous with consciousness. Enlightenment arises through, and as the result of, lived experience in the body–mind.

Although it is our human potential to be able to evolve beyond animal instinct, Taurus energy can be caught up in a driving desire for the satisfaction of pretty basic physical appetites and acquisitiveness. Taurus makes itself feel secure through such indulgent pursuit. Equally, at another register, the sign can be a powerful force motivating spiritual aspiration. To which level a person applies their Taurean energy is entirely dependent on their awareness and their

---

[42] Nahmad (1993), pp. 29, 34.

stage of maturity. A person's vibration may be coarse and oriented towards the physical plane, or refined and oriented towards higher planes of being. Mostly we are funny mixtures of the whole range.

Venus rules the Law of Attraction: the resonance by which like is attracted to like. What we like, what we value and what is attracted to us are reflections of qualities within us. The action of resonance is the energetic domain of Venus, which not only functions to connect higher and lower within the self, but also creates situations of resonance through the agency of other people and external circumstances. The agency of other people is what we commonly call *relationship*, and where there is resonance between people, we commonly call this love, attraction` or desire (when there is sympathy), and antagonism or aversion (when there is antipathy).

It is often through the agency of other people that we are able to find lost or forgotten aspects of ourselves that need to be worked on and integrated into our idea of self in order that we can make progress in life. Relationship presents us with a mirror that reveals what we are attached to in ourselves, but also what has been rejected; we love and reject the qualities of others accordingly, paying little regard to the enormous projections that take place between friends, relatives, companions, colleagues and lovers.

The desire and aversion we experience in our relationships are grist to the mill of the spiritual project of transmutation undertaken in Taurus. The energy of these reactions, when observed and 'owned' and seen for what they are, can be used to relate the lower nature to the higher self:

> Men have sought through physical expression to produce the inner fusion and harmony which they crave and this cannot be done. Sex is but the symbol of an inner duality which must be itself transcended and wrought into a unity. It is not transcended by physical means or rituals. It is a transcendence in consciousness.[43]

The quotation above is entirely categorical: what we crave in our sexual relationships 'cannot be done'. The necessary dissatisfaction and disenchantment arising from frustrated desire potentially serves the purpose of raising consciousness and fomenting spiritual aspiration. It is as if we have to reach a certain pitch of desperation before we get real about what might be an appropriate object for our love energy.

Attached as we are to our physical appetites (and Taurus, being a fixed sign, can become very attached indeed), the ultimate impossibility of their satisfaction is hard to swallow. Swallowing life's lessons is very much the domain of Taurus and the throat chakra. Something sticks in our craw; we cannot swallow it; we are choked; we reach to throw up. These are symptoms of rejecting what is happening in our lives: aversion. A secondary response to aversion can paradoxically be the desire to over-indulge in food, alcohol, drugs and cigarettes: we throw things down our throats,

---

[43] Bailey (1951), p. 385.

swallowing hard, to keep difficult emotions from rising out of our mouths and finding expression maybe in unruly or unseemly ways. We swallow rebellious feelings with mouthfuls of fat, sugar and carbohydrate; we swaddle our pain and sensitivities in layers of fat around our bodies. In these ways we avoid polluting our carefully constructed identities and our ways of being with difficult and potentially alienating feelings.

Dethlefsen and Dahlke write about swallowing representing integration and incorporation. Problems with swallowing or with vomiting are indications of unwillingness to accept (or downright rejection of) something that is happening in life.[44] Louise Hay's analysis concurs:

> The energy center in the throat, the fifth chakra, is the place in the body where change takes place. When we are resisting change or are in the middle of change or are trying to change, we often have a lot of activity in our throats.[45]

She suggests that problems with the throat indicate stifled creativity and a sense of inadequacy. A sore throat (being *inflamed*) suggests anger. Coughing indicates resistance and stubbornness. Hay relates tonsillitis and thyroid problems to not being able to do what you want to do.[46] If we cannot do what we want to do, we feel disempowered and separated

---

[44] Dethlefsen and Dahlke (1990), pp. 130-131.
[45] Hay (1984), p. 130.
[46] Hay (1984), pp. 130-131.

from that which we love. This can bring an experience of humiliation, which Hay thinks underlies thyroid symptoms: 'I never get to do what I want to do. When's it going to be my turn?'[47] There might well be very significant resentments behind symptoms arising in the neck and throat. When the neck is affected the Taurean quality of stubbornness comes to the fore; we speak commonly of a 'stiff-necked' attitude. Inflexibility is strongly represented by the immobility and fixity of view incurred by a neck complaint.

The quality of the throat chakra energy will be reflected in self-expression and the quality of the voice. When energy is balanced in the etheric vehicle, the head and the heart united, the voice is clear and resonant. Quality of being is reflected in the voice: an emphasis in Taurus can produce fine singers. Sound vibration has always been used to call the body into balance; spiritual practices have always included mantra or vowel song. Sound resonates through the whole body, making energy travel up and down the spine, thus re-membering the connections between the energy centres and our connections to the sacred directions. Sound can be used very practically to invoke this connectedness and inter-connectedness, and to call ourselves into the fullness of being. Working through the throat in this way is a good way forward for problems pertaining to Taurean, Venusian or second-house energies. As Venus is to the Earth what the higher self is to the personality, the potential of reviving and re-invigorating the throat may be truly illuminating.

---

[47] Hay (1984), p. 186.

Taurus tends to bestow the body with a certain stockiness and strength. As the sign of fixed earth, it often shows robust health and resilience. Its temperamental intransigence – phlegmatic to a fault – can offer great resistance, which can, of course, be both a blessing and a curse.

GEMINI
The Integrating Principle

$$\text{♊}$$

*The world materializes and man spiritualizes along the
same spiral. It is the breathing of the cosmos. With
the exhalation the spirit contracts, creates, and
involves or winds into matter; this is the creation of the
world by the breath of God. With the inhalation,
matter expands and evolves or unwinds into spirit.
Man is the heart and microcosmic controller of this
pulse. By becoming conscious he is inhaling – effecting
the return breath.*

> *We breathe in only to breathe out; this is true
of the universe no less than of man, who was created
in the same image. This is why the life of each person
is conceived, in so many mystical, religious, and
mythological systems, as the conscious unwinding of
the original coils of manifestation.*[48]

Gemini rules the lungs, and Mercury, the bodily process of
respiration. Respiration is, of course, the interchange
between without and within, self and not-self, which is

---

[48] Purce (1974), pp. 11-12.

absolutely fundamental to life. The first breath of life taken by the newborn, marks the moment of the soul's incarnation into form (the movement from the state of total dependence to independence of the mother's body). Breath reveals, paradoxically, both independence and interdependence; it defines the very parameters of self and not-self by crossing the thresholds of the individual body. In this repeated crossing back and forth – interweaving – between the bodily self and its environment, we are rendered simultaneously separate (differentiated, individual, independent) and contingent (interdependent, contiguous, co-existent). The breath shows us how we are woven into the fabric of life: 'We are the ebb, we are the flow; we are the warp, we are the weft; we are the web.'[49]

This paradox of unity and duality is essential to the human experience; it is fundamental to the development of consciousness, which relies on *duality* to realise *unity*. The experience of duality incurs the suffering of separative consciousness (the sense that we are separate from each other and from the web of being, existentially alone in Fortress Self); but occasionally the scales fall from our eyes and we have moments of piercing this veil of illusion – *seeing through* – and perceiving the Oneness that gives the lie to the illusion of duality. When god created the first human, so myth has it, he plucked a reed from the riverbed and by making holes in it fashioned it into a flute. Blowing into it, god is able to play the music of human existence; the winds of

---

[49] This phrase was shared with me and attributed to the Northumbrian monastics.

life pass through the flute and make all kinds of music: the variety of human experience. Rumi writes:

> A craftsman pulled a reed from the reedbed,
> cut holes in it, and called it a human being.
>
> Since then, it's been wailing a tender agony
> of parting, never mentioning the skill
> that gave it life as a flute.[50]

'Respiration' shares its root etymologically with the words 'inspiration' and 'spirit': *spirare*, meaning *to breathe*. Breath is the animating principle, the conduit of the holy spirit into our experience; it is that which calls us into life – inspires us – at all levels. Similarly, working with the breath will take us from the separative, personality perspective towards a greater awareness of spirit and connectedness. We have a tendency, of course, to breathe without awareness; much of the time this can mean we breathe shallowly, with very restricted lung capacity. The effect of shallow breathing is to create an undercurrent of anxiety; rapid, shallow breathing is associated with fear in our instinctual experience, an aspect of the fight or flight response. People are taught how to overcome panic attacks by mastering their breathing. When we breathe deeply and with awareness we are far more capable of soothing the Gemini-ruled nervous system and remaining calm and centred in the body, for the body rests more in its gravity line, relaxed and at ease, allowing a natural and full

---

[50] Rumi (1998), p. 44.

energy flow. We instinctively associate full breathing with wellbeing, and so cultivating the full breath will contribute towards wellbeing.

Many relaxation and meditation techniques begin with learning to focus attention on the breath, because the breath conditions so strongly the way we experience our bodies and our lives more generally. Re-training the breathing is a method of re-training the way we experience life, and thereby construct our realities. Gemini, Mercury and the third house of the birth chart pertain to how we encounter our immediate environments, and how we assemble our personal realities: the lens of perception.

The breath is the indicator of how we allow the flow of spirit, energy and vitality into our bodies and beings. Tension creates constrictions and blocks in the body that restrict the movement of the breath (spirit) in and out of our lives. Approximately 70 per cent of toxins are eliminated through the exhalation; holding on to the out-breath (an effect of stress) is, quite simply, a poisonous activity. Conscious use of the out-breath can be effective in releasing old memories and patterns that have been deeply internalised. In her book, *The Sorcerer's Crossing*, Taisha Abelar recounts the method by which she freed herself of her past by making a 'recapitulation' (as part of her shamanic training), which is a thorough and systematic remembering of the past and releasing it from the body with a special out-breath.[51] The breath holds enormous potential for healing.

The breathing will also show how we hold on to energy that is 'spent' and how we resist opening ourselves to the influx of the new. Resistance to change and attachment to old patterns (however unpleasant, limiting and harmful) may find expression in the breath. Breathing reflects how we let life flow into and out of our existences. With each breath, *prana* (vital energy) passes directly into the etheric vehicle and is mainly received through the heart centre. Thus, it is fair to assume that Gemini and the third house of the birth chart rule the heart chakra (though not the organ, which is ruled by Leo). Breathing is also therefore an indicator of the condition of the heart chakra; just as the breath must be allowed to flow fully in and out of the lungs, so love must flow into and out of the heart chakra if the heart is to be nourished, healthy, open and free of tensions. A block or tension in the heart chakra will be accompanied by a restriction in the breath, signalling the problem that is arising at a non-physical level. Working to bring awareness and fullness to the breath will encourage the heart centre to relax, release and open.

Gemini also rules the hands, arms and shoulders. This is interesting for two reasons: first, because of the relationship between the breathing and the arms; and second, because it underscores the idea of inflow and outflow between the self

---

[51] Abelar (1992).

and not-self that we have established as a Gemini theme. The diaphragm (ruled by Gemini) is the big muscle between the thorax and the abdomen that is moved up and down by the breath. It is connected to the shoulder blades and the arms through the thoracic spine. The muscles of the shoulders and the diaphragm connect to the twelfth thoracic vertebra: the breath, the shoulders and the movement of the arms are thus directly related to each other through the spine (ruled by the Sun). The diaphragm also marks the bridge between the higher and lower chakras (and the higher and lower levels of experience pertaining to them). The arms, hands and shoulders are our tools for receiving *from* the world and giving *to* the world. We give and take through the hands; the dexterity of the hands determines how we deal with and model the stuff of our lives; the strength of the arms and the mobility conferred by the shoulders condition our ability to give and take effectively.

The lesson of the breath for the arms is that just as the breath must be allowed fully in and fully out, so we must be generous givers and grateful receivers: our giving and taking must be in balance. It is a strong idea with us that it is more blessed to give than to receive, but this is nonsense and cannot be. It is blessed to give and to receive in equal measure; the more we give, the more we are able to receive; the more we receive, the more we can give.

The principle of Mercury is communication. Our arms and hands are our working and communicating tools; using them we become active and effective in the world. They are the communicators between self and not-self, bringing the world of not-self towards us and offering the world of self outwards. The arms and hands pertain to how we interact with our environments. Problems in the arms or hands could point to several mental–emotional states: the wish to retreat from the immediate environment; retraction from the human commerce of giving and receiving; the desire to resist 'reality'; or to a block in the ability to give or receive love.

In *The Healing Power of Illness*, Dethlefsen and Dahlke correspond the hands with the ability to act and comprehend. Astrology would strongly support this thesis as comprehension is very definitely the province of Gemini, Mercury and the third house. Louise Hay writes of the arms as expressing our ability to embrace life experiences. The *capacity* to do this she assigns to the upper arms; the *ability* to our lower arms. The distinction between capacity and ability is not sharp, but it is quite a useful one to make: capacity can be understood as referring to *how much* we can handle, and ability to *how* we handle it. How we handle things is also expressed through the hands:

> The hands grasp, hands hold, hands clench. We let things slip through our fingers. Sometimes we hold on too long. ...
> We [get] a handle on something. It's hands down. It's hands off, hanky panky. We give someone a hand, are hand in hand, it's on hand or out of hand, underhanded or overhanded. We have helping hands.

Hands can be gentle, or they can be hard with knotty knuckles from overthinking or gnarled with arthritic criticism. Grasping hands come from fear; fear of loss, fear of never having enough, fear that it won't stay if you hold lightly.[52]

It is notable that Gemini rules these pairs (the lungs, the arms, the hands) because Gemini is, of course, the sign of the Twins. Liz Greene (in *The Astrology of Fate*) develops the mythical background of the signs; in the case of Gemini she draws on the myth of the twins, Castor and Pollux, one of whom is mortal, the other immortal.[53] The myth of the twins portrays the relation between the higher and lower aspects of the self: the soul and the personality, and the spirit and the soul. This can be thought of as the level of alignment that exists between the higher self and the lower, personality aspect of self. The spiritual task of transforming energy from lower to higher is one of aligning the lower self with the higher. Gemini's rulership of the arms and hands is indicative of the services the two brothers must render to each other in dissolving the separative (polarised) relation that has existed between them for so long.[54]

The energy of fusion that comes through the sign of Gemini oversees the polarised interplay between seeming opposites. Through this interplay, consciousness arises. When the Sun is in Gemini there is a struggle for fusion between the soul and

---

[52] Hay (1984), p. 131.
[53] Greene (1997), pp. 189-196.
[54] Bailey (1951), p. 366.

the form (personality) life; when Gemini is on the ascendant the struggle is for fusion between soul and spirit. The heart chakra is the 'organ of fusion'. As the heart centre becomes active, the individual is slowly drawn into an increasingly closer relation to his soul … . He is drawn into a close service relationship with humanity. His growing sense of responsibility, due to heart activity, leads him to serve and work.[55]

When the heart chakra opens, energy is lifted from the lower chakras (below the diaphragm), concerned with instinct and personality, to the higher chakras (the heart, throat, brow and crown), which are concerned with *transpersonal* (group consciousness) experience and spiritual development. Emotional pain in the heart area (for example, fear of vulnerability, feelings of heartbreak, emotional numbness, etc.) points to the withholding of love that may be due to the fear of surrendering personality to the transpersonal realm of the heart: 'The love that you withhold is the pain you carry.'[56]

As we have said, human experience is quintessentially one of the interchange of spirit and matter, mind and body; we are the mode by which heaven and earth meet and make their exchanges. As Gemini governs the interplay between dualities, *its energy underlies all the other polarities of the zodiac*. Gemini has a restlessness and versatility that can manifest as anxiety or superficiality; it seeks stimulation and

---

[55] Bailey (1953), pp. 160-161.
[56] Attributed to Ralph Waldo Emerson.

change to such an extent that it can be in danger of skating over the surface of life without much awareness of the deeper levels of experience. A certain agility and nervousness is bestowed by Mercury, the orthodox ruler of Gemini. As Gemini rules the nervous system, manifestations of nervous illness – anxiety, depression, hyperactivity, over-/under-stimulation – will likely pertain to Mercury and the third house of the chart. The nervous system conditions our experience of reality: its impact on perception is that great. Learning some techniques for dealing with agitation, fear, anxiety and negative thinking will crucially improve mental and emotional health.

Mercury rules sensory perception (taste, touch, sight, smell and hearing), which describe how a person relates to the world around them. They may be resistant to something in their environment. Chronically, such resistance impacts upon the senses. Sensory impairment is a somatic restriction of the conveyance of the external to the internal. For example, tinnitus or hearing impairment may express the desire not to hear someone or something else. Sensory processing impairments can arise when the boundary between self and not-self is not clearly felt, rendering the sensory system overwhelmed (hyper-arousal); or when the boundary is so strong that stimuli from the outside are only weakly perceived (hypo-arousal). Our senses establish our connections with our own physical bodies, with the world and to the earth. Their operation defines our perceptions which in turn describe our reality. It is interesting to reflect on how highly individualised our 'realities' are – unnerving even!

What is made available to our senses in terms of experience shapes our realities. *Sensation is continuous with consciousness.* For example, if our sensory experience is derived from climbing trees, swimming in rivers and eating food we have grown ourselves, we will have a very different range of perceptions to that which arises from spending hours online, eating processed food and not going outdoors. Healthy development requires sense-rich experiences. Sensory pathologies will arise from restricted sensory opportunities because senses need nourishment. The personal realities resulting from lives of sensory malnutrition are impoverished, just as food lacking in leaves us hungry and malnourished. The information required for health is found in physical life; it is unavailable from virtual experience.

We are currently training the human sensorium to deteriorate as we spend more and more of our lives online. The upshot of this is that an increasing sense of *unreality* and disconnection pervade lived experience. The body, whose physicality is non-negotiable, speaks up for the necessity of living an embodied life, interacting with and nourished by experience in the physical world. It speaks up by presenting us with pathologies that express how we, as individuals, are suffering from cultural alienation from the physical, natural world: neurological dysfunction.

Mercury is the messenger of the gods, the planet of information and its processing, interaction and communication. It speeds around the Sun (travelling close to it), carrying energetic messages between the signs and planets and thus giving our experience coherence and congruency. With Venus and the Sun, Mercury forms the 'triad of personality'; its orbit is 88 days and it is never further than 28 degrees from the Sun. It determines the way in which we seek to integrate different experiences and energies, and thus how we learn and shape our realities. Mercury is the communicator – the pollinator, in a sense – between the self and the various elements of not-self. Like the breath and like the arms, Mercury has the function of weaving between and thus interrelating apparent polarities. Mercury is also the psychopomp, the guide of souls; he guides us into life (marked by the first breath) and takes us into death (marked by the last breath).

Mercury's rulership of sensory perception and the nervous system shows its sensitivity. It governs the reception and transmission of energy – of which information is one variety; it therefore requires a high level of sensitivity. This however has the tendency of producing an over-reactive, nervous disposition that is too much involved with its own stories and dramas to be able to see the wider context and meaning of experience. Depth and focus of mind can be limited under Gemini's influence due to the chatter of its 'monkey-mind'. Mercury and Gemini in the birth chart can indicate areas of over-sensitivity and physical weakness. As Mercury is so fast-moving, it is *impacted* upon by slower-moving planets (both natally and by transiting activity). Therefore, Mercury in the chart is an area that is likely to manifest a problem that is actually emanating from the domain indicated by the slower-moving planet. Mercury is the means by which the deeper meaning of the slower planet enters consciousness and makes itself available for healing and development: conscious integration.

The integrating principle represented by Gemini and its ruler suggests not only the traditional Geminian theme of communication, but also, more profoundly, of communion. Communion is an integrated state of being, facilitated by communication. The energy of Gemini is graphically illustrated in the idea of language, which it rules. Language is a definingly human gift, made by breath moving in and out of the body, vibrating the vocal cords. It consists of vowels (breath moving through the open mouth), which represent spirit, and consonants (breath moving through the partially obstructed mouth), which represent matter. So language is the interaction between spirit and matter. The making of language through this interaction is also the basis for making meaning. The former activity belongs to Gemini and the third house; the latter to their polarity, Sagittarius and the ninth house. We call realities into being in Gemini and the third house, and assume them as contexts of meaning and significance in Sagittarius and the ninth house. In the words of Neale Donald Walsh, 'Your thought about something is creative, and your word is productive, and your thought and your word together are magnificently effective in giving birth to your reality.'[57]

---

[57] Walsh (1997), p. 10.

Integration occurs between polarities under the auspices of Gemini. Information is sought in the third house, knowledge (particularly wisdom-knowledge) in the ninth. For example, astrology is a ninth-house matter and as such reflects upon, and provides context for, personal reality, assembled in the third house. Astrology details the interactions between our energy fields, showing us how intimately we are interwoven with each other, our tribes and environments (immediate, planetary and galactic). In this way it continually interrogates the third-house concern of what reality consists in for the individual, leading to continual reappraisal and reconstruction of that reality. The meaning-making function of the ninth house is redemptive: where there is meaning there is the possibility for faith. Problems with respiration, arms, shoulders, the nervous system and heart centre point to distortions in our perception of reality; they may well be illuminated by exploring these existential matters of perception, meaning, rationality and faith.

> We need not create our own meaning in this universe. The spontaneous motion of life toward unity is meaning in itself. The pain stuck in our bodies is stagnant meaning, which simply needs breath and awareness to move again. The meaning of life, the clear light of love and wisdom, rides through our body on our breath, more deeply and tangibly as we evolve.[58]

---

[58] Blackstone (1991), p. 88.

CANCER
Emotional Intelligence

You are in process of incarnation; you are following your chosen way. Is the house you are building yet lit? Is it a lighted house? Or is it a dark prison? If it is a lighted house, you will attract to its light and warmth all who are around you and the magnetic pull of your soul, whose nature is light and love, will save many. [...] Some are lost in the illusion and know not what is reality and truth. Others walk free in the world of illusion for the purposes of saving and lifting their brothers, and if you cannot do this, you will have to learn so to walk.[59]

Cancerian energy is the energy of belonging, reflected by the connection between mother and child. The mother is the vessel that carries a being from the world of spirit into the world of life in form; she is the symbol of continuity between past life and the present incarnation, and is represented in the birth chart by the Moon, Cancer's ruler. The mother is a

---

[59] Bailey (1951), p. 343.

bridge between lifetimes. Or, if a belief in past lives is absent, we can call the mother the bridge into this lifetime, the Moon describing the conditioning of early life, which is also completely valid. The Moon represents the memory of a past life that is impressing, or lodging within, the emotional body giving us all kinds of default emotional responses.[60] This is necessary for orientation but is also something we need to outgrow in order not simply to remain stuck in the conditions of an obsolete identity. Remaining within the orbit of the Moon is devitalising emotionally, spiritually and physically.

The Sun shows us where the centre of gravity for our current lifetime needs to be: this is where we are breaking new ground for consciousness and this is the path of growth and development. We need to move off of the Moon; it offers us resources for the journey we need to make towards the power and vitality of the Sun. This is not to say that the Moon is not of value, but that its value is released and its potential realised when it points us towards the Sun. This has its analogy in astronomy.

The Sun, we know, is the source of light, warmth and thus life on Earth. The Moon is a reflector of the Sun's light. It has none of its own. My reflection in the mirror is of me, but it is not me. The lunar consciousness (which pertains to our habits and emotions that keep us clinging to security, stuck firmly within the compound of the known) is ever the saboteur of our ability to find our way forward. It is

---

[60] It is interesting in this context to note that the Moon rules the limbic system, which is involved in the formation of memory and emotions.

essentially neurotic and obstructs the *way it is*; and it is strengthened by our departure from real-life encounters in the physical world in favour of the virtual realm, which is only ever a reflection of the real just as the Moon's light is only a reflection of the Sun. Our current evacuation of embodied experience (I am writing this during the Covid pandemic) is a danger for us: the human task it is to bring spiritual forces to the physical world, *not* to the panoply of attention-harvesting devices to be found online! Quite simply, we need to be connected to each other and to physical reality, just to be OK.

The cultivation of lunar consciousness makes us very susceptible to unhelpful emotional reactions (e.g. fear, worry, irritation) that thrive when we are ungrounded and not strongly present to our physical experience (we know what fantastical states the mind and emotions can whip us into, especially in the middle of the Moon-ruled night). There is a distinction then to be made between fantasy and reality. Negative emotions and states of mind, when we get stuck in them, challenge the body's immune response and ultimately make us sick.

It is through the umbilical connection that we first receive nourishment and the Moon rules matters pertaining to feeding, nurturing, the maternal feminine and the experience of home. Anatomically, Cancer rules the womb, the breasts, oesophagus, stomach and alimentary canal, and the lower ribs. These mostly soft parts of the frontal body pertain to receptivity, nourishment and vulnerability. These qualities are also the gifts of the sign, though negatively can manifest as defensive touchiness, moodiness and impressionability.

Cancer is cardinal yin energy belonging to the watery triplicity. The power of yin is often underestimated, even denigrated, in our culture. Yin energy is passive, receptive, yielding and containing. The womb, a liminal place between worlds, is the first 'home' we know. Like the calyx of a flower or the cauldron of the goddess in Celtic mythology, it is a seemingly magical vessel where creation is made manifest. It is an intensive environment, a place of protection, nurture and peace, allowing the foetus to develop and grow in optimal conditions. Peace and protection are preconditions for the work of development; if we cannot find them without, we must certainly cultivate them within. Cancer and the fourth house describe the home in its mundane reality; the less obvious aspect of 'home' is that it is the space for inwardness, inner searching, psychological journeying and the cultivation of awareness. There is a correspondence between the home as a private space and the inner life. The fourth house of the birth chart signifies the place of sanctuary, contemplation and meditative work – working towards conscious self-development – as well as signifying our dwelling places.

The womb, the home and the inner life are all places of creativity and the development of potential, which can be given full self-conscious, outward expression in Leo and the fifth house. Physical or emotional problems pertaining to creativity and the development of potential are likely to be expressed through the womb. Commonly these manifest as fibroids, menstrual problems and conditions sufficiently uncomfortable as to be treated by surgical removal. What happens to unresolved issues pertaining to a body part when that body part is removed? Our drive to eradicate symptoms can perpetuate illness, for it interrupts the dialogue the intelligent body is attempting. A symptom, rightly regarded, is the first sure step towards healing: 'at one and the same time a signal and a vehicle of information.'[61] It shows us what needs healing and how; it is simply an attempt to come to consciousness. Unresolved issues deprived of their primary site of expression find another appropriate lodging in the body or are driven into the outer world of events and circumstances. This is by no means to say that it is inappropriate to intervene surgically, as, of course, it may well be necessary to do in many situations.

Having outgrown our umbilical connection to the mother, nourishment is sustained through the breast. The breasts describe the relationship to mothering, nurturing and giving to dependants. Louise Hay makes the remark that part of this mothering process is letting the thing that is nurtured grow up. To create a state of dependency in offspring, 'smother-love', is as pernicious as neglect. A major issue of maternity is knowing when to hold on and when to let go. The womb must deliver the babe; the nursing infant must outgrow the breast; the childhood home must release the young adult into independence. Rejection of, or clinging to, the role of mother are conditions that, if held chronically, tend to manifest

---

[61] Dethlefsen and Dahlke (1990), p. 10.

through the breasts. As the breasts are also the visible – and, in our culture, highly sexualised – expression of femininity, they will often suggest how a woman relates to her feminine sexuality (a matter which is conditioned through the experience of the female line of her family).

The vulnerability of the Moon can lead it to be excessively self-protective; it armours itself either by attempting to bind others to it in pseudo-umbilical connections of emotional co-dependency, or by fleshing itself out through over-eating, or by more subtle forms of psychological armouring that may manifest in the body as painful lumps in the breasts, amongst other things. Cancer – indicating the need for nourishment – can create guzzlers and gorgers. We drown our sorrows and we stuff our faces, feeding ourselves up against the emptiness inside or stuffing down disruptive emotions. Similarly, nourishment can be refused or feeding patterns disrupted by a dysfunctional relationship with the feminine: witness the range of eating disorders increasingly being expressed by pubescent girls and boys, and adults alike. Such imbalances reflect feelings being choked back and suppressed, particularly the craving for love and an overwhelming sense of need for nurturance, safety and belonging.

The relationship with the personal mother, or with the maternal feminine in general, needs to be interrogated when we encounter problems such as these. Often there is a lingering sense that the mother – *or importantly, the motherline* – was in some way unreliable (either under-protective or over-protective), leaving the Inner Child with the desire to be held, nourished, nurtured and unconditionally loved (i.e. all-powerful and entirely irresponsible). Snarl-ups in Cancerian energy can tend to create such patterns of maternal/infant manipulation and control, which hold people in thrall to infantile modes of relating in many aspects of their adult lives. While this is unavoidable to some extent, the cost of this regressive mode to the development of consciousness hardly needs to be elaborated. The Moon's 'pull of the past' is very familiar to us: another aspect of our individual and cultural journey towards fully adult expressions of wo/manhood. As I have said, the personal mother and father are bridges we walk across from one lifetime to another; they orient us in our current lifetime by echoing realities we have known in past lives. If we try and stay on the bridge we can impede and obstruct the authentic expression of our true identities. We do not have to sever our connection with parents, but we do need of necessity to separate from them as we become adults.

To nourish ourselves we have to swallow, and Cancer rules the oesophagus and the stomach. The oesophagus does the swallowing and the stomach receives and holds (or fails to receive and hold) what is swallowed. What we can swallow is common parlance for what we can 'allow'. Swallowing, allowing and receptivity are registered through the stomach and oesophagus. A healthy stomach can receive and contain a whole range of foods. The primary function of the stomach is the yin function of receptivity:

It takes in all the impressions that come from outside and receives whatever is to be digested. The ability to receive requires openness, passivity and willingness (in the sense of self-surrender). With these properties the stomach represents the feminine role. ... The feminine principle expresses receptivity, self-surrender, susceptibility and the ability to receive and contain.[62]

Problems with the stomach show that there is an inability to receive and assimilate what is going on in the experience of life. We use the expressions 'I can't stomach it', 'I can't swallow it'. Dethlefsen and Dahlke relate stomach problems principally to problems around the ability to feel, and the realm of feelings:

If we drive out of our consciousness the capacity to feel, this function descends to the bodily level, where it is the stomach that now has to take in and digest not merely the impress of our physical food, but our psychological feelings too.[63]

Often, the psychological feelings we are less ready to express pertain to our aggressive drives, which become in the environment of the stomach literally corrosive. The over-production of acid, causing ulceration of the stomach lining, indicates that a person is engaged in digesting the stomach itself ('It's eating me up!') rather than entering into conflict

---

[62] Dethlefsen and Dahlke (1990), p. 131.
[63] Dethlefsen and Dahlke (1990), p. 132.

and dealing with the cause of the 'acidity'. This line of thought encourages Dethlefsen and Dahlke to suggest that those who suffer with their stomachs are unwilling to express aggression outwardly and enter into open conflict.[64]

The possibility of Cancer and the Moon energy in the birth chart is *conscious* sensitivity and *conscious* emotional intelligence; the self-awareness arising from such consciousness creates the willingness and openness to accommodate feelings, impressions and experiences and make these available to the purposeful vitality of the solar energy. The Moon indicates, by sign and house, a weak place in the body. It is where we are conditioned by the past and by habits that will inevitably create blocks in consciousness, which then seek to come to our attention through physical manifestation. As the Moon is the fastest-moving body in the solar system it is impacted, astrologically, by all other bodies: everything *impresses* the Moon. Its susceptibility to register impacts makes it capable of creating continuity, by synthesising and relating the past to the present. However, identification with the Moon energy creates low vitality and, ultimately, frustration, because it is identification with a former mode of being (a memory) which is compromising and undermining the requirements of the present experience. The Moon gives us resources and experiences on which to build towards the Sun energy: that is its usefulness. It is all a matter of becoming conscious of our regressive modes and being willing to learn to re-route our energy into conscious,

---

[64] Dethlefsen and Dahlke (1990), pp. 132-133.

responsible, purposeful modes of activity. Dethlefsen and Dahlke sum this dynamic up in a characteristically uncompromising, indeed rather tetchy, comment on sufferers of stomach problems – though let us not forget that we all have a Moon to work with in our birth charts and we are all learning to deal with our emotional reactions; the need for love and belonging are entirely valid (though we have to supply these for ourselves once we are adults):

> What stomach sufferers need to learn is to make themselves aware of their own feelings, to get to conscious grips with their conflicts and consciously to digest incoming impressions. Furthermore, ulcer patients need not only to become aware of, but actually admit to, their desire for infantile dependence and maternal security and their longing to be loved and cared for – even (indeed, especially) if these desires are well-hidden behind a façade of independence, competence and pride. In this, as ever, the stomach speaks the truth.[65]

---

[65] Dethlefsen and Dahlke (1990), p. 134.

LEO
The Courage of Consciousness

When we realize that our primary destiny is to become fully ourselves, we can accept any circumstance that brings us closer to that goal. Illness is part of our dialogue with our wholeness; it is part of the healing process itself. Pain naturally brings our attention to those aspects of ourselves we have wanted to ignore. Above all, pain and illness are a request for our own love and care.[66]

The opening quote pertains strongly to the healing issues constellating around the sign of Leo because it brings together the themes of *becoming fully ourselves,* illness as a path of consciousness and the necessity of love. Leo, the Sun and the fifth house of the birth chart are about individual consciousness of *self* – selfhood – and the purposefulness, power, creativity and flow of love that are released when we learn, and align with, who and what we are. Through Leo, the Sun and the fifth house we become aware of our uniqueness:

---

[66] Blackstone (1991), p. 114-115.

the particular qualities and *beingness* that we embody as individuals: the eros of uniqueness. Leo lends these qualities a certain distinction, which beckons the attention of others and earns the individual recognition. It is crucial that the Leo Sun or Leo rising individual receives this recognition, but to do so they must cultivate and *reveal* their individuality. The Sun must shine, and must be seen to be shining! Suzanne Rough has remarked that without receiving recognition some part of the Leo person dies. [67] If an individual's Sun energy (the placement of the Sun in the birth chart) is not identified, the lifeforce will not be sufficiently engaged to ensure wellbeing.

It is a question of where a person's centre of gravity falls. Recall that we are souls using the vehicle of the personality (a body, some predispositions and life circumstances) in order to break new ground for consciousness. If we stay stuck in the conditioning of early life (or past life – astrologically, it is the same thing) we are prone to simply repeating patterns. Then we are like actors identifying ourselves with the role we are playing, forgetful of the fact that we are actors with a life beyond this one of the current role. This is the lunar consciousness, discussed in the previous essay. Our lifetimes are a process of remembering that our little, temporal lives are held by the great life of our soul forces: remembering we are actors playing a role. This remembering is redemptive and deeply healing. Our centre of gravity, our orientation, needs to be in the solar consciousness for us to be whole and well. This allows us to use our challenges more effectively, to bring

---

[67] https://www.dkfoundation.co.uk.

soul force into the context of our daily lives, creating fracture lines whereby the other worlds can potentise the physical world. When I say 'other worlds' I am referring to all that is non-apparent in our normal realm: past, future, present, above, below, cosmic forces, karmic forces, ancestors, etc.[68]

It is a challenge for most people to move into their Sun energy. It is often new and untested. We are attracted towards it because it beckons and excites us, and rewards us when we respond. The solar path is pleasurable but it is not easy. Responding to the call of the Sun increases vitality, personal power and a sense of purpose. The Sun rules Leo, and for all of us, no matter which sign the Sun occupies in our charts, indicates (by sign, house and aspect) the qualities we need to cultivate if we are to develop full self-awareness, fulfil our potentials and activate our purposefulness, vitality and health.

To speak of coming to consciousness is really to speak of the project of human life at large. We are formations of energy that, coming to earth, manifest in bodies; it is through our sensate bodies that we experience the world, and through sensation that we come to consciousness: 'Just as letters and numbers are formal vehicles for the ideas which underlie them, so everything *visible*, everything concrete and functional, is purely an expression of an idea, and thus a mediator of the invisible.'[69] As consciousness arises through

---

[68] There are very many different descriptors of other worlds; I'm just alluding to some possibilities.
[69] Dethlefsen and Dahlke (1990), p. 5.

the body (the physical form that clothes the unseen human energy pattern), we can see that what we call illness (unwanted symptoms and sensations expressed by the body) is the body manifesting a process that is occurring within these energy patterns. The manifestation is a signal to consciousness of what is happening at less tangible levels.

Bodily symptoms are, at bottom, an expression of the attempt to come to consciousness, and coming to consciousness is the fundamental purpose of taking human form. They point to where and how our soul life is impeded. The body is the interface between the other worlds of past, future, present, of cosmic and ancestral forces, because these other worlds are available to consciousness through bodily experience. The soul journeys over many lifetimes in its quest for an increasingly inclusive consciousness. It operates through form (the body and the personality) – that is to say, it *manifests* – in order to acquire experiences and developmental opportunities. According to Hilarion, the law of self-expression means that *one must express* internal essence:

> Man descends into physical matter in order to learn about himself. If he refuses to allow out that which is within, how is he ever to learn what he is really like? The law thus calls for expression of the internal essence. ... The function of earth life is such that one's entire *environment* takes up and reflects back the essential traits that are within.[70]

---

[70] Hilarion (1982), p. 25.

That is really something on which to ponder! The outward world, as we experience it, is an expression of the inner situation. The Gospel of Thomas spells out the same reflection with even greater clarity:

> If you bring forth what is within you then what is within you will save you. If you do not bring forth what is within you then what is within you will destroy you.[71]

Coming to consciousness relies upon a truthful encounter with our physical experience and all that manifests in the 'worlds' we inhabit; we are manifesting what we are – 'the essential traits that are within'. The sign of Leo and the placement and condition of the Sun in the birth chart signal where and how the soul is operating through the personality; that is to say, Leo and the Sun represent the current identity being assumed in any one lifetime.

Orthodox astrology tells us that the Sun represents identity, purposefulness, vitality and power potential. Certainly, if we learn to identify the Sun energy in our lives and orient ourselves towards its requirements, we will, wittingly or not, be drawing ourselves into alignment with the higher self, and it is this alignment that is the source of any power, purpose or vitality we may acquire. Failure to orient ourselves towards solar energy, however, will result in futility, decreasing vitality

---

[71] Gospel of Thomas, verse 70.

and a radical lack of confidence. Obviously, then, the astrologer concerned with personal or spiritual development always gives a thorough delineation of the Sun in the chart. The challenges and difficulties we face in life are always useful to the extent that they reveal shortcomings in consciousness, which serve to point to the development that needs to take place. That development will always be centralised and synthesised by the Sun, which is, then, the lynchpin of any consultation.   A birth chart is the picture of a predicament: it shows where we have been (what we already know, resources we already have) and the pull of that past upon us, and where we are heading and the developmental requirement to gain the power to accomplish self-actualisation. There is a dynamic tension between the past and our potential. We can use our challenges to work with this tension, oriented towards our rightful identity – when we know what that identity is, as described by the Sun.

The Sun is the central organiser of the individual's life force just as it is the centre of our solar system. The Sun is the principle that organises and integrates all of the other energies in the birth chart, because it is the centre around which they must orbit. The Sun is our source, our star: the representative of the stellar level (which pertains to higher consciousness) in our small corner of the cosmos. Seeking to align ourselves with our solar energy is essential to our wellbeing: it is the key to the contribution we, as individuals, need to make to humanity and to Gaia in the development of planetary consciousness.

In Leo we become conscious of self and demarcate our individuality, but this is not an end in itself. Leo is in polarity with Aquarius, the sign of group consciousness and communal endeavour. The trajectory of Leo is to become self-conscious in order to affiliate and give the gifts of self to the group. Self-serving uniqueness, individuality as the be-all and end-all, is a *stage* in development, not its goal. Leo rules the heart, just as Aquarius rules the circulation: they make sense of each other. Indeed, they require each other to the extent that they are unimaginable without each other. We know that opposite signs are continuous with each other, just as the yin and the yang are continuous and inseparable. However, it is not so easy for us to accept, as a practical reality, the notion that self-consciousness is contingent upon group consciousness, or that the group develops awareness only to the extent that its members have self-consciousness.

Pursuit of selfish desire (masquerading as individuality) in our consumerist culture is one reason for our diminishing sense of meaningful community; at this time many people are engaged in instigating new group formations or reinvigorating old modes of communality as we seek to locate ourselves in constituencies and communities that bestow political power, shared responsibility, security and the meaningfulness conferred by common vision. This is not argued as a historical point, but offered rather as an observation based on the principles of astrology: the pursuit of selfhood (Leo) can only be taken so far before it implodes, at which point it registers a hunger for communal context, shared meaning and 'tribal' identity (Aquarius). Collectively this is a point that we have reached.

The dangers of selfhood taken too far are obvious: self-importance, self-indulgence and autocratic isolation. Carlos Castaneda's teacher, Don Juan, was of the opinion that self-importance was both the sorcerer's supreme enemy and the 'nemesis of mankind' (and he could be describing negative Leo):

> Don Juan's argument was that most of our energy goes into upholding our importance. This is most obvious in our endless worry about the presentation of the self, about whether or not we are admired or liked or acknowledged. He reasoned that if we were capable of losing some of that importance, two extraordinary things would happen to us. One, we would free our energy from trying to maintain the illusory idea of our grandeur; and, two, we would provide ourselves with enough energy to enter into the second attention to catch a glimpse of the actual grandeur of the universe.[72]

The point is made in Alice Bailey's *Esoteric Astrology,* that often people are convinced they are self-aware when in fact they are simply oriented towards self-satisfaction and operating as the dramatic centre of their own universe. There is a distinction to be made between self-awareness and

---

[72] Castaneda (1993), p. 37.

selfishness: 'the only truly self-conscious person is the man [or woman] who is aware of purpose, of a self-directed life and of a developed and definite life plan and programme.'[73] We are all to varying degrees *glamorised* by self and the 'dramatic I'. The antidote to this glamorised self-perception is authentic awareness of the deep presence (sometimes referred to as the 'I Am' presence) that runs steadily like a river behind the desires and dramas of the 'dramatic I': Self, soul, the witnessing presence. The Uranian vision of Aquarius and the expansiveness of Jupiter (the esoteric ruler of Aquarius) help illuminate the path towards authenticity and awareness of the environing group. Self-discipline is then required to walk the path thus illuminated; without such discipline an 'unexpectedly futile life' results. The lion, Bailey remarks, must emerge from its lair.[74]

In the body, Leo rules the heart, the spine and the sides of the body. It also rules the eyes. Some astrologers make the distinction that the Sun rules the left eye of the female and the right eye of the male, while the Moon rules the right eye of the female and the left eye of the male. The symbol for the Sun (☉) is obviously eyelike, and seeing is the product of illumination (which is a function of the forces of light and life that flow from the Sun). The eyes are traditionally understood to be the seat of the soul. As the Sun in the birth chart represents the current project of the soul functioning through the personality, there is an evident equation between Sun, soul and the eye. Sylvia Brinton Perera makes the point

---

[73] Bailey (1951), p. 288.
[74] Bailey (1951), p. 310.

that 'in Sumerian poetry the expression "the eyes of life" is used to suggest seeing that is full of love and gives vitality'.[75] Good vision results from allowing in light (the Sun, consciousness, openness). Maybe 'the eyes of life' can be regarded as the seeing that arises from fully-realised Leo energy: open-hearted, vital and aware. In a very basic sense, problems with the eyes manifest in not seeing clearly and resistance to clear vision: a rejection, or at least an obfuscation or glamorisation, of consciousness. Practitioners of the Bates Method of vision improvement have observed that vision worsens at particular times of life: around age eight, adolescence and early adulthood.[76] This comes as no surprise to the astrologer, ever mindful of the Saturn cycle, the seven/eight-year cycle which challenges the current identity at around age 7, 14, 21, 28, etc. Saturn marks the great staging posts in the journey of life and the process of maturation, and Saturn it is that sets up a great challenge to the Sun, as conditioned reality (ruled by Saturn) attempts to establish limits to the innovations of new consciousness.[77]

When we talk about heart and spine we are colloquially referring to courage. Someone who is not very hearty or who lacks backbone is one who retreats, who seems to weaken in the face of life's challenges. This is precisely someone who lacks a sense of self, who makes no claims on behalf of 'I' or

---

[75] Perera (1981), p. 31.

[76] Schneider (1994), pp. 189-190.

[77] Esoterically, this challenge is figured as the face-off between the Angel of Presence (or the Solar Angel) and the Dweller on the Threshold (which represents all unresolved personality contents).

who cannot adapt themselves to current life circumstances. Problems arising in the heart function or the spine reveal this basic question of courage, or self-value. The words core, *coeur* (heart) and courage are etymologically linked, which serves as a reminder that coming to consciousness is not simply a matter of waking up, but of activating our core qualities (the deep authentic self) and our courage. This is the willingness to show who we are, to become adaptable and stand upright in the face of life's challenges. The strength to do this – to occupy our full stature, stand in our own power – are the gifts of Leo and the Sun.

The spine, more than any other body part, expresses the ideas of connectedness and alignment. It *literally* connects our various body parts, allowing them to function as an integrated whole, just as the Sun organises the solar system. A healthy spine holds the vital organs in their right places and in right relation to each other; it is also the line along which the etheric energy centres, the chakras, are situated. Chiropractic has established a system of practice where all symptoms can be treated through their connection to the spine. The spine aligns above with below, within with without. Only the human spine is upright: we are connected to the vertical axis, the polarity of heaven and earth, *as active participants in their interchange*.

Hilarion proposes the spine be divided into three, representing the three worlds of experience (or what he refers to as the three facets of the soul): the lower spine, from coccyx to the eleventh thoracic vertebra, are the physical vertebrae; the tenth thoracic to the seventh cervical are the emotional vertebrae; the sixth cervical to the atlas are the mental vertebrae. When energy is flowing through the spine uninhibitedly there is balance between the three worlds; the blood supply to the nerves is optimal and the subtle energy of prana (from the Sun) optimally supplies the chakras. All is well. Any resistance to life will create an energy block in the spine that may manifest through another part of the body (chiropractic and osteopathy are rich in the knowledge of how the spine refers pain outwards, which can then be related back to particular vertebrae).

Correspondences between vertebrae and symptoms manifesting in particular parts of the body, and between vertebrae and planes of being will obviously furnish us with very fruitful lines of enquiry and many opportunities to come to consciousness about the conditions and beliefs surrounding our symptoms. However, the bottom line will always be to relate the spine – and the level of vitality in general – to the Sun and its requirements for development in the current incarnation. This delineation will need, in turn, to be related to those elements in the chart that are impeding expression of the solar energy (particularly to Saturn and the Moon, representing the undertow of past-life identity).

What is it that gives us the courage to enter into the fullness of life and the fullness of our beings? The heart is our source of heartiness, as simple as it seems. The strength that comes from having a strong heart gives us the conviction to call ourselves into being. Writing of the heart, Louise Hay touches on the issues of love and drama that we have connected with Leo:

The heart, of course, represents love, while our blood represents joy. Our hearts lovingly pump joy throughout our bodies. When we deny ourselves joy and love, the heart shrivels and becomes cold. As a result, the blood gets sluggish and we creep our way to anaemia, angina, and heart attacks. The heart does not 'attack' us. We get so caught up in the soap opera and dramas we create that we often forget to notice the little joys around us. We spend years squeezing all the joy out of the heart, and it literally falls over in pain.[78]

Heart problems urge us to look at how we are relating to love, joy, pleasure and creativity, for they indicate some impediment to the experience of these qualities, which of course, correspond to the fifth house of the birth chart. If one is over-burdened by the stress of work and the seriousness of life, it is very unlikely that the Leo/fifth-house energies of pleasure and play are going to be flowing. In fact, they are going to be badly snarled up by restrictive and joyless beliefs in duty, responsibility and the importance of self. The heart, so much an indicator of the real self, has a way of calling us back to ourselves:

> Under normal circumstances we are unaware of our heartbeat: we can hear and feel it only under the stress of emotion or illness. Our heartbeat comes to our conscious attention only when something is

---

[78] Hay (1984), p. 133.

exciting us or when deep changes are afoot. ... Heart symptoms force us to 'listen to our hearts' once again. Heart patients are people who only want to listen to their heads, and in whose lives the heart figures far too little.[79]

The negative expressions of Leo, the Sun and the fifth house reflect selfish, fearful and attached states of being connected with life lived from the solar plexus as the control centre. The project we share is to lift the energy from the solar plexus, by transforming it and refining its vibration, to the heart centre. This is a movement from 'my will' and self-satisfaction to 'Thy Will' (or the will of life, *the way it is*), and respect for the working out of a greater level of being within which 'I' find my true context:

> I am reiterating the necessity to recognise the stimulation of consciousness as the objective of all the astrological influences because the outstanding theme of Leo is the activity of the self-conscious unit in relation to its environment or *the development of sensitive response to surrounding impacts* by the one who stands – as the Sun stands – at the centre of its little universe.[80]

In psychological parlance, Leo energy corresponds to the Inner Child, just as it corresponds to the creative activity of conceiving and child-rearing. Very often it is as children that

---

[79] Dethlefsen and Dahlke (1990), p. 200.
[80] Bailey (1951), p. 294.

we have established patterns of defence and resistance that condition our bodies at subtle levels that manifest later as pain; consciously interrogating our memories in connection with these energetic patterns allows the voice of the Inner Child to be heard, so that we can release the old defence and the ancient belief behind it and free ourselves to enter more fully into the present and authenticity. Judith Blackstone notes that 'this is a process of literally coming to our senses', which is precisely what life would have us do.

> As we become more integrated, the sense of 'I' takes on an unmistakable fullness and cohesiveness. ... This 'I' which expresses itself in the deepest current of our experience is the same 'I' which emerges in everyone. As we grow toward our center, we grow (very gradually) toward the basic identity of the whole... .[81]

The cycle of the Sun gives us our year and our seasons, marked by the equinoxes of spring and autumn and the solstices of midsummer and midwinter. These are a reflection of the stellar level working upon the planetary body of Earth, calling the spirit of Gaia into consciousness, just as the Sun calls us individually into consciousness. 'Illness' and imbalance manifest in the planetary body just as they manifest in our own bodies, showing where and how consciousness has been derailed, where the forces of materialism are overwhelming the forces of light (to borrow terms from *Esoteric Astrology*). It is human beings that help

---

[81] Blackstone (1991), pp. 47, 71.

receive and transform stellar energy and channel it down into the body of Earth; the more aligned and conscious we are as individuals, as societies, as nations, etc., the more help and healing we can bring to Gaia. The Sun's journey as it transits the birth chart shows us where our conscious focus may be in general matters of everyday concern. The energy released into different areas of the chart by the lunation cycle (conjunctions and oppositions of Sun and Moon, i.e. the New Moon and the Full Moon, respectively), indicate areas of our lives that will be drawn to our attention and where we can usefully focus and decisively put the increase of energy to effective use.[82]

---

[82] Stephen Arroyo makes useful remarks on the energy released by lunation (1992), pp. 192-193.

VIRGO
Bodily Intelligence

*I was an unseen treasure and I longed to be known, so
I created the world that I might be known.*[83]

Virgo pertains particularly to the health of the body, to diet,
hygiene, routine and the use of functional energy. Douglas
Baker points out that Virgo, as the second earth sign, refines,
organises and systematises the 'crude matter' of Taurus.[84]
Like Gemini, Virgo is ruled by Mercury, and while Gemini deals
with the interplay, or oscillation, between dualities, Virgo
deals with their blending. In Gemini, spirit and matter are
polarised; in Virgo, spirit is subsumed within matter and one
begins to sense the quickening of the spirit within form. Form
is the vehicle for spirit just as the pregnant mother's body is
the vehicle for the incoming soul. Virgo energy is the energy
of gestation and it is in Virgo that we begin to discern the
presence of spirit or soul within our personality lives and

---

[83] *Hadith Qudsi,* quoted in 'A hidden treasure' by Pir Zia Inayat-Khan,
http://www.sevenpillarshouse.org/article/a_hidden_treasure/ (accessed
Aug. '21)
[84] Baker (1975).

bodies. Virgo attunes us to our senses and sharpens them, encouraging discernment, discrimination and analysis: qualities which lead to our ability to find spirit within matter.

> Lives in Virgo emphasise the search for the Self. The Self is lost in the dross of material living. Only by sifting carefully, layer by layer, can the precious radium of spirituality be identified.[85]

Virgo oversees the quickening of bodily intelligence through bringing attention to physical experience, and the gestation of soul awareness through the medium of the body. The symbology of Virgo concerns the whole goal of the evolutionary process: the revelation of spiritual reality that has been hidden, shielded and nurtured by physical reality. Virgo rules the 'blinded stage' of ritual, that which precedes the gift of light, where one is left in quiet and darkness to grow receptive to the movements of spirit. This is the time in the vision quest before the vision comes; in Virgo we grow receptive and quiet, discerning in our stillness the presence and dynamics of spirit as it moves within and around us. This is a place of waiting and becoming alert to the kindling of soul life within the body.

In Christian tradition, form life (life pertaining to the body and the personality) is thought to obstruct and obscure the life of the spirit. Spirit is seen in some religious interpretations as being enmired within form. However, it is *by virtue* of

---

[85] Baker (1975).

manifesting in form that we develop consciousness of any kind, because 'matter guards, cherishes and nurtures the hidden soul.'[86] The body and worldly existence are not obstructions to spiritual life but its enablers, the mode through which spiritual reality is revealed and made known.

The lesson of Virgo is that form and spirit should not be polarised or perception limited by false dualities, but that the presence of spirit must be perceived within form. This lesson has a big impact on notions of the body and health. The body (as I have said) is a bridge between the Seen and the Unseen, the place where different worlds coincide (past, present, future; above, below; cosmos; ancestors), their interface and their interpreter. Problems in the body, Virgo teaches, are problems that exist at more refined levels beyond the gross physical, in the Unseen. The body does not register pathology without an aberration arising within consciousness. An aberration may simply be something that is seeking to be included in consciousness, arising for the purpose of healing and wholeness. The body is the index for consciousness and will only be healed by being understood as such.

If symptoms of illness are masked without being healed (for example, through suppression by drug treatments), then the message the body brings is impeded in getting through to the personality. If the personality concedes to listen and discern patiently (like the neophyte in the blinded stage of the ritual), there is the possibility of the message being heard and

---

[86] Bailey (1951), p. 252.

integrated within consciousness. When this happens, healing can take place. To this extent, healing, health and self-renewal are contingent upon our receptivity to symptoms we may consider 'pathological'. Although this is simple, it is not easy. It needs to be learned, and understanding the 'poetic' expressions of bodily symptoms and sensations is a great place to start learning.

Virgo rules the sixth house of health, work and service. These matters relate to the way in which we use functional energy. For this reason, Virgo and the sixth house also govern the habits, routines and organisation of everyday life. As such, Virgo can have a rather mundane focus. It sees a job that needs doing and is willing to do it. Its practical, vocational sensibility is that of doing and serving. At its worst, it is a dogsbody uninspired by vision or aspiration, and at best, the willing and effective worker whose intelligent spirit emanates through even the most humble tasks. Virgo can be the diligent, careful apprentice, or the over-fastidious hypochondriac. Its concern is very much with the details of the daily round and if this preoccupation is unrelieved by higher vision, Virgo can be overwhelmed with drudgery, pettiness, perfectionism, obsessiveness and a fear of disorder.

Virgo, it is evident, bears a strong relation to the critical, rational faculty and is close in this sense to that other Mercury-ruled sign, Gemini. Gemini and the third house condition the mental style – the mode of thinking and communicating; Virgo and the sixth house condition the *modus operandi* – the mode of working and doing. Gemini, as an air sign, pertains to thought, whereas Virgo (earth) pertains to materiality. This is reflected in the major bodily processes ruled by Mercury: respiration (the lungs are ruled by Gemini) and digestion (the small intestine is ruled by Virgo). Both these processes are of assimilation and discrimination. Digestion is like breathing, only it involves dense matter: it is the coming to earth of the process we discussed in relation to Gemini.

In the small intestine food is split into its constituent parts (analysis). What is beneficial is absorbed into the blood and what is not is released into the large intestine where water is extracted from indigestible material before it is eliminated as waste. The small intestine represents our conscious analytical thinking, while the large intestine (ruled by Scorpio) represents the unconscious content of our beings and our own personal underworlds. In Traditional Chinese Medicine (TCM), the small intestine is partnered with the heart: 'Some would say that the small intestine is able to separate what is useful from what is not useful on the physical level while the heart does so on an emotional level.'[87]

Virgo rules not only the small intestine, but also the gallbladder and the solar plexus (third chakra), and the pancreas, which is the physical manifestation of the solar plexus chakra. Disorders of these areas register imbalances of the Virgo energy of discernment, discrimination and analysis. When undue focus is given to details we tend to cling to our

---

[87] Hill (1997), p. 25.

routines, fearing disorder and loss of control; when we lose the overview, the big picture, we cannot access the meaning behind our mundane activities and we cannot plan ahead; this brings stress into the functioning of the Virgo-ruled areas of the body. We can become overly fastidious, perfectionist, obsessed with hygiene or order, or we can manifest disorders of the small intestine, gallbladder or pancreas. Virgo diseases and imbalances seem to pertain to this loss of the vision that supervises and organises our everyday lives, making us fussy and fearful and overburdened by drudgery. Work without meaning *is* drudgery; work with meaning can be inspired activity. Problems with digestion suggest that a person is overwhelmed by experience, by information and details; somehow they are taking in too much to process.

This idea is confirmed in *The Healing Power of Illness*, in which Dethlefsen and Dahlke write that disorders of the small intestine arise as problems of processing and becoming overly analytical:

> Disorders in the region of the small intestine should ... raise the question of whether we are being too analytical, for it is in the nature of the small intestine's job to analyse, to split apart and to go into detail. People with disorders of the small intestine incline for the most part towards excessive analysis and criticism: they are always finding fault with things. The small intestine is also a good indicator of any fears that we may have for our own survival. ... A fear, that is, of not

being able to get enough out of things, a fear of going hungry.[88]

Such agitations can cause constriction and tightness and lead to sluggishness in the activity of the small intestine that can in turn lead to toxicity. This is signalled by irritability, rashes or spots on the skin. Another symptom is diarrhoea: 'When we are afraid, we no longer take time to analyse incoming impressions. Instead we let them all through undigested.'[89]

In TCM the gallbladder puts into action plans made by the liver. The role of the gallbladder is to collect the bile produced by the liver and to release it into the small intestine to help with the breaking down of fats for digestion. In common parlance, the words 'gall' and 'bile' are related to audacity, anger and resentment. Malfunction of the gallbladder may relate to frustration, aggression and control. When too much bile is released it causes acid attacks and potential ulceration; it rises up causing acid to be tasted in the mouth. We use the expression 'it leaves a bad taste in my mouth' to signify disappointment and revulsion, and the reasons for these emotional responses should be considered when acid is causing a problem in the body.

A common problem associated with the gallbladder is gallstones. Steroids, too much fat, alternatively too little fat or irregular meals, can lead to gallstones developing and obstructing the bile-ducts in the gallbladder. Perhaps also the

---

[88] Dethlefsen and Dahlke (1990), pp. 134-135.
[89] Dethlefsen and Dahlke (1990), p. 135.

kind of worry and reticence that prevent us from putting our plans into action may, over a long time, result in gallstones, the pain of which may reflect the pain, disappointment and resentment of our failure to stand in support of our plans. Plans are simply directions we long for the journeys of our lives to take us in; it is hard sometimes to follow through on these plans, they can seem audacious or we fear they might not come off. Is it better to live with the disappointment of having never 'gone for it', or to go for it and fall flat on our faces? When we chronically withhold support for ourselves in doing the things we long to do, we block our progress with the wet blanket of unlived life. Dethlefsen and Dahlke put gallstones down to blocked 'aggression':

> Energy needs to flow. If energy is prevented from flowing, an energy-blockage results. If an energy-blockage finds no outlet for some time, the energy has a tendency to solidify. Deposits and stones within the body are always manifestations of congealed energy. Gallstones are fossilised bits of aggression.[90]

They make the point, parenthetically, that aggression need have no negative connotation, any more than the words 'bile' and 'teeth' should have negative connotations. Aggression is, after all, the energy of self-actualisation (see the essay on Aries).

---

[90] Dethlefsen and Dahlke (1990), p. 141.

The pancreas has two roles in digestion: it releases digestive juices and it produces and releases insulin, which is needed to digest sugars. The disease most commonly associated with the pancreas is diabetes, where a problem with insulin production means that sugars are not digested. The diabetic condition causes the 'acidification' of the body, which results eventually (and often with alarming speed) in coma. In Louise Hay's tabulation of diseases and 'probable causes', she notes the causes for diabetes being, 'Longing for what might have been. A great need to control. Deep sorrow. No sweetness left.'[91] The control issue is notable in that it is also associated, as suggested, with the gallbladder and is arguably a key feature of matters pertaining to Virgo, the sixth house and the solar plexus.

Dethlefsen and Dahlke correlate love with sweetness, and aggression with acid; when sugars are excreted without being absorbed, the sweetness (or love) in life is passing us by and we are held in thrall perhaps to a nostalgic longing for love. If we are wondering where the sweetness in our lives has gone, maybe we need to reconnect to our vision, or our context of significance/meaning in life, and ask why we are neglecting the positive aspects of our lives. Self-pity, nostalgia and objectless, omni-directional longing can glamorise us, obscuring the truth of our situations. It may be, for example, that when we are flooded with a craving for sweetness, we are in a state of clinging to an obsolete idea, object or relationship. The condition of attachment creates a thralldom

---

[91] Hay (1984), p. 162.

that circumscribes our development; it can make us feel safe even as it inhibits our freedom.

The solar plexus chakra governs these kinds of attachment. Neediness in relationship – so often related to issues of control and fear of freedom – is an imbalance in the solar plexus. Through the solar plexus we develop balanced emotional responses:

> The solar plexus is associated with the great pleasure that comes from deeply knowing one's unique and connected place within the universe. A person with an open [solar plexus] chakra can look up to the starry heavens at night and feel that he belongs. He is firmly grounded in his place within the universe. He is the centre of his own unique aspect of expression of the manifest universe and from this he derives spiritual wisdom.[92]

The solar plexus reflects our capacity for good, appropriate self-regard. Low self-esteem makes us feel punched in the guts, because the solar plexus is not functioning optimally where there is an issue of this kind. The sense of belonging, groundedness and self-respect that reflect a healthy solar plexus result from the intelligent awareness of the fusion between spirit and matter that Virgo presides over. It gives rise to appropriate, balanced emotional affiliations and a sense of order and purposeful activity in life. When these

---

[92] Brennan (1988), p. 75.

conditions prevail, the Virgo energy is flowing harmoniously, and an individual can operate effectively: contributing, serving, helping and balancing the requirements of the physical vehicle.

Matter, the body and physical health are key themes of Virgo, thus it is the sign with the strongest tendencies towards 'somatisation': expression through physiological conditions in the body. It also tends to *identify* with such conditions, often addressing them with treatment regimes prescribed by therapies that share Virgo's detailed, analytical, intelligent approach to life.

LIBRA
Resolving Polarity

Libra governs balance. We only know balance by going in and out of it. It is not a place you can pitch your tent. We know balance because we have lost it, not because we have it. This is a bit like health, peace or ease: generally we only realise we had it when it is gone. The experience of ease and harmony are also under the rulership of Libra. Aries, in polarity with Libra, rules strife. Aries and Libra describe the relationship between the warrior and the peacemaker, self and other, me and you.

Libra rules the bladder, kidneys, urethra and the skin. The kidneys are organs of discernment, eliminating what is not good and retaining what is good for us; they restore the blood to equilibrium. The skin is our boundary with the world; the largest organ of excretion, it is also our sheath of protection and, as we receive through it the sensual impacts of the world outside, a great source of impressions and perceptions. Here Venus is involved in balancing, sensing and bringing the inner (self) into relationship with the outer (other).
Problems such as eczema, psoriasis, cystitis and kidney weakness pertain to Libra and the seventh house. Libra,

symbolised by the scales, rules balance and equilibrium, and has been called the 'place of judgement'. It is associated with fairness, judicial processes, advocacy, aesthetics and partnership. In Aries we come to consciousness through the will to be. In Libra, consciousness is derived from the will to relate. The Aries–Libra polarity is concerned with striking the balance between the developmental requirements of the self and right regard for the other. The glamour that Aries tends to fall into is self-assertion without due regard for other; the glamour of Libra is over-regard for other to the detriment of self.

These cardinal signs are marked by the astronomical events of the vernal and autumnal equinoxes. It is the intersection of two celestial circles that marks the global moments of equinox: the circle of the Sun's apparent path around the Earth (the ecliptic) intersects with the circle of the celestial equator of the Earth. These intersections are defined as 0° Aries and 0° Libra.[93] The vernal equinox in Aries heralds the season of growth and the waxing power of the Sun; the autumn equinox is marked by increasing darkness and a turn inwards. From this point on we experience the waning of the Sun, which is then once more reborn at the winter solstice, time of greatest darkness. Libra is, like Aries, a fulcrum, where we tip into a new solar phase. At this time earth energy begins to contract, witnessed by the yellowing of leaves and the slowing of growth in the natural world. Earth

---

[93] When these celestial circles are furthest apart, we experience the shortest day (winter solstice) and the longest day (summer solstice): 0° Capricorn and 0° Cancer, respectively, in the northern hemisphere.

energy – and our own – is now taken inwards and when the Sun transits Libra we often take on new projects and return our attention to things that may have drifted over the outward time of the summer.

Libra carries this quality of drawing in, accompanied by attention and intelligence; we are mentally alert and active as we embark upon the next phase of the journey. This alertness and attention pertain to the air quality of Libra. Libra, the descending sign, falls towards the nocturnal – the inside, the invisible – as we are moved from outwardness to inwardness, back towards wholeness and balance. Libra looks out towards the other, overseeing the process of relating – *weighing* one thing with regard to another, which requires an awareness of relationship, in its broadest sense. (This is where its Venusian concern with aesthetics comes from: it is able to see one thing in relation to another, a quality fundamental to forming aesthetic judgements.) This awareness is mental (airy), and Libra is the cardinal air sign (Aquarius is fixed air, Gemini mutable).

Libra has rulership of the kidneys, bladder and urinary system, the fallopian tubes, the lumbar area, the skin and the sense of balance. With Aries, Libra rules the adrenal glands, which are positioned at the top of the kidneys, and are the physical manifestation of the root chakra. The root chakra expresses the Aries–Libra polarity, combining the will to be of Aries, and the ability to come intelligently into relationship of Libra. A healthily functioning root chakra senses, assesses and responds appropriately to the immediate environment.

The rulership of the kidneys by Libra is curious: what can be the connection between the cardinal air sign and the distinctly watery bladder and kidneys? And why are the adrenals, positioned *above* the waist, associated with the root chakra, which governs our connection to the Earth and is located at the base of the spine? This is rather mysterious and perhaps serves to remind us that the chakras form a highly complex energetic system (of which I, certainly, have only a very rudimentary grasp). In TCM the kidneys rule all the lower orifices, suggesting an energetic connection between the two areas of the body. The root chakra's rulership by Aries and Libra together suggests that its function might pertain in some way to resolving polarity.

To interrogate first, airy Libra's rulership of the watery kidneys. Most obviously, the kidneys are paired organs (like the lungs, ovaries and testes) and therefore have an affinity with relating and partnership themes (air). In embryonic development the kidneys first manifest in the region of the neck, at the opening, significantly, of the air passages. They then migrate down into the sacrum, rising to their final position in the lumbar region. The kidneys are not embedded in surrounding tissue and retain a certain mobility: they are responsive to the movements of the diaphragm during breathing (another association with air). The affinity between the ear and the kidney is commented upon by Walter Holtzapfel as he notes the ear-like shape of the kidney. Writing from an anthroposophical perspective, Holtzapfel points to a correspondence between the form of the whole kidney/bladder region and that of the ear/throat region. He also remarks that if the ear of a newborn baby is missing or malformed, the kidney on the same side is likely to bear similar damage. Further, shortage of breath is symptomatic of many diseases of the kidneys. In Holtzapfel's view:

> Once we are aware of the relationships between the kidneys and bladder region and the upper air passages, we are no longer surprised by Rudolf Steiner's statement that the kidney is the regulator of the air element in the organism.[94]

It is interesting to think about the ear's positioning and function in the sense of hearing (governed by Mercury and Saturn). We hear because something earthly (not-self), separated from the earth, resounds in the medium of air: it vibrates and thereby become audible. We hear when our ear bones are moved by resonance. Our hearing mediates external qualities into internal experiences: our ears are set externally on our heads but develop inwardly into the inner space of the head. Hearing represents the internalising quality that is potential when the human being encounters the world. Through this discussion we will see that this relational experience of self/not-self is crucial to the energetic work of Libra and to the resolution of the Aries–Libra polarity.

The adrenal glands (ruled, as noted, by both Aries and Libra) govern stress responses (fight, flight, freeze or faint), which are fundamental to our ability to survive. In a sense they

---

[94] Holtzapfel (2013), p. 64.

measure our reaction to what is in our environment. This suggests the Libran weighing process. It is interesting to note that the stress reactions of asthma and eczema are treated by cortisone drugs mimicking the secretions of the adrenal glands. If the body's air system is truly regulated by the kidney function then we should consider that the root of lung problems may be in the kidneys. This interrelation of body systems reflects the complicated nature of holism: we seek to analyse – to reduce things that only exist in complex relation to each other to their constituent parts. This discussion of Libra forces us both to analyse (take apart) and correspondingly, to synthesise (bring together), which is perhaps fundamental to the gesture of Libra. It is not a great leap from this point to suggest that Libra acts in overseeing apects of our physical *relationship* to the earth, the environment and to each other; its co-rulership of the root chakra is, in this light, comprehensible. Our grounding, our belonging to the body of the planet, to place and to each other is sustained by an awareness of Libran relating. Further discussion of the kidneys will follow later.

Libra is the seventh sign of the zodiac whose cusp is the descendant. The ascendant–descendant axis correlates to the line of the horizon: all that lies below it is unilluminated, in nocturnal darkness, and in some sense is private or inward; above the horizon is the diurnal realm. Robert Hand, writing about the horizon, describes a person lying in a field with their feet pointing south towards the position of the Sun at noon:

The horizon represents your eyes or your skin. Everything above the horizon is in front of your eyes or outside your skin. You can see what is 'out there' objectively; you perceive it is other than yourself. But what is below the horizon is behind your eyes or inside your skin. You cannot see it; you can only deduce its presence. ... [Y]ou are unaware of it, because it is so much a part of you. ... The horizon can be the boundary between what we perceive as inner and outer... . The descendant is where planets ... [pass] from the outer realm to the inner. ... [I]t relates to the kind of impression the not-self makes upon the self.[95]

The skin, ruled by Libra – with some influence of Saturn (these things are complex), defines and contains us, and sensitises us to all that is not-self. Paradoxically the self, with which we are in our culture so obsessively concerned, is all that we cannot see; a kind of phantom whose presence can only be deduced. If it were not for the presence of other beings, could the self be said to have an existence at all? Somebody passes through the field of our gaze and looks in at us – we are seen. If we are not acknowledged at this point it feels strange: Did he see me? Am I here? Am I dreaming? Of course, we *are* dreaming in a sense, and when we are acknowledged by the other, the dream becomes real; by virtue of relating we flower to a fuller reality: we can feel ourselves to be real in connection with the other. A truth is captured in the words, 'Because you see me I know I am alive.' This process of coming into awareness of

---

[95] Hand (1981), p. 249.

self through relating to not-self belongs to the air realm: it requires thought and reflection.

Disruptions to the relationship between self and other, inside and outside, me and my environment, show up in the skin in a variety of ways: coloration, sensation, rashes, inflammation, infection, psoriasis, eczema, dermatitis, etc. The condition of Libra, Venus and the seventh house of the chart will be pertinent to the nature of the challenge.

The sense of balance or orientation, is an 'organ for the perception of the connections between the centre of the earth and our own body'.[96] The relevance of this idea of balance to the root chakra is perfectly clear. Uprightness is fundamentally and characteristically a human quality. It is the quality that allows us to weave together the above and the below, to mediate between heaven and earth. Uprightness is established by the sense of balance. It requires a gravitational field in which we learn to discern up from down, back from front and left from right (the planes of our physical human existence). Through balance the human 'I' finds orientation in space and makes a connection with the world around. In this way we establish a standpoint and a location in physical and social space.

Try balancing on one leg and closing your eyes! We balance by sensing the space surrounding us; our balance arises through our relationship with the environment: self coming

---

[96] Aeppli (2003), p. 12.

into relationship with not-self. This view of balance suggests that a certain strength of will is required to project ourselves energetically into the environment. The Aries–Libra polarity is resolved through their healthy interaction, the will of the self in harmony with due regard for other.

The Sun, exalted in Aries, is in its fall in Libra. Maybe this is because in Libra, coming into relationship with other, the more naïve sense of self that was born under the impulse of Aries is in some way destabilised. Meeting the other initiates us into a deeper sense of self, foisting upon us the realisation that we are necessarily contingent upon the other as we require a witness to concur in our belief that we exist. It seems that we are here to bear witness to each other's existences: for I can hardly see myself at all, I see only you. We lend each other context and can only embark on stories of selfhood together: we call each other into being.

In the western medical model the kidneys filter the blood and body fluids, also regulating the acid–alkaline balance of the blood and blood pressure. In Traditional Chinese Medicine (TCM) they hold the fundamental constitutional energy inherited from the parents, called *jing*. *Jing* is form-giving essence, animated by *shen* or spirit, while *qi* is the flow of energy. *Jing* is irreplaceable; when it is exhausted, we die. It governs all aspects of growth, development and reproduction. 'The kidneys', writes Sandra Hill, 'are the base, the root and the deep structure of the body.'[97] In TCM, the kidneys govern

---

[97] Hill (1999), p. 27.

the water element in the body, which in turn governs fertility and the ability to have roots, and therefore rootedness (water descends, thus finding the deepest level). The emotion belonging to the kidneys in this model is fear, which has the effect of uprooting us: impelling us to fight or flee. Weakened kidney energy suggests unexpressed or unacknowledged fear. Failure to release negative emotions and shocks can debilitate kidney function. Just as the kidneys filter the blood, the discerning judicious energy of Libra oversees the sieving of experience, releasing what does not serve and retaining what truly belongs to the self.

Lack of grounding, weakness in the root chakra, causes us to feel uprooted, stressed and disoriented. We fall out of relation to reality, our perceptions become unreliable. Our uprightness (that fundamentally human quality) is disrupted. In this state we are susceptible to danger, physically, psychologically and spiritually: deeply unbalanced. Stress reactions and fear are then likely to register in the physical body, leading potentially to debility in the kidneys.

Dethlefsen and Dahlke, writing about the meaning of kidney illness, refer to not letting water flow under the bridge – 'hanging on regardless'. The common symptom of kidney stones can be understood as the retention of what should have been eliminated: of substances that contribute nothing. The healthy function of the kidneys – and of Libran energy – is to bring blood pressure, blood *ph* and body fluids into right balance. This balance is reflected in human relationships, where we are constantly discerning between what is self and what is not-self, attempting to come to a real and workable balance so that healthy relating is possible. We learn, through experience, that difficulties with partners are, in truth, the projections of difficulties within ourselves. Astrology is a wonderful illustration of this truth, for Libra, Venus and the seventh house describe the *conditioning factors* surrounding an individual personality's experience of partnership issues; they describe the partner, but only by inference.

The conditioning factors belong to the individual as inner qualities (whether a partner is present or not) and are merely the lens through which the partner is seen. We have the choice, at a certain level of awareness, either to persist in our projections or to attempt to withdraw them. Dethlefsen and Dahlke remark that true love is a process of withdrawing projections.[98] The failure to resolve projections is like the kidneys' failure to retain vital salts and proteins or to eliminate substances that are present in the blood to an excessive extent. Kidney malfunction is a failure to recognise what rightly belongs to this body, just as relationships cannot evolve healthily when we resist withdrawing our projections.[99] The Libran discernment of self and not-self, holding these poles of being in an appropriate balance, is clearly relevant to an understanding of kidney function.

In TCM the kidneys store the will. This is interesting as in astrology the will is the province of Aries, reminding us that the seeming polarity that exists between opposing signs is

---

[98] Dethlefsen and Dahlke (1990), p. 174.
[99] Dethlefsen and Dahlke (1990), p. 176.

actually the contraction of a continuum: astrological polarities belong to each other in subtle and meaningful ways. Again, as noted earlier, we can analyse and take apart, but we also need to synthesise and put together what has been taken apart. Sandra Hill describes the kidneys' connection to the will in a way that helps us understand Libra's rulership of the root chakra:

> The will, which is stored in the kidneys, is a deep evolutionary urge, a push for the individual to fulfil his or her unique potential. On a more mundane level it is the will to live, the will to survive, the will to continue the species, the sex drive, an energy which in most spiritual traditions and in many different ways can be transformed from a basic reproductive urge to a means of spiritual growth. Its relationship, via the kidneys, to the lower parts of the trunk, to the spine and to the brain make it impossible not to draw parallels with the Indian concept of kundalini, which from its seat at the base of the spine, inspires the transformation and transmutation of evolutionary energies.[100]

The virtue of the kidneys is seen as being wisdom: 'grounded and earthed wisdom which is based on the will to live, and on the reality of circumstances'.[101] There is a balanced willing at work here; it is not blind impulse but has more a flavour of

---

[100] Hill (1999), p. 54.
[101] Hill (1999), p. 45.

pragmatism: the work of Aries and Libra in collaboration. When the energy of the kidneys is out of balance there are symptoms of premature ageing, sterility, retarded growth, dark bags around the eyes, salt cravings, split hair, hair loss, oedema, lower back pain, premature greying, urinary problems and lethargy. The associated emotions are lack of willpower, panic, depression, paranoia, fear and overwhelm.

The axes of the birthchart (the horizontal axis of ascendant and descendant, the vertical axis of midheaven and nadir) form a cross of matter. The ascendant pertains to the emergence of the self, while all the other angles bring the self into relationship with reality through various forms of not-self (the mother, family and home at the nadir, the partner at the descendant, and the father and the impersonal world at the midheaven). The horizontal axis, ruled by Aries and Libra, is the axis of self-learning and modification as we discover ourselves through the mirror of relationship. It works in concert with the vertical axis, anchoring us in our places of rooting and belonging at the nadir, and of aspiration, aim and ambition at the midheaven.

Saturn is exalted in Libra because it is through the work of a healthy Saturn that we are able to find stability and reality amidst the shifting forces in the world of form, and hold better the balance that Libra pursues. When we are flung between the oppositions of self and not-self, glamorised and blinded by projections, we are in the realm of delusion where individuation is stymied and lifeforce wasted. In resolving the polarity, grounded in truth and reality, we are open to the evolutionary flow of our own lifeforce. This is beautifully illustrated by the existence of what TCM calls the Gate of Life, which is the acupressure point situated on the spine at the midpoint (the point of balance) between the kidneys:

> We have seen that the fire of the gate of life provides the energy for all transformation and transmutation within the body and is the basis of metabolism and immunity. ... Symbolically, the gate of life is said to provide the link between your inherited energies and tendencies and your ability to transform and transmute them in order to fulfil your potential. It is your link with both your origin and your possible evolution.[102]

---

[102] Hill (1999), p. 72.

SCORPIO
Reaching to Hell

*I knew that infinity was pointing out to me, through
the vivid recollection of those forgotten experiences,
the intensity and the depth of my drive for control, and
thus preparing me for something transcendental to
myself. I knew with frightening certainty that
something was going to bar any possibility of my being
in control, and that I needed, more than anything else,
sobriety, fluidity, and abandon in order to face the
things that I felt were coming to me.*[103]

Scorpio shares its traditional ruler with Aries: Mars. Mars in
Aries is concerned with the outward, dynamic, fiery
expression of the will. In Scorpio, Mars operates more
covertly. Scorpio, sign of fixed water, takes Mars to the
emotional level, which, in Scorpio, is deep, dark and brooding.
Scorpio and eighth-house energy is concerned with the
mysteries: sex, death and rebirth or regeneration. Mars and
Scorpio rule the male sex organs, Venus and Scorpio the
female. Scorpio concerns our most intense (and often most

---

[103] Castaneda (1998), p. 172.

private) experiences and emotional states. Scorpio's reputation for smouldering sexuality is fuelled by its hallmark characteristics of intensity, jealousy, resentment, obsession and interest in power play. Scorpio has the capacity to intensify whatever principle moves through it. It submerges planets and drags them down to the depths where all non-essential, extraneous matter is removed. Mars in Scorpio, therefore, is more concerned with penetrating the darkness within, exploring the psyche, sexuality, power dynamics and the occult, than it is with the extroverted gung-ho adventuring of Mars in Aries.

The modern ruler of Scorpio, since its discovery in 1930, is Pluto, the planet furthest from the Sun. As the slowest-moving of the planets (its orbit around the Sun taking 248 years), it packs the greatest punch. Pluto is the higher octave of Mars; if Mars represents the personal will and desire-nature of the individual, Pluto describes a much stronger force, the will of life, or what we might reasonably call *necessity*. Dane Rudhyar describes Pluto as reducing things to essentials.[104] It operates ruthlessly and relentlessly to shake us free of whatever in us is non-essential (impure, obsolete or inauthentic). It provides therefore the possibility of rebirth and regeneration. Pluto oversees the radical pruning operations of consciousness – and radical healing in the body! Its principle is *transformation*.

---

[104] Rudhyar (1975), p. 63.

Because its activity is radical and thoroughgoing, it brings many challenges into consciousness: it insists on change at the deepest level by killing off what is outmoded, of which we are often fearful of letting go. The more we hold on to the obsolete or the inauthentic, and cling fondly to old modes of being and cherished identities, the more forceful Pluto's activity will be. Pluto's effects are often registered in the body simply because its challenges are too much to be accommodated by conscious levels of being. Pluto and Scorpio pertain strongly to the unconscious, and what is unconscious will be projected externally or seek manifestation in the body. Projections hook on to *agents* in our external worlds through which to enter into our experience. Pluto can come at us, externally, in such forms as violent attack, criminal or psychotic behaviour, sexual encounters, fascinating or seemingly powerful 'others' and social or political intrigues, etc.

Pluto takes us into areas we would never volunteer to go, where we have to confront the poverty of rational consciousness, the limits of willpower and the insistence of our instinctual drives. Pluto brings us into relationship with what Jungian terminology calls the Shadow: that which has been repressed, disowned or rejected. The contents of the Shadow are not all negative; human beings have a persistent tendency to disown their fullness of spirit. We reject our brilliance, our power, beauty and vision just as readily as we reject our aggression, compulsiveness and ugliness. Jung used the expression, 'For a tree's branches to reach to heaven its roots must reach to hell.' We seem to have trouble reaching

133

to either extreme, keeping ourselves instead within a narrow band of familiar conditioned ordinariness that we find stultifying but safe.

Scorpio and Pluto are designed to push us into extremes where we are brought face to face with the deeper, often darker, truths that form the underbelly of our narrow band of ordinariness. Wherever Scorpio and Pluto are placed in the natal chart there is a concentration of experience that forces us to penetrate into the underbelly and get acquainted with that which is usually hidden. The effect of this focus in the chart is to purge this area of experience of its non-essentials. When Pluto is active or a planet in Scorpio is activated, that which *was* hidden is forced up from the underbelly and erupts through the surface. Pluto oversees processes of elimination at every level. Whether this is the elimination of toxins through a boil, the elimination of pressure through volcanic activity or elimination of waste material through excretion and, ultimately, death, it is Pluto activity that is involved. Elimination is the pre-requisite for regeneration, for which Pluto sets the stage. Hence, Scorpio is associated with transformative processes, because, with Pluto, it effects the kind of radical clearance that makes room for change: 'Pluto registers that a time has come for the possibility to move from one level of consciousness and activity to another; he then produces the conditions required for such a passage or transmutation.'[105] Scorpio and Pluto bring healing through elimination and purification.

---

[105] Rudhyar (1975), p. 65.

Mythologically, the planet Pluto is represented by Pluto, the god, known to the Greeks as Hades. Liz Greene is the commentator par excellence on the associations between mythology and astrology, and she writes at length about Pluto in *The Astrology of Fate* from the perspective of depth psychology (embracing themes of necessary forgetfulness/repression, the discovery of one's own poisonousness, power and sexuality), exploring different mythologies.[106] Greene makes the point that the word 'Pluto' in Greek means 'riches', suggesting that we can be enriched by our Plutonic descents to hell. The 'depths' are often figured as the place of deep fecundity – germination processes (also ruled by Pluto) take place deep within the dark fruitfulness of the earth – and in the alchemical model, the *nigredo* (or black) stage represents contact with the *prima materia*. The *prima materia* is the dark, rich, inchoate material of the Unconscious, the rejected stuff that can be transmuted into gold. Pluto, it should be noted, is associated with conditions of blackness within the body.

People experiencing Pluto energy are often thrust into dark experiences that confound rationality and exceed all notions of fairness. This energy shakes us free of ancient conditioning often by creating experiences of loss and trauma that can cut through conditioned consciousness. People in the throes of a Pluto crisis talk of the 'dark night of the soul', being

---

[106] Greene (1997). Sylvia Brinton Perera's *Descent to the Goddess* (1981) is a remarkable telling of the Sumerian myth of Inanna's descent to hell, which is illuminating as a study of initiatory Plutonian crisis.

abandoned by god, or the feeling that life has forgotten them. Plutonian crises force us to integrate the rejected parts of ourselves and to go on a quest for higher meaning. Indeed, people often embark on a crusade to find god just so that they can tell him what they think of him! At some point on this crusade some of the richness that comes from integrating forgotten aspects of self is likely to be felt; one finds oneself changed, richer, deeper and, through the humiliation of the Pluto experience, more respectful of life and its processes. The 'treasure' of the descent to hell is described in the following way by Rudhyar:

> If this meeting [with the Shadow] is courageously and unfalteringly experienced, the Shadow is transformed into God-in-the-depth, the God of the mysteries, the 'living' God who polarizes God-in-the-highest, and thus reveals the essential unity of matter and spirit, and also of failure and success ... or Potentiality and Actuality.[107]

We might, in the context of health and healing, add to this that encountering the Shadow reveals the essential unity of health and sickness, of healing and wounding, and of growth and decay.

Scorpio rules the organs of elimination and reproduction: the large intestine, rectum, gonads, appendix, prostate gland and pelvic area. The gonads are the manifestation of the sacral

---

[107] Rudhyar (1975), p. 71.

chakra, which pertains to sex, power and creativity. Mars rules the sweat glands (and as they operate as eliminators it seems justifiable to attribute them to the eighth house and Mars in Scorpio, rather than in Aries). Pluto rules hidden cell changes, destruction of tissue, boils, sexual disorders, toxicity caused by impaired elimination, haemorrhoids, violent attacks (arising within or outside of the body) and, as noted, conditions of blackness. These are often conditions of purification and purging. Bowel problems and many menstrual conditions and sexual difficulties are Plutonic in origin.

Hay relates the large intestine to releasing the past; the genitals to the power principles, male and female; the pelvis to change; boils to anger; and cancer (hidden cell changes) to deeply held resentment.[108] In the case of cancer, the cause and the problem are often extremely well hidden and pertain to mental–emotional patterns that are so deeply conditioned and their effects so normalised that the patterns are effectively banished from consciousness. We cannot deny, however, the destructiveness of those patterns for we know how deadly some cancers can be; the diagnosis of the condition is the return of the repressed pattern. The diagnosis heralds the beginning of the medical battle, but it is also the call of the spirit to the personality to bring light to what has been banished into the outer darkness of consciousness, to bring love to those aspects of self that are most despised and rejected.

---

[108] Hay (1984).

Much is said in alternative approaches to health about taking responsibility for our wellbeing. And our health and wellbeing *are* our responsibility, but we have to be careful that we do not suggest that there is any blame or judgement involved. A physical symptom will reflect the truth of ourselves and it may be very painful facing that truth. What is needed in learning to take responsibility for ourselves is not judgement and blame, but love and courage. We all have darkness and limitation; we all have Pluto and Saturn in our charts; we are learning together to face the truth of ourselves and each other in order to bring ourselves into right relationship with ourselves, each other and our world, indeed all of Life. Fear and judgement kill.

Pluto conditions fall into three related areas: passion, change and power. By 'passion' I am referring to the powerful human emotions pertaining to the Scorpionic themes of sex, death and transformation – lust, envy, anger, resentment, denial, fear, etc. All of these have positive counterparts, which can be considered as the gifts of Scorpio and the eighth house. Guilt should perhaps be mentioned in this regard, which represents the unconscious attempt to camouflage the real issue – not only to hide our shame from others but also to conceal our difficult natures from ourselves.

The positive aspect of passion may be said to be a penetrating awareness of deep emotional states, the ability to see things in their wholeness – light and dark – and to give ourselves in a committed, joyful way to the ebb and flow of life. Scorpio teaches us nothing if not how to roll with the punches. The problematic aspects of passion show themselves when our emotions become distorted by our attachment to them, or our identification with them. Being a fixed sign, Scorpio has the tendency to hold on very hard to old patterns of thought and emotion. It is renowned for resentment and fear of rejection. It feels very deeply and despite seeming powerful and self-assured to others, it is an extremely emotionally sensitive sign.

Getting stuck in old patterns produces toxic emotions; toxicity will be commensurate with resistance to change. Symptoms will tend to show up as Plutonic processes or in the Scorpio areas of the body – bowel, pelvic area – and will describe, of themselves, the nature of the emotional pattern in which the person is stuck. People get stuck when they are fearful of change; to some, any change is a change for the worse, in which case it is always better to stick with 'the devil you know'. However, the body knows the truth of the situation and will bring to light what has been hidden, by creating an apposite and precisely descriptive difficulty. Symptoms may often involve the elimination of toxic materials: the boil bursts through the skin depositing its cargo of toxins safely on the other side of the body. The surface level of existence erupts and the contents of the Unconscious are dumped within the conscious realm to be dealt with; thus, Scorpio asks us to face up to the truth of ourselves and so move to a more integrated level of being:

> The most fundamental meaning of all Plutonian
> processes is that they force us, often relentlessly, to

devaluate or abandon all that is a manifestation of *surface* living and to plumb as profound a depth of human experience as our mental, affective, and spiritual condition can withstand.[109]

Scorpio challenges are radically transformative. Alice Bailey gives the keynotes of the sign as test, trial and triumph; the trials of Scorpio arise, esoterically, as the 'serpent of wisdom' (the soul) seeks to overpower the 'serpent of evil' (personality/form life).[110] Energetically this is a matter of raising energy from below the diaphragm to above it. For trauma to be transformed into wisdom there needs to be humility in the face of powers far greater than the personal will. This implies the need to develop a more adequate understanding of power. We need to have an appreciation of our personal power *and* of its limitation. Personal power comes from our capacity to hold and channel the power of life moving through us: it is not ours. Issues of power are, of course, in the province of Scorpio and the eighth house.

In *Anatomy of the Spirit*, Caroline Myss argues that there are three underlying principles to health:

1   Biography becomes biology
2   Personal power is necessary for health
3   You alone can help yourself to heal

---

[109] Rudhyar (1975), pp. 72-73.
[110] Bailey (1951), pp. 206, 212.

Personal power comes from a certain level of honesty and authenticity; from being, to some extent, in our true line. Myss writes:

> Power is at the root of the human experience. Our attitudes and belief patterns, whether positive or negative, are all extensions of how we define, use, or do not use power. Not one of us is free from power issues. We may be trying to cope with feelings of inadequacy or powerlessness, or we may be trying to maintain control over people or situations that we believe empower us, or we may be trying to maintain a sense of security (a synonym for power) in personal relationships. Many people who lose something that represents power to them – money, or a job, or a game – or who lose someone in whom their sense of self or power is vested – a spouse or lover, a parent or child – develop a disease.[111]

These connections between power and other people are relevant here as Scorpio and the eighth house pertain to 'relating consciousness', especially to the intimacy of emotional and sexual relating. It is worth considering whether Scorpionic conditions are expressing fears and attitudes pertaining to a person's source of emotional intimacy. Scorpio urges us to accept responsibility for our personal power, and to refrain from abusing it or undermining

---

[111] Myss (1997), p. 45.

it; it also urges us to bow to a far greater power than our own: the power of necessity – the *way it is*.

Scorpio and Pluto bring to light what has been excluded and rejected – the marginal aspects of ourselves and, crucially, what we may have inherited from our ancestors. We exclude aspects of ourselves when we deem them transgressive, unacceptable, challenging or disgusting. Exclusion from power gives the Shadow a peculiar kind of potency and, when activated by transit or progression, we experience a rude, terroristic incursion as the Shadow makes a raid on the personality. This happens in our social and political lives just as it happens in our close relationships and within our own bodies and beings. The Shadow's raid on the personality is never a revenge attack or a punishment, it is simply the only way the being knows how to move towards wholeness. The Shadow's raid expresses a readiness for integration and healing, arising from the dark, fertile depths of life.

> We have no reason to mistrust our world, for it is not against us. Has it terrors, they are *our* terrors; has it abysses, those abysses belong to us; are dangers at hand, we must try and love them. And if only we arrange our life according to that principle which counsels us that we must always hold to the difficult, then that which now still seems to us the most alien will become what we most trust and find most faithful.[112]

---

[112] Rilke (1993), p. 69.

SAGITTARIUS
Quest for Meaning

Sagittarius is ruled by Jupiter, the Greater Benefic, which is the largest planet in the solar system. It is more than twice the size of all other non-stellar matter in the solar system *put together*. Jupiter is a mighty planet, a great gaseous body whose gravitational pull protects us from the huge amount of cosmic debris whirling around in the asteroid belt (between the orbits of Mars and Jupiter). These astronomical details indicate the astrological energies associated with Jupiter: Jupiter is abundant, excessive and a source of buoyancy and protection. The natural house of Sagittarius and Jupiter is the ninth, which rules matters concerning foreign places and cultures, big ideas, dissemination of knowledge, higher knowledge (wisdom-knowledge as opposed to information and factual knowledge, which belong to Gemini, Mercury and the third house), law, philosophy and religion. The quest for a framework of meaning is a ninth-house matter, as is the study of astrology (for example), religious thought and the spiritual path. Gemini energy encourages the search for variety and experimentation; it governs the interplay between extremes. Its opposite sign, Sagittarius, encourages the search for meaning; it governs fusion, focus and one-pointedness.

It is in the ninth house, through the energy of Sagittarius and Jupiter, that we seek to expand and attempt to find a context of significance for our experiences. This search for personal development and spiritual meaning is a quest to transform intellect into intuitional intelligence, which is intelligence illuminated by the spirit and capable of discerning meaning, purpose and the principles underlying phenomena. Sagittarius has this quality of drawing things together, by utilising one-pointed focus, and thus making sense of them.

This energy can serve a priestly purpose and the matter of creating shared meaning through ritual, for example, pertains to Sagittarius, Jupiter and the ninth house. For this reason, religion and the religious instinct are ruled by Sagittarius. Religion, etymologically, means 'to bind together'; when things are bound together in right relationship, meaning arises and creates wisdom and faith. The religious instinct and the desire for meaning, in the therapeutic perspective of Carl Jung, are the most crucial in human experience. The unsatisfied religious instinct leads to faithlessness, which undermines an individual, leading to psychic disturbance and, fundamentally, disease:

> I have frequently seen people become neurotic when they content themselves with inadequate or wrong answers to the questions of life. They seek position, marriage, reputation, outward success or money, and remain unhappy and neurotic even when they have attained what they were seeking. Such people are usually confined within too narrow a spiritual horizon.

Their life has not sufficient content, sufficient meaning. If they are enabled to develop into more spacious personalities, the neurosis generally disappears....

The majority of my patients consisted not of believers but of those who had lost their faith.[113]

The role of faith and meaning in good health are almost totally unrecognised by mainstream *and* alternative health practitioners. Lack of faith constitutes being out of contact with truth (for it is when our energies and expectations are somehow false or inadequate – alienated from the *tao* of the *way it is* – that we experience loss of faith). Not many healing modalities have, as yet, developed perspectives for dealing with loss of faith; shamanic healing stands out as an exception, with its techniques for responding to soul loss. Spiritual and religious practices, such as private and public ritual, offer people ways of working through crises, but such practices need to be authentic and vital. At this time, many of the practices and rites of passage and intensification available to us are offered by religious institutions that are themselves visibly ailing, corrupt and inauthentic.

Without a context of significance and meaning, illness and other life challenges come to us as 'random misfortune'. We are unlucky, in a meaningless universe. Our inadequate perceptions of life cause us to suffer. Our suffering then potentially drives us to seek out a system of meaning, and in

---

[113] Jung (1983), p. 162.

this way we may find we are on a path of personal growth or spiritual development. It is for this reason that Sagittarius is esoterically considered to rule the Path of Discipleship. The experience of Sagittarius and the ninth house is to quest for a meaningful religious vision that provides an appropriate context for framing our experiences, thus redeeming the suffering and illness arising from loss of faith. Law and higher education are ninth-house matters, like religion, in as far as they too provide expansive systems for understanding principles.

Many of the diseases pertaining to Sagittarius, Jupiter and the ninth house are, however obliquely, related to crises of meaning and to the thwarted desire for freedom and expansion, which is a key feature of the energy. They are largely conditions of excess (a response to the unsatisfied hunger for meaning): weight gain and obesity; addiction; over-indulgence in food, alcohol, drugs and sex; liver disease, such as hepatitis and cirrhosis; bilious attacks; tumours, growths and swellings, etc. Jupiter represents the urge to expand: whatever it contacts, it augments. This can be experienced positively as joviality, buoyancy, optimism and magnanimity; or negatively as lack of realism and discipline, over-indulgence and the tendency to want to buy friends and favour with shows of largesse. Sagittarius brings abundance and opportunity, but it is the individual's response to these (and responsibility towards them) that conditions whether they are perceived negatively or positively. Obviously, an inadequate framework for meaning might cultivate negative responses. The person who is willing to learn and to grow is more likely to be able to find the opportunity concealed within the challenge than one who is stuck in a more restricted mode of operation. The more 'spacious' (to use Jung's word) we can be, the better able we are to transform difficulty into opportunity. This is very much the gift of the Sagittarian and their famous optimism.

Sagittarian energy is the energy of moving outwards. Like the archer, firing her arrows, Sagittarius motivates us towards aspiration, extension of the self and energetic expansion. To stay still and resist growth or movement is, of essence, unhealthy. Sometimes people who are living ostensibly healthy lives become ill. This attracts comment. We cannot understand why someone who is a textbook example of healthy living can be diagnosed with serious illness. It seems to us most unfair. What is less obvious, and what we often fail to see, are the ways in which life is urging someone to grow and move on, which they may be strenuously resisting. Life requires us to go on the journeys we are designed for. If we do not journey willingly, the energy of expansion can start manifesting in the body. It is through journeying that we acquire a meaningful perspective on our lives. The poet Rilke expresses this beautifully, using the Sagittarian motif of bow and arrow in the first of *The Duino Elegies*:

> Is it not time that, in loving,
> we freed ourselves from the loved one, and, quivering,
> endured:
> as the arrow endures the bowstring, to become in the
> gathering out-leap,

something more than itself? For staying is nowhere.[114]

Sagittarius/Jupiter ask us to expand. If we are to expand positively and usefully we must have purpose and direction. Basically this is the journey of development that occurs in Sagittarius: a person learns to move on from aimless globetrotting and roaming around, to pilgrimage; from ambition, to purposeful direction. The Sun, by sign and house placement in the birth chart, indicates what, for the individual, constitutes purposeful activity. This is the primary consideration for the direction of a person's energies; other factors will, naturally, add layers of description to the Sun's requirements, but the Sun, as the representative of the stellar level and the organiser of all other energies in the chart, has to be the principal focus.

An examination of Sagittarius, Jupiter, the ninth house and the ruler of the ninth house will indicate the nature and function of the individual's system of meaning. They show where and how a person wishes to expand outwardly in their life. Jupiter's placement in a chart points to the area of life in which a person experiences least restrictedness; in this area they experience opportunity and unboundedness. Focus on this area of life can often work to restore their faith in life and bestow a sense of buoyancy and optimism.

Sagittarius rules the liver, thighs, hips and sciatic nerve. Jupiter rules the blood. Together, the last four signs of the

---

[114] Rilke (1964), p. 61.

zodiac (Sagittarius, Capricorn, Aquarius and Pisces) rule the legs: thighs, Sagittarius; knees, Capricorn; lower leg and ankles, Aquarius; and, feet, Pisces. Working up from Pisces, the feet represent the individual merging with the collective; the ankles and lower leg describe issues with the community and one's sense of the future; the knees show one's relationship with authority, humility and responsibility; and the thighs indicate the context of meaning and how one wishes to move forward in life.

In *Body Signs*, Hilarion suggests that the upper leg is symbolic of the higher self and the lower leg the personality; the knee is the articulating joint between the two and the point at which, potentially, they come into alignment. He writes about the leg as being a constant reminder of the human goal in earth incarnation to draw the lower self into alignment with the higher self. When energy flows between higher and lower, the higher is given the practical experience of the lower, and the lower is infused with the wisdom of the higher.[115]

The hips allow movement in all directions and represent the freedom of soul consciousness; there is a natural right to travel in any direction if we operate with the understanding that we must pay our karmic dues: 'The hip bone ... represents the creative forces which have made humanity and have set it free to find its own way through reality.'[116] Problems in the hips may indicate that the way ahead is unclear: we feel

---

[115] Hilarion (1982), p. 16.
[116] Hilarion (1982), p. 16.

unguided or we have lost the path. Hilarion asserts that a problem in the femur head is an indication that there is a problem between the soul and the higher levels, indicating a need for greater alignment. This can be addressed by seeking greater alignment at a lower, perhaps more accessible level, by observing how the personality is serving the requirements of the soul. Again, this is an issue of purpose and direction.

The motive force of the body (the energy for dynamic movement) comes from the hips and thighs. If a person wants to expand and move forward but has no sense of direction or purpose, if the path is unclear or the journey is in question, then a problem with the hip or thigh may express this predicament. An impulse for movement gives a strong energetic message to the upper leg; if it is not acted upon, the energy is held, eventually creating a block. If conscious recognition is given to such a situation then energy can be released through appropriate activity; for example, by bringing the body into movement – anything really that allows the energy to be discharged and its flow reinstated, will be helpful and may allow the issue to shift at a more refined level.

Expansion can come through any appropriate ninth-house matter: studies at a higher level, dissemination of information, spiritual practices, seeking of wisdom, foreign ideas or foreign travel. All of these things serve to open up personal frames of reference, allowing new contexts of meaning to emerge and replace obsolete models or outgrown ideas or teachers.

Astrologers examine Sagittarius and Jupiter in a chart to discover how a person relates to issues of abundance/poverty, optimism/pessimism and faith/cynicism. At the risk of being over-simplistic, material wellbeing, at one level, is the ability to attract energy, represented by money. It pertains to a certain kind of consciousness that possesses the confidence that money spent is money gained.

Energy/money needs to flow. It is the contraction caused by holding on (through fear or insecurity) that creates an energy block that can result in 'poverty consciousness' (one can even be wealthy and believe oneself to be under-resourced).

These issues also relate to the upper leg, which provides not only the power to expand but also the power to stand on one's own feet, supported by the goodness of life. Stress in the thigh can relate to financial matters. The sciatic nerve, running from the sacrum to the foot (communicating between the creative centre – the second chakra – and the earth), particularly relates to being able to support oneself emotionally and financially. Sciatica manifests fear of poverty or being under-resourced now or in the future.

Holding on to things – money, status, possessions, views, memories – creates attachment, which, over time, produces blocks in the flow of energy. Chronically, holding on can create growths in the physical vehicle that manifest accretions or accumulations of energy that exist at subtler levels. This can be extremely pernicious, as in the case of malignant tumours where the holding on is accompanied by resentment and poisonous emotions; or it can be less dangerous and manifest as a non-malignant growth or swelling. Louise Hay makes the following remarks:

> Swelling of the body represents clogging and stagnation in the emotional thinking. We create situations where we get 'hurt', and we cling to these memories. Swelling often represents bottled-up tears, feeling stuck and trapped, or blaming others for our own limitations.[117]

Growths and swellings manifest old hurts. Weight gain is a way of shielding oneself against hurt; a fleshy protection against the assaults of life; and love is sought through over-eating. Overweight might, in some manifestations, express the fear of not having 'enough'. Suffering from lack of abundance and opportunity may also be a response to the painfulness of life without faith and trust. Life without a context of significance is a pretty bizarre dance between the horizontal and the vertical! Without faith, the interminable pattern of eating, sleeping, defecating and cleansing can easily seem absurd, even futile. The eighteenth-century Japanese Zen master, Issa, captures this absurdity perfectly in a haiku:

> One bath
> after another –
> how stupid.[118]

---

[117] Hay (1984), pp. 145-146.
[118] Issa (1763-1827) in Stryk and Ikemoto (1981), p. 103.

The gift of context offers the transformation of absurdity into meaning. It allows us to take an overview of life rather than getting stuck in the mundane details (redeeming the routine nature of much of our lives) and it facilitates planning. In the Chinese system of medicine (TCM), the liver (ruled by Sagittarius), is the body's planning centre. Stagnation of energy in the liver will result in disorganised behaviour or overly meticulous planning. Liver is ruled by the wood element in TCM and its energy moves vigorously upwards and outwards, conforming to the western astrological model of Sagittarian mutable fire: '[Wood] is a powerforce that is often likened to the release of an arrow from a bow, or a coiled spring released.'[119] Its associated emotion is anger and its virtue humanity. Anger results from lack of 'freeflow', a quality required by liver energy for healthy functioning. Sagittarians require activity and space; there is a tendency to become stir-crazy when restricted. According to Sandra Hill, lack of freeflow is at the root of all liver pathologies.[120] Outbursts of force and violence, sudden migraines and attacks of bile or nausea can indicate liver imbalance, suggesting that motivation and overview are needing attention. Well channelled, the energy of anger can be utilised effectively to move us on and break through old blocks and patterns.

Interestingly, in TCM the liver has a key role in expansion and projection, facilitated by its role of storing the 'hun' or soul:

---

[119] Hill (1999), p. 46.
[120] Hill (1999), p. 34.

The liver has the ability to expand, to move, to project, to see into the distance, and all these attributes are made possible by the hun. The hun allows dreams, imagination, clairvoyance, astral projections – and at the same time they depend upon the blood of the liver to hold them, to stop them floating away. ... If the blood is weak, the hun may fly off and have difficulty returning; the body may continue to function, but the consciousness is no longer there.[121]

This relates back to the problem of soul loss that arises through lack of faith, which is fundamentally the challenge of Sagittarius. Jennifer Harper writes that the hun thrives on 'having a sense of purpose and vision; without these it becomes discontented and despairing, stagnation of liver *qi* contributing to this loss of aspiration and motivation.' It thrives on compassion and vision.[122] The crossover between the Chinese analysis of the liver and western astrology's understanding of Sagittarian energy is compelling, and is made more so when we think of the liver's role in the detoxification process. Detoxification relates to excess and imbalances associated with negative expressions of Sagittarius:

Addictions are closely related to the liver, be they related to alcohol, drugs or food. The emotional tension that gives rise to addictions is felt in the liver. As the liver is a powerful detoxifying plant, it becomes

---

[121] Hill (1999), p. 51.
[122] Harper (1997), p. 177.

a dumping ground for those poisonous aspects of our being which we feel we cannot express: hatred, envy, rage, jealousy and self-disgust. If these emotions accumulate in the liver, they will weaken it and impair its function.[123]

Sagittarius, concerned with friendliness and joviality, often conceals these primitive emotions and stores them up, weakening liver function, causing perhaps biliousness and nausea and, over time, creating digestive problems.

At the most basic level, the remedy for challenges afflicting the areas of the body ruled by Sagittarius (and the ninth house and Jupiter) is vision and a broad horizon, and the meaning, freedom and fullness of life that result from vision. Sagittarian energy bestows 'the power to make progress upon the path and to walk the Way'.[124] Finding and walking the path (and walking our talk) are the rewards of the ninth house, which teaches us that faith in life comes through acceptance and openness to our experiences: we have to learn to love the journey and, in this way, we experience growth, possibility, freedom and joy, which are the positive manifestations of Sagittarius. The path we walk must be a path with heart:

> Ask yourself, and yourself alone, one question. ... Does this path have a heart? All paths are the same: they lead nowhere. They are paths going through the bush,

---

[123] Harper (1997), p. 176.
[124] Bailey (1951), p. 191.

or into the bush. In my own life I could say I have traversed long, long paths, but I am not anywhere. … Does this path have a heart? If it does, the path is good; if it doesn't, it is of no use.[125]

[125] Don Juan Matus in Castaneda (1968), p. 106.

CAPRICORN
The Search for Dharma

Capricorn rules processes of *Initiation*. In the human body it rules the knees. It is through recognising the need for humility, represented by kneeling, that we can proceed to initiation. In kneeling we are giving respect to a power higher than ourselves and a purer will than our own: we are taking our place in the order of things, appreciating the laws by which we are governed:

> Capricorn rules the knees and this is symbolically true, for only when the Capricornian subject learns to kneel in all humility and with his knees upon the rocky mountain top to offer his heart and life to the soul and to human service, can he be permitted to pass through the door of initiation and be entrusted with the secrets of life. Only on his knees can he go through that door. As long as he arrogantly stands where he has not earned the right to stand, he can never safely be given the information which is imparted to all true initiates.[126]

---

[126] Bailey (1951), p. 169.

The knees from an esoteric point of view are connected to initiation and progress upon the spiritual path. Knees, like all other things belonging to the earth realm, break if they do not bend. Life requires of us a certain flexibility, agility and pragmatism; it requires us consciously to observe the way things are, the *way it is* (the *tao*, the laws of life) and to adapt ourselves accordingly. The lower leg symbolises the lower self (the personality life) while the upper leg symbolises the higher self (the soul life). The knee is the communicating joint between lower and higher. Problems occurring with the knee joint indicate that communication between soul and personality is troubled, suggesting a need to address the spiritual perspective, or integrate material and spiritual concerns. Debility in the knees can stop a person in their tracks. Serious damage to the knees shows that an individual is at a critical phase of development and there is a need for special effort to re-establish contact between the personality and the soul. If chronically disregarded there is a danger of separation between the soul and the personality that may result in the soul permanently losing contact with part of its vehicle: soul loss. The knee expresses the need for *alignment* between the personality life and the informing soul. The higher energies of the soul must be grounded through the personality and expressed through the body:

> By bringing the lower end of the femur into contact with the ground in the act of kneeling, the individual is literally making contact between the earth and that

part of his anatomy which designates the link between his lower and higher selves. This represents the most significant part of his soul-structure, for without this link nothing of value can be learned from an earth incarnation. By touching the earth itself with the symbol of the higher/lower link, one is symbolically stating the importance of the link with respect to earth life.[127]

Capricorn is cardinal earth and is ruled by Saturn. Saturn was called the Black Sun by the Chaldean astrologers and it is significant that this is a symbol for melancholy; Capricorn natives are often marked by the tendency to depression and seriousness. They can seem to carry the weight of the world upon their shoulders and it is characteristic that as children they can seem old beyond their years. These are reflections of the energy of Saturn that operates through a process of *crystallisation*. Crystallisation is the concretising faculty: it causes contraction, constriction, limitation and hardness. It is the process by which forms and structures are created. Saturn creates structure. Structure asks for commitment; it enforces limitation, discipline and focus.

Structures do not last forever. They can be long-lived but they are never permanent. Just as Saturn creates structure it also puts it under pressure, eventually making it brittle and prone to shattering. When the structures of our lives come under pressure we have to review and rebuild them or accept

---

[127] Hilarion (1982), p. 17.

the possibility of collapse. In reviewing them, we are being asked to define our commitments, to understand what is serving us in our lives and what has become anachronistic and lacking in authenticity. Transits of Saturn will tend to unearth for conscious consideration those things that are no longer serving. This can be very uncomfortable for we are often extremely attached to, and identified with, the familiar ways and forms of our lives, even when we acknowledge that they are unhelpful to us. To bring inner change in response to these transits, conscious co-operation must be engaged; this implies that we accept our condition and our responsibility for it.

Saturn is known as one of the lords of karma, the teacher through pain; it fulfils this role by teaching us the relation between cause and effect. The 'blows of fate' that befall us and enact our karma are often felt to be misfortunes. However, if we resist the view that what happens in our lives befalls us from the outside and, instead, experiment with the idea that what happens in our lives is an expression of who we are (our conditioning, our needs, the effects of our thoughts and actions, the lessons we are here to learn, the outworking of our karma), then a transformation is possible. What feels like a hard knock can, potentially, be transformed into an opportunity for growth; the blow we experience is actually an effect of our own behaviour, or of decisions we ourselves have made in the past. In the words of Jung, 'Who looks outside dreams; who looks inside wakes.' We may not enjoy receiving our lessons, but our difficulties are our opportunities to develop – and life requires this of us: that we develop consciousness and transform energy.

Alice Bailey describes this learning process in Capricorn:

> Capricorn is an earth sign, and in it we have expressed the densest point of concrete materialisation of which the human soul is capable. ... When crystallisation has reached a certain degree of density and so-called 'hardness', it is easily shattered and man, born in Capricorn, then brings about his own destruction; this is due to his fundamentally materialistic nature, plus the 'blows of fate' which are the enactments of the law of karma. Again and again, a certain measure of concreteness is achieved, only again to undergo destruction, prior to the release of the life and the rebuilding of the form.[128]

And Saturn, despite its dark reputation as the deliverer of painful lessons, is, if we accept the principle of cause and effect, the bringer of opportunity. To recognise that our struggles are opportunities requires a certain willingness and detachment. Certain laws pertain to life on earth and we suffer if we do not live in accordance with them. This is not to say that the universe is punitive, simply that it works in particular ways. Fire, for example, burns. It is indifferent to us and does not burn us as a punishment; it is simply in the nature of fire to be fiery. We suffer through how we react to

---

[128] Bailey (1951), p. 158.

life; we can choose to bring consciousness and self-understanding to our suffering (seeing how we have participated in creating it) and then, at the very least, it becomes useful and we can begin to work with ourselves.

Capricorn creates the need for effort, strain, struggle and striving. It is often symbolised by the mountain goat: the creature that through persistent effort and steady attention attains its goals. Through this energy of perseverance the tests of discipleship and initiation are taken in the sign of Capricorn. Capricorn is free to choose its goal: it can be oriented towards material ambition *or* towards spiritual aspiration. It is a sign that can tend to be fixated upon worldly success and the desire for status, financial comfort and security. But if we recall the symbolism of the knee, the requirement of Capricorn is to bring the higher and the lower into communication. Non-alignment of the physical and the spiritual aspects of life will result in strain. This will manifest either through events (the individual's ambitions being foiled and plans for life coming undone), through the mind (efforts being derailed by negative mind states) or, very commonly, through the body (for example, the knees giving way).

Capricorn corresponds not only to the knees but to the joints in general, the skeleton, bones, nails, teeth, hair, bone marrow, spleen, cartilage and tendons. As a generalisation we can say that it rules the bony structure of the body and those things that lend it mobility (joints, cartilage, tendons). Diseases and conditions corresponding to Capricorn are such as rheumatism and arthritis, skeletal disorders (including fractures), dental problems, gallstones and depression.

The skeleton represents the inherent structures we live by. Strains and breaks within this structure indicate an inability to integrate at a more refined level (than the physical, which is after all, the most dense level of energy) changes we are required to make in the structuring principles of our lives. Saturn brings structure by asking for a commitment in a certain direction (for example, we marry, we enrol at university, we take out a loan) and these decisions involve us in concrete commitments and arrangements. Yet life requires that we keep changing: the structures we implement through the decisions we make come increasingly under pressure until we are forced to amend them to suit present circumstances. If we resist the process of change and amendment then the structures may break down. As noted, Saturn makes structures of all kinds increasingly hard through crystallisation, so that eventually what was once strong and serviceable in our lives becomes brittle and is easily shattered.

Capricorn people, cautious and conservative by nature, tend to be attached to their structures; they get set in their ways. Wherever Saturn is in the chart will be a harbour of this conservatism. The consequent rigidity and stiffness may manifest in a lack of physical mobility. Stiffness in the joints is an indication that we are becoming bogged down in our views, stuck in a rut and resistant to something within us that is attempting to change. In *The Healing Power of Illness*, Dethlefsen and Dahlke note that the healing of a joint often involves forcing it to an extreme position so it can find a new midpoint. A similar healing process is often witnessed in life when we are slow to change. If we consistently abdicate responsibility for some aspect of our wellbeing, for example, eventually we will have a problem that forces us to take notice.

It is necessary to explore what function the symptoms of an illness or condition are serving. There could be, for instance, a link between rheumatism and suppressed aggression. In the view of Dethlefsen and Dahlke, 'Pain is always the result of some piece of aggression. ... Anybody who suffers from aches and pains should always reflect on just who those pains were really intended for.'[129] This statement calls for some qualification; the word 'aggression' is loaded. I think it is more useful to think in terms of thwarted drive, desire or impulse, rather than aggression. Bodily symptoms require nuanced understanding because they contain unconscious material that is seeking to come to our conscious attention. Pain suggests some urgency to this.

Louise Hay often has something pertinent to say on the aetiology of physical symptoms and their relationship to inner experience.[130] She associates the knees with forgiveness, tolerance and compassion. These qualities are the hallmarks of the humility and respect that is linked with Capricorn. Our knees reflect that status of pride and ego, to which of course, we cling with great attachment. Hay relates rheumatism and

---

[129] Dethlefsen and Dahlke (1990), p. 212.
[130] Hay (1984).

arthritis to feeling victimised and unloved, to chronic bitterness and resentment. Here again, manifesting in the body, is aggression, thwartedness and the life-denying gesture of resentment turned in upon the self – perhaps because at some time in our lives it was unsafe to express protest or desire to an authority figure. Remember, Saturn is the expression of conditioning over many lifetimes; it appears to us as 'reality'. It is the main challenge of our lives to see through this conditioning and move beyond the patterns of restriction it has created. We sometimes believe we have been badly done to or have had a hard hand of cards to play, and from the perspective of separative personality consciousness this may certainly be true.

The extent to which we hold these beliefs indicates how much we are resisting responsibility for our lives; there is a need for us to accept the circumstances of our lives for therein is our great opportunity – the learning our lives are designed to give us. Who knows, we may well have *elected* to incarnate specifically in order to engage with the very learning situations that in our lives we reject. In any case, we are here to journey and not to stay still. Capricorn ailments enforce stillness: they speak of our unwillingness to journey. The joints, according to Hay, show how readily we integrate changes in the directions our lives take. A journey of any length requires us to change direction many times.

Physical immobility corresponds to a certain inflexibility of outlook. It is usually fear that makes us cling to familiarity, resistant of change. We dig our heels in when we feel threatened – we lock our knees; we feel threatened when we are confronted with the new. Life on earth is for the development of consciousness, and we cannot develop consciousness without expanding into the new and giving up our old ways of being. This is a fundamental requirement and, essentially, is not up for negotiation. Rigidity, fractures, dental problems and other conditions associated with Capricorn all point to fearfulness in the face of change, sticking in some pattern that is, for the purposes of consciousness and the soul, outgrown. Aggression is a typical fear response: hence the aggression turned in upon the self of the rheumatic patient, the aggression projected out into the world of the accident victim, etc. The activity of Saturn and the energy of Capricorn will effect restructuring on all levels. Bend or break.

The conditions of Capricorn seem often to be *chronic*: they develop over time. This is unsurprising since Saturn is the deity, Chronos: time. Time is characteristic of personality consciousness in the earth realm and the physical ailments associated with Capricorn and Saturn point to the manner in which we are dealing with the earth experience as human beings. Our humanness requires that we integrate spirit and matter, drawing them into energetic alignment through our beings. Material needs must be respected and attended to, but they must be held in balance with the spiritual side of our natures. Capricorn expresses a need for integration and alignment: the ill-aligned joint will become inflamed; the ill-aligned bone will break; tendons and cartilage are designed to hold the skeleton in alignment. Humanness is defined by being held in a creative tension (an alignment) between heaven and earth. The lesson of Capricorn for the body and the soul is principally one of alignment and flexibility.

If we are perpetuating structures, responsibilities, commitments, ways of being, relationships or practices that no longer serve and have become *inauthentic*, then a transit of Saturn or the influence of Capricorn will work to see them off. In this way Capricorn and its ruler invite us, somewhat forcefully, to review the ways in which we are emotionally, psychologically and physically *attached* – and they then attempt to prise us from the objects of our clinging. Finally, it should be remembered that Saturn is the indicator of the conditioning of the mental level over lifetimes, giving rise to a mindset and a highly conditioned perception of 'reality'. The ailments of Saturn and Capricorn may express really deep work in overthrowing and outgrowing the stultifying effects of conditioning, that will also have been repeated in the early life (often somewhat painfully, and perhaps involving the 'father'). Saturn represents fear and inhibition. These are really hard to overcome, because it is emotionally painful to confront these places; and also because the sense of reality that we are cleaving to is hard-wired into us. Suzanne Rough of the D. K. Foundation has described Saturn as the 'perimeter wall around our reality'.[131] Bumping into that is painful; but staying stuck inside a prison made of our perception will, ultimately, prove to be far more injurious.

---

[131] Teaching, consultations and many resources are available from www.dkfoundation.co.uk.

Why do you stay in prison
when the door is so wide open?

Move outside the tangle of fear-thinking.
Live in silence.

Flow down and down
in always widening rings of Being.[132]

---

[132] Rumi (1990), p. 36.

AQUARIUS
The Blood is the Life

Aquarius, we are told, governs the blood system and its circulation. By means of the blood the lifeforce is distributed throughout the entire human body. It is, therefore, the symbolic task of the liberated Aquarian to dispense spiritual life throughout the fourth kingdom in nature.[133] Aquarius is in polarity with Leo. As Leo rules the physical heart it makes sense that Aquarius rules the circulation, taking the gift of Leo and distributing it to the collective, represented by the body. In astrology we often refer to the metaphor of scaling the mountain of experience in the sign of Capricorn and, from this vantage point, having a detached overview, dispensing the gifts of our experience to humanity in the sign of Aquarius.

Aquarius is the sign of world service, of fellowship, community and the ruler of the New Age. It is a sign that urges us beyond the limits of self-interest and self-consciousness; the rationale of Aquarian energy only really makes sense if we bring ourselves into a context of community and shared endeavour. If we stick, eyes down, to a restricted, egocentric or superficial view of life, the energy of Aquarius is likely to see us develop a

---

[133] Bailey (1951), p. 142.

rather shallow sense of service. In *Esoteric Astrology*, Alice Bailey refers to the 'faithful employee, the adherent and worker in some business within whose limits all his interests are confined and to whose welfare all he has is consecrated'.[134] She describes the average Aquarian as one who has put all his wares in the shop window, behind which there is little to be found.[135]

Aquarius without vision and a sense of communality cultivates his or her own servitude (which can be strongly tinged with egotism – a way of drawing attention to self) rather than visionary world service. Experience in Aquarius, ruled by the disruptive, unpredictable, trans-Saturnian force of Uranus, is designed to shake us out of our isolated, ego-bound view of life. The glyph for Aquarius, two jagged lines like an electrical charge, illustrates the peaks and troughs of experience that are likely to beset the Aquarian:

> Aquarius is pre-eminently a sign of constant movement, of changing activity and recurrent mutations.... The Aquarian can experience the depths of depression and of self-depreciation or he can know and pass through the exaltation of the soul and the sense of spiritual power which soul control gives, and know them to be the interplay and the action and reaction which are necessary for growth and

---

[134] Bailey (1951), p. 142.
[135] Bailey (1951), p. 136.

comprehension. The law of such action and reaction is the law with which he works.[136]

It is important to recognise that Uranus is the first planet whose orbit lies beyond that of Saturn. Saturn, as the most distant planet observable to the naked eye, describes the limits of consciousness. It is the wall around our conditioned, separative reality: the mindset, beyond which is outer darkness. At the collective level: consensus reality. Uranus, 'that mysterious and occult planet',[137] can be seen as the reality of liberation belonging to the higher self that is accessed by breaking through Saturn's wall. Suzanne Rough has described Uranus as the 'ambassador of the right direction'; and a very unruly, eccentric ambassador it can be.[138] As it has the task of breaking through the Saturn problem (the reality with which we are totally, slavishly identified), we can perhaps appreciate why it has to operate in such a disruptive fashion. And while its force breaks up our comfortable, habitual patterns – doing whatever is required to shake us out of our limitation and fear-thinking – it does create enough freedom for us to sense how we might do things differently, pointing us in the right direction. Bailey describes Uranus as the 'urge to better conditions'.[139] Stephen Arroyo, in *Astrology, Karma and Transformation*, remarks that Uranus is not *necessarily* experienced as

---

[136] Bailey (1951), p. 142.
[137] Bailey (1951), p. 138.
[138] www.dkfoundation.co.uk.
[139] Bailey (1951), p. 139.

destructive, but only manifests in this way when there is resistance to its influences.

The effects of Uranus manifest in the body as accidents, cramps and spasms, shocks, circulatory disorders, disorders of the autonomic nervous system and the body's 'electrical' systems and problems pertaining to the pituitary gland. Aquarius rules the ankles, so difficulties arising here indicate that Uranian energy is requiring us to reassess the mobility, direction and the flexibility with which we respond to the conditions of our lives (as the ankles mediate between the ground we walk on and our legs, which carry us forward).

Orthodox astrology regards Uranus as the higher octave of Mercury (as Neptune and Pluto are the higher octaves of Venus and Mars respectively). This reminds us that Uranus impacts upon the perception: 'Uranus, at its best, is the great liberator, the awakener, the illuminator which stirs up the person's inner and outer life with such intensity that things are never the same afterwards.'[140] While Mercury governs communication, rationality, sense perception and the lower mind, Uranus corresponds to intuitional perception, refined intellect and innovation. Aquarius is, potentially, visionary, futuristic, humanitarian and brilliantly cerebral. However, the full potential of Aquarius can only be released through the deconstruction of the paradigm established by Saturn, and this requires some alignment between the personality and the soul.

---

[140] Arroyo (1992), p. 40.

The Aquarian function of destroying the paradigm and expanding the vision, forces a person to integrate a new understanding – a new sense of reality – and to develop a more authentic, autonomous response to life. Uranus effects liberation. The sign and house Uranus occupies in the chart shows the area where liberation is being sought, its element indicating the *level* of experience at which liberation is required (e.g. Uranus in water indicates liberation is sought at the emotional level).[141] This work of vision and integration is, in the etheric vehicle, undertaken by the brow chakra; Aquarius rules the brow chakra and the pituitary gland, which is its physical counterpart. The pituitary gland is sometimes referred to as the master gland of the endocrine system because it represents the control centre of that system. Esoterically considered, the brow chakra – also known as third eye – is the translator of high-vibration, spiritual energy (Bailey refers to it as 'soul force'),[142] distributing it for use in the lower centres. It is interesting to note that Pisces rules the crown chakra and the feet (the body's connections to heaven and earth), and Aquarius rules the brow and the ankles/shins (the points at which the heaven and earth connections are mediated for use by the rest of the body and its energy system).

---

[141] Fire corresponds to the higher mental (intuitional) level, earth to the physical, air to the lower mental (cognitive/intellectual) and water to the emotional.
[142] Bailey (1953), p. 45.

Aquarius, governing the brow, conditions the control centre of the vitally important endocrine system.[143] This might suggest that Aquarian energy is working to impel the control centre towards a higher vibration and, hence, to reorient it towards a vision of life that is beyond the separative consciousness of Saturn. This is an aspect of how Aquarius works in polarity with Leo: Leo generates supreme self-consciousness and individuality, which, in Aquarius, must be converted into group consciousness and contributed to the collective. This conversion from self-server to group-server requires a radical shake-up of the control centre, so that it is energetically oriented to the group rather than merely to self. As Leo rules the heart and Aquarius the brow, there is the suggestion that resolving the polarity (consummating the energy of one in that of the other) is bringing the head and the heart into right relationship. The symbolism of the body is always uncannily instructive. The feeling and emotion of the heart must be brought into right relationship with the intuitional intelligence of the higher self.

The heart and circulation must be open and free from blockages in order to be healthy. The etheric counterpart of the blood circulation is the circulation of *prana* (lifeforce energy, *qi*): a problem arising in one indicates a problem, correspondingly, in the other. That problem will relate to a disconnection from, or imbalance in, the heart energy, and it

---

[143] See the essay on Pisces for more about the endocrine system. If we consider the glands to be the physical manifestation of the subtle energies of the chakra system, we might think of hormones as being spiritual substances effecting energetic change within the body–mind.

will result in lack of vitality, withdrawal, detachment, loss of feeling or consciousness (whether at the physical, emotional or spiritual level). If blood does not circulate fully there is a loss of feeling in the extremities. This will be accompanied by a certain loss of consciousness at higher levels. The heart (Leo) must be strong for the circulation (Aquarius) to be sound, and likewise, the circulation must be unimpeded for the heart energy to be discharged fully.

When Leo–Aquarius energy fails to flow it can manifest as blood clots, brain tumours, hardened arteries, epilepsy (and nervous disorders) and heart attacks. These diseases are indicators that there is personality-level resistance to the requirements of the higher self, and that the love energy of the heart chakra is compromised. Through such shocks, Uranus is functioning to refocus the will, to create *willingness* rather than *wilfulness*, and to reorient the efforts of the personality. The personality gets easily and deeply attached to its ways; it dislikes reorientation, as we all know. Accepting the defects of personality and turning our efforts towards higher aims is uncomfortable and requires a large amount of self-acceptance and love: the heart must be strong. The commentators on the meanings of illness, Dethlefsen and Dahlke, are not using astrological models in their work, and yet, when they write about heart disease they could very well be describing the work of Uranus and the Leo–Aquarius polarity:

> It is precisely on those people who are not prepared to be dragged by 'any old emotion' out of their familiar

rut that such rhythmic disturbances tend to descend. In such cases the heart becomes disturbed because those concerned lack the confidence to let themselves be disturbed by their emotions. They cling on to their reason and their familiar way of life and are not ready to have their established routine disrupted by feelings and emotions. They do not want to have the harmonious regularity of their lives disturbed by emotional outbursts. Yet in such cases the emotion simply somatises itself, and the heart then starts disturbing them on its own account. The heartbeat goes wild and so forces those concerned literally to 'listen to their hearts'.[144]

I have mentioned that injuries to the ankles and shins will be expressive of Uranian energies. Interestingly, Louise Hay regards lower leg problems as indicating fear of the future. Aquarius and the eleventh house of the birth chart represent the future. Lower leg injuries also indicate a poor earth connection (lack of grounding), which typifies the cerebral, detached and spaced-out functioning of Aquarius and its ruler. A twisted ankle can serve to remind us that we are lost in our heads, that we are not present in our bodies, that we are fearful or that we are failing to integrate higher and lower, or self and group (for example, finding ourselves separated from friendship circle, support network or community group).

---

[144] Dethlefsen andDahlke (1990), p. 212.

It is hard for many of us to accept the idea that accidents that hurt us are generated within our own energy fields. It is a very objective and courageous person who is able to hold the view that they have some culpability for an accident that resulted from carelessness on someone else's part. Energies operating through us that are repressed from conscious realisation have little scope but to affect us from the outside, and it is the contention of astrology that we meet ourselves in the events, circumstances and people we attract to us. As the body–mind is an electromagnetic field, we engage in magnetic attractions and repulsions: what we attract *is,* in a real sense, who we are. Jung contended that we awaken to the reality of ourselves when we look *within* for the source of our experience; when we look at our experience as purely external to us, we remain in a sense, in a dream. This perspective has great pertinence to the idea of the 'accident'.

The bolt from the blue, the accident or the sudden paralysis could well be the workings of Uranus upon a recalcitrant personality. It is always useful, whatever your view, to *experiment* with the idea that what comes at you apparently from the external world *might* be word from a messenger at a higher level of your being. 'The body always tells the truth.'[145]

These admittedly unwelcome messages from a higher level present us with the opportunity to align our personalities with that higher level. In this way, the accidents and illnesses of Uranus are encouraging us to break through the bondage of

---

[145] Dethlefsen and Dahlke (1990), p. 207.

Saturn and come into a freer, more authentic way of being: they are signals of an urgent need for freedom. This is a movement from incarceration towards liberation expressed by the Saturn/Uranus interface. Uranus urges us towards liberation and originality; it points up our identification with tradition and the Law of the Father (authority in all its guises), and spells out to us the cost of this unquestioning adherence to inauthentic being. The iconoclastic interventions of Uranus always represent the severing of attachments for *developmental* purposes. And ultimately, the purpose of development is to bring soul and personality into alignment, to infuse personality and everyday experience with soul force.

Alignment and integration, we have established, are functions of the brow chakra through which we are awakened to spiritual vision. The energies flowing through Aquarius, so potent for us at this point in the world's turning, are working to bring about this alignment and integration – to balance the heart and head in right relationship, to relate the centre to the periphery, the individual to the group, the node to the network and the point of intersection to the web at large. The idea held out by the Leo–Aquarius polarity is that we belong to each other. There are many hearts, one life; many centres, one web.

> The ajna [brow] centre is the organ of the integrated personality, the instrument of direction and is closely related to the pituitary body and the eyes, as well as to all the frontal areas of the head. ... Today, the goal is

that of a ... higher fusion – that of soul and personality.[146]

---

[146] Bailey (1953), p. 200.

PISCES
The Gravity Line

You and I
are mostly water.
Last year
most of each of us
was in the ocean.
We circulated together
in the Atlantic
or Pacific perhaps,
for we are mostly water.
And that water was lifted
by sunshine heat,
by the impact of photons
cascading down
beating upon the ocean's face.
And every photon
comes from the sun,
from the belly of the star;
you and I were stars last year.
We chased each other
in the turbulent heart of the sun.[147]

---

[147] From David Brazier's poem 'Where were you last year?'

Pisces rules the top and the toes: the crown chakra (manifesting in the pineal gland) and the feet. These points are our connections to heaven and earth, and it is entirely appropriate that Pisces should govern these areas where the seemingly separate body of the individual interfaces with the impersonal, transcendent realm of pure spirit (heaven) on one side, and our planetary home, characterised by dense matter (earth), on the other, because Pisces is ruled by Neptune, whose principle is *unity* and transcendence. If we are to be open to the spiritual energies coming through the crown, we must have our feet firmly anchored on the earth. If we do not, how can the crown energies be transmitted into the earth? It is through our feet that we connect not only with the earth but also with the rest of humanity in complete equality; and through our feet we meet the whole world and connect with our spiritual journeys as we 'walk the path'.

Our connection with the earth through the feet facilitates the flow of earth energies into our bodies/energy fields and out into the cosmos. Pisces' rulership of the crown and the feet demonstrates this two-way traffic of energy flow between higher and lower, subtle and dense. Facilitating this flow, interweaving cosmic and earth energies, is what makes us human: this is what humans are for.

We are receivers, transformers and transmitters of energy, and the centres conducting and distributing energy are the centres along the spine in the etheric body: the chakra system. This is the system by which energy is received from heaven, transmitted down the spine, through our feet and into the earth; and likewise received from the earth, transmitted up the spine and outwards to the higher (or more refined) levels. Humans are, notably and significantly, upright units working in this huge job of energy transformation and interchange between higher and lower. This is in a sense an impersonal process, but one that benefits from our personal willingness and consciousness. It is also a process by which we refine our beings and come to consciousness.

We can be *more* or *less* co-operative with it. Co-operation will, of itself, ensure improvements in our health, wellbeing and development. The process is governed by natural force and natural law, so working with it rather than against it, will bring us into alignment with natural force and law, and this, of itself, has healing effects. So how can we co-operate with the process of energy transformation? There are, amongst others, two simple approaches: care of the body, and care of the mind. When we eat, we are also transforming energy. Eating natural foods and keeping the body active and flexible, and being aware of where energy gets stuck and stagnant (and getting it moving) will help considerably in taking care of the body. Care of the mind may take the form of practising meditation, spiritual practices, addressing difficult mental patterns and ensuring that we are not overloading our minds with information, intoxicants, virtual 'experience' or trash TV, etc. Cultivating a healthy body and mind helps us to connect with what is *real*[148] and come into our gravity line: the right

---

[148] The question of what constitutes reality is a pressing one for our times, human experience having very suddenly become exposed to, and

relation between above and below (that flows through the Sun-ruled spine), which allows us to access more energy and for our vibrational rate to rise, making us better transformers and more truly our human selves. This process belongs to our individuation. We need to become ourselves so that we can transform energy most effectively; in this way we are of service – service being the keynote of Pisces.

Becoming ourselves involves allowing the authentic expression of the personality as the vehicle for the soul. The symbiotic relation between soul and personality (alluded to in the matrix of the birth chart) is depicted in the glyph for Pisces: two fishes (soul and personality) connected by the vital silver thread that binds soul and personality together throughout the cycle of manifest life. Spiritual activity is the conversion and transmutation of the lower self into the higher self: the contribution of Pisces (in consort with Virgo) is in keeping soul and personality in connection with each other, and with heaven and earth, both inspiring *and* grounding the human being. Thus it oversees a process of spiritualisation – that is to say, a refinement of vibrational energy.

Pisces is the dreamer of the zodiac. Its energies are diffuse, unboundaried, undifferentiated. It has the urge to merge, and an idealistic – sometimes totally unrealistic – longing for transcendence or *oneness*. Pisces and Neptune confer powers of imagination, inspiration and artistic talent (especially pertaining to music, dance, poetry and film and photography,

---

dominated by, 'virtual reality', comprised as it is merely of traces and reflections of reality.

i.e. arts of ephemerality and illusion). There is a mediumistic quality to Pisces: impressible, suggestible and psychically sensitive. It needs its opposite sign, earthy, discerning Virgo, to stabilise its far-out energies. Pisces does the dreaming, Virgo does the digging. Dreaming without digging is pie in the sky; digging without dreaming is mere drudgery. Diggers and dreamers need each other and, working together, Virgo–Pisces have the willingness, effectiveness and the inspired vision for transformative activity and meaningful service.

The pineal gland is located in the centre of the head and is active in infancy until the will-to-be is sufficiently established. It has a role in anchoring us in our physical incarnation.[149] Descartes called it the 'seat of the soul' and Christine Page (a medical doctor with an esoteric bent) suggests in *Frontiers of Health* that it may act as a hormone regulator, releasing neurotransmitters (e.g. melatonin) in the brain; as melatonin is produced in darkness and during meditation, Page considers the light-sensitive pineal gland to be involved in allowing impulses of the soul to enter the physical brain. Page writes that the pineal connects to the electromagnetic force of the earth's core.[150] In this picture, the pineal gland holds us in the gravity line.

Esoterically, spiritual forces pour into the individual body through the crown chakra and are distributed by the chakras along the spine. The chakras are externalised in the glands of the endocrine system: the interface between physical and

---

[149] Bailey (1953), p. 145.
[150] Page (1992), pp. 222-223.

spiritual energies. The crown is like the ascendant in the birth chart, as it is through the ascendant that all the energetic forces of the incarnating being are poured from the first breath until the last. We should also remember that the spine is ruled by the Sun around which all planetary forces are constellated, just as it is around the spine that the energy centres are constellated. These correlations are significant correspondences that help us understand the mysterious processes that are at work in and around us.

It is no surprise that Neptune, as the ruler of Pisces, rules the crown. Neptune is spiritualising, refining and de-limiting. It longs for unity and the merging of all beings in the cosmic sea of interconnection. Its work in individual consciousness is to erode the personality perspective, which is boundaried, separative, dualised. In our individual bodies and minds we can readily become disconnected (from the natural world, from our own natures, from each other, from heaven and earth) and, thus hopelessly forgetful of our spiritual realities. Neptune urges us towards remembering and reconnection; it inspires us with glimpses of a vision of oneness where – Neptune is the higher octave of Venus – all is cosmic love. Stephen Arroyo writes:

> Neptune dissolves the old highly ordered patterns of consciousness. Thus, we are made aware of the limitations of our usual perceptions and of the fact that there exists something greater and more comprehensive than what we have presumed. This intervention in our lives of a more unified (however

185

insubstantial) 'something' is received by some people as a profound spiritual mystery or as an act of 'grace'.[151]

Diseases associated with imbalances of the crown chakra all pertain to a relationship with this transcendent interconnectedness and finding the will to live. Depression might be said to express disconnection and loss of will due to low activity in the pineal gland. The various forms of dementia also relate to this loss of will, disconnection, alienation and struggle to engage with the present. A withdrawal from connection and engagement (perhaps due to shock, grief, loss of meaning, etc.) impacts upon the functioning of the energy centres. When the individual chakras are in a condition of 'livingness' they are able to remove blockages within the energy system: '[T]he livingness of the individual centres which, through the potency of their life, themselves are effective in destroying all hindrances and obstructions. They can "burn up" all that hinders their radiance.'[152]

Epilepsy can be seen as a response to an overloaded crown chakra. Like a tower without a lightning conductor, a kind of combustion takes place in the energy-body. The whole energy system needs to regulate and ground itself as it receives massive hits of highly refined energy, which burn it out. The 'gravity line', achieved potentially in Pisces, seems to present itself as this lightning conductor, offering a kind of

---

[151] Arroyo (1992), p. 44.
[152] Bailey (1953), pp. 185-186.

healthy balance through the right relationship of the crown to the feet, of heaven to earth: we need our connections to be in balance if we are to be well.

Pathology is associated with withdrawal from either pole or from both. Epilepsy may express withdrawal from the earth pole – perhaps responding to refined artistic impulses, seeking escape, or connection and relationship with spirit or with those in spirit. Schizophrenia is another condition where there seems to be great openness to spiritual and non-material realms without grounding and the gift good grounding brings: the ability to stabilise the energy system and to reality-check. We all exist on spectrums the extreme ends of which are pathological. We are all subject to depression, loss of meaning in life, loss of will, mental impairment due to psychological and emotional states. Many of us also exhibit the propensity to over-indulge (in drugs and alcohol, for example) when we are struggling with life.

A strong emphasis in Pisces or a strong Neptune (conjuncting Sun, Moon, inner planet or angle) will weight our position on the spectrum towards the pathological (i.e. the non-normative). This is difficult to handle, of course, but there are great gifts associated with Pisces/Neptune: inspiration, imagination, idealism, compassion, empathy, connection to 'mystery'. The artist, the musician, the mystic, the visionary, the shaman, the therapist and the healer are Piscean characters who are able to see through into another reality and bring that vision to be shared in the human realm.

Our culture does not value these gifts and abilities very highly at the present time. They do not fit into a materialistic, mechanistic view of reality. They do not fit into a market economy, are not readily branded and traded: they don't make commercial sense. The unfortunate effect of this attitude is a massive waste of human creative potential and an astonishing loss in cultural terms, but also in the more nebulous terms of human relationship to the natural and spiritual environments; it is these relationships that are proving to be vital for human sustainability.   We belong to the earth not just as residents occupying a house, but as a vital part of the earth's energetic systems, its body and being; part of *anima mundi*. We have lost our cultural sense of this truth at this time and this impacts upon the Pisces/Neptune people severely. They are left to valorise their gifts and potential in isolation, without the general validation of others and 'the world'.

Small wonder that Pisceans, as it has been observed, make the best alcoholics! Perusing a list of disorders associated with Neptune gives a sense of where we are at in dealing with this energy in our social and cultural world: depression, dementia, epilepsy, Parkinson's Disease, hallucinatory disorders, delusion, paranoia, drug-related disorders, conditions of toxicity, addiction, schizophrenia, psychosis, disorders relating to mind–body disconnection, diseases of the lymph system, diseases of the immune system and diseases evading diagnosis.   Neptune brings nebulousness and confusion: boundarylessness, susceptibility to infection and parasites, and a tendency to have a leaky energy field. All are themes of Piscean challenge and imbalance.

The condition of the feet is expressive of how we cope with being connected to the earth, gravity and the incarnation process. Toes can resist contact with the earth, for instance, curling up into hammer toes, to resist connection. The arch of the foot can be flat and earthbound or held very high, straining away from the earth, etc. Pisces governs through the feet our intention to progress, to be self-supporting, to find our direction and clarity of intention. There are many practical and illuminating metaphors pertaining to our feet: 'stand on your own two feet', 'standing your ground', 'I'm putting my foot down!', 'best foot forward', 'digging your heels in', 'getting cold feet', 'I can't stand it!, 'I understand'.

These metaphors bring us clearly into the realm of the will-to-be associated with the pineal gland. Through the sole of the foot we connect to the whole world and everything in it, one and all: collective planetary experience. As all the nerves and meridians end in the feet, it is through the feet that connection can be made with the whole person too. In this way, through the law of correspondence, the foot is a microcosm of the whole person, just as the whole person is the microcosm of the mighty cosmos, *the Body of Stars*. It is this quality of correspondence, the microcosm's relationship with the macrocosm that seems so specially the domain of Pisces.

In relating the crown to the feet, heaven to earth, macrocosm to microcosm, Pisces helps facilitate our right alignment, swinging us into the gravity line, which is the place of grace. We can open to spirit to the extent that we are able to be grounded and rooted in the energy of the earth. Neptune's visions and dreams are a curse if we can't 'keep it real'; when we are in our gravity line, grounded and authentic, Neptune brings us blessings and inspiration that are redemptive.

> It seems to me that the key to forming a right relationship to the Neptunian force in our lives is to realize that no satisfaction or liberation will come from our constantly seeking the ideal for which we yearn in the outer world, and that it will only come when we accept responsibility (Saturn!) for making our lives ideal through our own creativity and devotion. In other words, we have to turn within, we have to live the ideal in order to make it real.[153]

---

[153] Arroyo (1992), p. 45.

CHIRON
The Wounded Healer

Chiron, the Wounded Healer, was the leader of the centaurs, and the hybrid planetoid body that took his name was discovered in 1977. Chiron, unlike the rowdies he led, was a highly cultivated being and an exceptional healer. He was mentor and guide to the solar heroes, teaching them astrology, music and the healing arts. His acolytes included, fatefully, Hercules: it was one of Hercules' deadly poisoned arrows that wounded Chiron's thigh in an accident, leaving him unable to recover and yet unable, being the immortal son of Saturn, to die. He has to learn to live with the wound.

From Celtic legend we know the Fisher King, charged with keeping the Holy Grail, who has also been wounded in the thigh (or, in some versions, the genitals), too sick to live and too sick to die. He is forever growing weaker and is unable to father a child to whom to pass on the duty of keeping the Grail; as he weakens his realm becomes increasingly arid, until it is a wasteland. His palace, full of riches, has retreated to the subtle realms and can no longer even be reliably found.

There is no one who walks this earth unwounded. The pain of that wound is signified by Chiron in the birth chart, and it is intense and difficult. The house and sign occupied will be a place where the person cannot recover from wounding and yet neither can they die to, or give up on, this aspect of life. Instead they have to learn to be with pain, shame and difficulty, which will bring them back time and again to the unavoidable wound. This process cultivates considerable awareness of the area of life concerned, allowing talent, creativity, wisdom and compassion to arise. In Kahlil Gibran's words, 'Your pain is the breaking of the shell that encloses your understanding. ... It is the bitter potion by which the physician within you heals your sick self.'[154]

Our preoccupation with our own wounds is, however, boring and limiting. We have to learn to look after ourselves without *dwelling* in pain. Pain is, in a sense, information coming in an uncompromisingly dense and intense form. We can learn from it; it helps to bring our feeling lives to life; it is what has evaded the anaesthetic of our ways of being. To this extent it is a useful guide. And Chiron, as wound and as mentor, guides us towards what we need to give back to life, community, companions. The wisdom and compassion which are the potential gifts of Chiron emerge when we take our focus off ourselves, stop endlessly licking our wounds, and start giving back.

The particular wisdom Chiron brings, arising out of difficulty, is the key to the contribution our souls are longing to make to life. Suzanne Rough describes Chiron as 'spokesman for the soul's intention regarding the process of incarnation'.[155] The world is hungry for the deep awareness and compassion that the wounded healer bestows.

---

[154] Gibran (1980), p. 61.
[155] www.dkfoundation.co.uk.

Chiron's orbit, between Saturn and Uranus, is the 'rainbow bridge' between the planets of our separated personality consciousness and the outer planets that call to our connected, timeless soul existences – the transpersonal planets, which also signify the collective. Chiron weaves together the experiences of our limited, amnesiac personalities and the limitlessness of soul, drawing us ever back to our soul's intention, which will ultimately serve evolution (evolution being, in the words of Castaneda's Don Juan Matus, the 'product of intending at a very profound level'). Intention is an activity of the will. It requires determination and clarity.

A prominent Chiron (i.e. in the first house, conjunct the Sun, Moon or an angle, or the most elevated planet in the chart) is the mark of someone particularly engaged with working with the energy of wounding, recovery, healing and the cultivation of compassion. This might happen as a purely personal process, but as Chiron is the cornerstone of the spiritual identity, there is an urge to serve by guiding and mentoring, bringing healing and restoring a sense of spiritual connection to others.

Chiron was the first to be identified of the hybrid heavenly bodies known, appropriately enough, as the Centaurs, which combine the characteristics of asteroids and comets, found between the Asteroid Belt and the Kuiper Belt (beyond the distant orbit of Neptune). It has a highly elliptical orbit: taking, for example, fifteen *months* to transit Libra and eight *years* to transit Aries. Its orbit is also very erratic and chaotic;

just as it whistled into our solar system, it may one day whistle out again, and so it offers us a particular and present opportunity. It is in the nature of opportunity to open and then to close; opportunity does not endure.

Chiron Through the Signs

Keynotes for the expression of the *predicament* presented by Chiron in each sign of the zodiac and for its positive potential. (A similar message will be carried by Chiron's placements in the houses, e.g. for Chiron in the first house read Chiron in Aries.)

Aries　　　Stuck in Fortress Self, overcoming isolation and selfishness. Challenge of authentic will. *Self-actualising, self-authorising, expression of effectiveness. Appropriate initiative; right action.*

Taurus　　　'Hungry', discomfort with physical appetites, overcoming poverty-consciousness and worthlessness. Challenge of embodiment. *Establishing conditions for thriving life. Appropriate values; right use of resources.*

Gemini　　　Restricted communication, overcoming ideas about cleverness/stupidity. Challenge of perception. *Awareness of thought and word as both product and productive of perception. Appropriate communication; right speech.*

Cancer Needy, overcoming dependency. Challenge of belonging. *Fostering life, emotional intelligence, self-nurturing. Appropriate emotional bonds; right regard for family.*

Leo Poor self-regard, alienated, overcoming egotism. Challenge of seeing the Inner Child. *Finding the eros of uniqueness, charisma and creativity. Appropriate creativity; right self-expression.*

Virgo Pedantic, in servitude, overcoming anxiety. Challenge of sensitivity. *Cultivating body intelligence and sense of vocation. Appropriate respect for body; right livelihood.*

Libra Indecisive, in thrall to other, overcoming loss of self. Challenge of finding the Middle Way. *Being alongside other and retaining sense of self. Appropriate regard for self and other; right relationship.*

Scorpio Intensity, overcoming personal drama. Challenge of power. *Opening to awareness of depth and nature of power, emotional healing. Appropriate regard for the mysteries of sex and death; right force.*

Sagittarius No sense of horizon – lack of opportunity, puerile tendencies, fearing meaninglessness, overcoming fundamentalism. Challenge of questing. *Seeking and seeding faith in life, context of meaning adequate to experience of life. Appropriate understanding of opportunity; right direction.*

Capricorn   A cog in the machine, weighted down, overcoming obedience. Challenge of true authority. *Appropriate responsibility and status; right authority.*

Aquarius   Alienated, withdrawn, overcoming disconnection. Challenge of humanitarianism. *Finding ways of doing things differently, comradeship, visionary idealism. Appropriate ideals; right relationship to group.*

Pisces   Martyrish, disembodied, in retreat from life, overcoming selflessness. Challenge of cosmic connection while being on physical plane. *Cultivating personal boundaries and using physical vehicle for inspiration, healing. Appropriate level of renunciation; right belief.*

CASE STUDIES

Bringing the Stars
Down to the Ground

The Body as Ally

But if we can reconcile ourselves with the mysterious truth that spirit is the living body seen from within, and the body the outer manifestation of the living spirit – the two being really one – then we can understand why it is that the attempt to transcend the present level of consciousness must give its due to the body.[156]

What a strange relationship we have with our bodies. The dominant religious paradigms around the globe see the flesh as something to be transcended, the physical realm being denigrated as the place of corruption. In my Christian upbringing the body was the site of suspect desires; one's responsibility was to keep it clean and chaste until one could gloriously vacate and leave it behind with the rest of the hell-bound mire of earthly life. In general cultural terms, in these days of consumerism and social media, the body is the cosmetic avatar of selfhood: primped, preened, endlessly photographed, even photoshopped to look like a caricature of

---

[156] Jung (1961), pp. 253-254.

itself – the body as my shop window, my product and my brand. Both of these approaches, the religious and the cultural, see the body as a *thing* dispossessed of spirit and spiritual value, around which considerable anxiety constellates. Unwanted expressions and sensations in the body–mind exacerbate this anxiety; we label them 'symptoms', which send us running off to the doctor, just as former generations resorted to the priest. In our fear, we cling to our symptoms, recounting them to others and often according them more tenderness than we generally do the lumbering, cumbersome inconvenience of our bodies. Another fear response is, of course, to slam the lid on sensation and refuse to consider what the body is manifesting.

Through this exploration of the *Body of Stars* there is an invitation to come into the presence of the body *as an ally*. 'Once you start approaching your body with curiosity rather than fear, everything shifts.'[157] We are here together living lives *in form*, clothed in matter, animated by spirit. The matter of our bodies reflects our thoughts, beliefs, feelings and choices; the body is a mirror to show us what is going on with us and how we are reacting to our experience of life, which is an opportunity for growth, self-realisation and self-actualisation. The body manifests the self. Astrology, as we use it in the western world, is a tool for delineating and understanding this great preoccupation of *self*: our identities, and how individually they relate to and interact with all other

---

[157] van der Kolk (2015), p. 273.

aspects of lived experience. Identity is anchored fast to the body. The body ties us into an experience of physical reality and individuality, which is crucial as the basis of our consciousness.

Bessel van der Kolk writes from his experience of working with trauma, suggesting that the past gets impressed in the core of trauma patients, 'in the safety of their bodies'.[158] What we can see looking at astrological case studies of people dealing with health challenges (physical, mental and emotional), is the way in which the past, as conditioning, *is* written into both the experience and expression of the body. This constantly mirrors to us what has happened, both in terms of our perception and in how we are reacting to it. The body is offering a reflection of the subtle conditions (e.g. thoughts and feelings) that are keeping us gripped in patterns of habitual response, unfree. In this way, the body is raising them to conscious awareness, to give us a choice in every moment – to stay locked down in the fear-based prescriptions of the past, or to move towards spaciousness, love and healthy development: freedom. Fear or love: past patterning or authentic response in the present moment. This choice requires us to be aware of the default tendencies, so that we can move away from them to embrace the challenges of growth and wellbeing:

> In order to know who we are – to have an identity –
> we must know (or at least feel that we know) what is

---

[158] van der Kolk (2015), p. 127.

and what was 'real'. We must observe what we see around us and label it correctly; we must also be able to trust our memories and be able to tell them apart from our imagination. Losing the ability to make these distinctions is one sign of what psychoanalyst William Niederland called 'soul murder'. Erasing awareness and cultivating denial are often essential to survival, but the price is that you lose track of who you are, of what you are feeling, and of what and whom you can trust.[159]

When soul life is uninhibited by the prohibitions of past conditioning, the body will move towards increased health and wellbeing. The birth chart presents a picture of the developmental prerogative of a person's life. Saturn and the Moon are expressions of the past-life inheritance and the early-life conditioning, representing as they do, Father and Mother. The Sun describes where and how a person's soul is attempting to develop in the current lifetime; the ascendant and north node will give further information as to how the authentic identity can be supported. When legitimate evolution from past to present is suppressed, soul life is not being supported, and this will be registered in the physical vehicle of the soul: the body.

The body links each of us to the cosmos and describes how the cosmos comes to ground and gains expression in our embodied lives on earth. As we have seen, every part of the

---

[159] van der Kolk (2015), p. 134.

body is a living physical expression of subtle planetary energies, of which we are each emissaries in very unique and particular ways. Our bodies are the vehicles of spiritual forces; while our bodies and personalities are temporal and short-lived, the forces of soul and spirit they carry are eternal. And while we live on earth, our bodies are the index of these spiritual forces and how they are working through our physical, mental and emotional lives.

Health challenges will express aspects of our lives that are not fully conscious. These may well relate to past-life/early-life experience that conditions us in particular ways, and is inhibiting the authentic unfolding of identity in this lifetime. This is helpful to the extent that it can make us conscious of how we are dealing with our conditioning, enabling an orientation towards more progressive, authentic modes of being. Thus, illness initiates review. The failure to identify what is progressive and authentic in terms of developing the current identity makes for a lifetime starved of vital nourishment and denied the joyful, constellating energy of the Sun, which calibrates the whole energy field in terms of vitality. This failure will be registered by the body as unwellness: we are not without assistance in steering towards a more progressive direction. That is the whole point of the present work.

Unwanted sensations in the body, mind or heart are messages to us of the ways in which we are going against the grain of self, against *the way it is,* and how we are seeking to reorient. The reorientation we are unwittingly seeking is to move away from the impediments of conditioning that are the negative effects of the Moon and Saturn, and to identify the path of purpose, growth and vitality, as signified by the Sun.

We need to carry an awareness of who we have been, from whence we come and the resources and areas of experience already acquired and accomplished. Not to do so would be to start at zero, *tabula rasa*, in each incarnation. The capacities we inherit mentally and emotionally from Saturn and the Moon, though they tend so strongly to hold us in patterns that are not helpful in the present, are not to be disdained. Although they signify the pull of the past, they are crucial to our fulfilment *when they are brought into service of the Sun and the solar identity*.

All planetary principles, even the Sun, operate in many registers, some of which can be considered negative or unhelpful to the trajectory of personal development (as signified by the Sun and the nodes of the Moon). When the personality has identified how to evolve, by orienting positively towards the challenge of the Sun, then Saturn and the Moon have much to provide. Their aid comes in terms of enabling, empowering and nurturing the individual's lifeforce, as they operate consciously within a developmental context of significance and self-understanding.

Evolution (likewise a spiritual path) is not a motorway we can access and simply zoom along avoiding any further snarl-ups! Even when we have a sense of our authentic identity, we are still susceptible to the challenges of conditioning – of course we are. However, we will hopefully have an idea about *how to engage* with our challenges usefully and meaningfully, to serve the unfoldment of our consciousness/identity, which will in turn be of service to others and to life in general. The opportunity to live a human life is defined by its necessary commitment to physicality: life in a body amidst countless other bodies, sourcing sustenance and stability from the great body that is Earth. Our bodies are not mere carnal adjuncts to the non-physical aspects of our beings but are fundamental to the arising of any kind of consciousness *at all*. It bears repeating: the body is an index of consciousness; sensation is continuous with consciousness.

Our lives now are the product of many hundreds of years of the body (and physical life in general) being polarised with spirit: fallen and damned. There is much to rectify and reclaim here, for the physicality of our experience is the precondition of conscious existence. It is sacred. This is a truth to which we must bow. If our health challenges draw us closer to it, then they will have served us well. Climate crisis and the multifarious ecological problems, which reflect how the human family is dealing with physical life, are expressions of 'disease' in the planetary body. There is a correspondence between individual illness, collective illness and planetary illness. Learning to understand and take responsibility for physical life and deeply to appreciate its significance is scarcely optional. Pathology is our greatest teacher in developing this appreciation. Our suffering need not be pointless, if only it is allowed to be raised to consciousness *through the body*, making the body our most important ally:

204

'Everything pertaining to the soul is expressed and revealed in the body.'[160]

Introducing the Case Studies

'Storming the Citadel', Case A, is the story of a person with neurological birth defects. It is a complex medical picture and shows the incontrovertible importance of the physical level of expression to raise issues of conditioning to consciousness. We do not struggle to acknowledge that genetic factors can influence our health, but to suggest that the issues and struggles of our ancestors are medical factors is less likely to meet with common consent. And yet, what really is the difference between the two statements: essentially, it is semantic. This case study raises this issue of the ancestral inheritance and how we, as individuals, are charged to deal with our lineage.

Cases B and C both pertain to motherhood and distinctively female experience as the mode through which the deep summons of the self to authentic expression is mediated, shown here in very different ways. The injunction towards freedom and authenticity is felt in a dynamic tension with the desire to repeat the pattern of the past (the Moon) as it is central to the memory of a former identity. It is interesting in both cases to observe the ways in which the body seeks to prevent mere repetition of the former identity: we are

---

[160] Steiner (2004), p. 33.

programmed to evolve. In the words of Matthew Sanford, 'Consciousness does not abandon us. It is only denied.'[161] The deep wish of the self is for us to *become ourselves*.

In Cases D and E we see examples of how the angles of the chart (descendant and IC, respectively in these cases) receive the pressure of soul force to liberate the authentic identity through a conjunction with Uranus. Case E, particularly, pertains to unacknowledged and troublesome experience imported from the family line, and the client has generously furnished us with some of that context. Both of these cases show how useful midpoints between planetary significators can be, in describing what is showing up in the body and what is suggested in terms of steering the personality towards the rightful identity in this lifetime.

Mental and emotional health is addressed in Cases F and G. Although the experiences of these clients is distressing and impactful, they are very common – indeed endemic – expressions of anxiety and depression, and the kind of depression and emotional pain that arise out of the failure to live according to one's own design. Conformity and consensus are mighty drivers in our culture – astrologically they are both functions of Saturn. Creative potential is sacrificed on the altar of conformity; if we merely conform we cannot evolve. And if we cannot evolve, we are stuck, and stuck energy stagnates, creating conditions for illness.

---

[161] Sanford (2006), p. 168.

Case H is one of medical complexity. It is interesting for its demonstration of how Virgo and sixth-house influences tend to *somatise* – get translated into bodily expression as symptoms, which are then very readily identified with and begin to dictate *reality*.

I have entitled Case J, 'The Pressure to Overcome the Past'. I am grateful to this client for allowing me to share some of her back-story. This involves an early traumatic event pertaining to the parents (Saturn and the Moon), which is expressed with poetic acuity in the chart. Medically, this is a case of multiple sclerosis. The nodal axis of the Moon, expressing the trajectory of evolutionary development over many lifetimes, is worth drawing attention to in this case. The south node shows where we have already acquired experience by sign and house placement; the north node indicates the direction of growth. Dane Rudhyar goes as far as to refer to the south node as the anus and the north node as the mouth, which certainly disposes a person to go for growth, rather than stick with the tried and tested![162]

The last two studies, Cases K and L, show how aspect configurations within the charts (a t-square in Case K, a yod in Case L) form the basis of the health picture. This alludes to the great importance of aspect configurations as illustrative of the major challenges of a lifetime. The two studies provide a very interesting contrast in that the charts bear great similarities and yet manifest in totally different ways through

---

[162] Rudhyar (1991), p. 257.

the body. These charts might be shown as a warning to medical astrologers tempted to make hard and fast interpretations of astrological indicators. The body is eloquent and nuanced in its expression. It is a bold astrologer who would seek to make a medical diagnosis on the basis of a chart alone (clearly this is not something I even attempt, my drive being to delineate the developmental dilemma that I see as giving rise to the physical challenges); the ways in which planetary principles show up in the body are many and various.

These charts both demonstrate how houses, as well as signs, can indicate body zones/parts. There is an equivalence between, for example, Leo and the fifth house: they can both indicate the spine (as in Chart L); or between Sagittarius and the ninth house: they can both indicate the liver (as in Chart K). If Leo rules the ninth house in a chart, how do we know if it is indicative of the spine or the liver? My answer to this is to ask the client!

Diane L. Cramer refers to the different conditions tending to arise through the cardinal, fixed and mutable crosses in her excellent book, *How to Give an Astrological Health Reading*. She supplies a system of assessing which quadruplicity is emphasised. When I apply this to Cases K and L, Case K is predominantly fixed and Case L predominantly mutable. The fixed cross, Cramer contends, tends to affect (amongst other parts) eliminative organs, and to manifest in chronic illness; this accords with Case K as far as it goes. But the digestive and metabolic issues in the case would, on Cramer's system, accord with mutability, which is low in the chart – but it *is* the quadruplicity of the Sun, so may point to the solar energy being under-utilised perhaps. Case L is predominantly mutable but the symptoms pertain to joint pain, which Cramer would see as a cardinal condition (cardinality is the lowest count in the chart here). This manner of exploration hardly yields conclusive results (in my hands, at any rate).[163]

Some systems of astrological diagnostics are so exhaustive and detailed (for example, Eileen Nauman) that pages of analysis are produced and, even so, can seem to overlook a major energetic challenge in the birth chart (for example, the Moon conjunct Neptune, which we could simply assume was likely to express debility in the body part ruled by the house or sign placement). Having said this, I am stunned by her analysis of vitamin and mineral deficiencies on the basis of astrological significators; and the midpoint analysis she offers is rich pickings for any astrologer interested in health. I guess there are horses for courses.

The work I offer here is not intended to result in diagnosis or prescription. My intention here is to offer insights on the basis of the developmental context of a lifetime, and to enquire into the extraordinarily rich and mysterious nature of the body and somatic experience, so as to make a meaningful interrogation through the lens of astrology.

---

[163] The cardinal, fixed and mutable crosses are of evolutionary significance according to Alice Bailey, see *Esoteric Astrology* (1951).

I am overwhelmed with the feeling that my body has been waiting for me to stop neglecting it, waiting for me to quiet down and listen.[164]

---

[164] Sanford (2006), p. 193.

Case A: Storming the Citadel

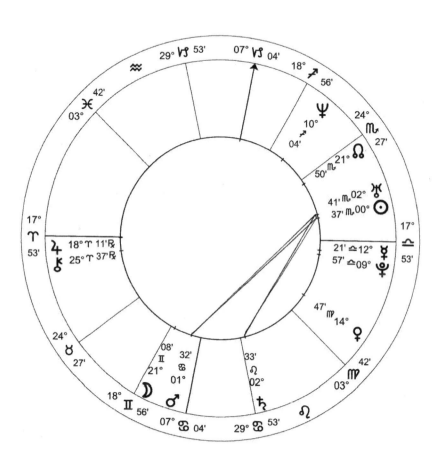

Symptom Picture

Case A's is a complex medical picture: genetic birth defects (a neurological issue with her spinal cord and issues with the nerves of one eye), connective tissue disorder, auto-immune disease with both immune deficiency and immune over-activation. These have had a major impact on her life, including having to give up work and independent living, being physically very dependent on help and being able to do mental work for limited periods only. In one episode of illness she nearly died, and lost the ability to walk. Although her condition is now stable, she is severely impacted.

Nervous system	Mercury conjunct Pluto in 6th
Spinal cord	Leo/Sun, Aquarius/Uranus
Eye	Sun, Moon
Birth defects	IC (square Pluto, quincunx Neptune)
Connective tissue	Saturn
Immune system over/under-activation	Mars
Lymphatic fluids	Moon
Thymus	Gemini, 3rd house

Purpose – the Path of the Sun

Sun in Scorpio in the seventh house. Development arises through cultivating depth awareness; this is a lifetime for attuning to relationship and acknowledging the needs of the 'Other'. Learning to be authentic emotionally and in order to create relationships in which there is freedom for both parties to be themselves is purposeful (Sun conjunct Uranus).

Undertow – the Pull of the Past

Saturn in Leo in the fifth house; Moon in Gemini in the third. This person has inherited a strong sense of individuality, of themselves as the one around whom others are constellated. The unconscious assumption is that if she is not the centre of attention, things will not work out. Autocratic tendencies are associated.

She is nervy, mentally stimulated, and focused on exchanging ideas and feeding the mind. The tendency to be dominated by the mind needs to be overcome in this lifetime (Moon in air).

Analysis

Birth defects suggest that experience from past life is being carried into the current lifetime. What is below the threshold of consciousness makes its way into the body. What has been denied and repressed in our experience – unconscious material – has nowhere else to go, ultimately, but into the body. Here, it comes to our attention through pathology eventually, which is a signal of our desire to change: our longing for wholeness and wellbeing. Maybe there is past-life trauma or trauma in the ancestral line that is seeking to be healed in this lifetime. The family lineage is indicated by the IC, the lowest point in the chart: the tap root. Case A's IC is in Cancer, the sign indicating family and the motherline, ruled by the Moon. Chronic immune conditions may be an expression of unprocessed trauma.[165] Healthy immune function is based on one's ability to discern physiologically between self and not-self: it hinges upon the self/not-self relationship polarity, which in astrology is expressed by the Aries–Libra polarity. We might expect to find this self/not-self theme prominent in the chart. Deb Shapiro poses the question, 'How have you become an enemy to yourself?' to people experiencing auto-immune disease. [166] 'Why have you become an enemy to yourself?' might also be a relevant enquiry.

The condition of the Moon (by sign and house placement and its relationship to the other planets) is a key indicator for weakness in the body in every chart. This is because it is fast-moving and therefore absorbs the impact of all the other planets. In Case A's chart it is in Gemini in the third house, pertaining to rational processes and communication; in the body Gemini indicates the arms, shoulders, lungs and nervous system. It also rules the thymus gland, and the Moon rules lymphatic fluids, which are part of the immune system. The thymus produces and releases T-cells, vital to immune function, into the blood. The thymus gland is the physical manifestation of the heart chakra. Case A's Moon makes few aspects with other planets, most notably there is a wide, dissociate conjunction with Mars in Cancer (the ruler of the chart). The Sun is in the 7th house indicating that it is purposeful for Case A to come into one-to-one relationship with others, whether as business or romantic partners, in a

---

[165] In *The Body Keeps the Score*, the trauma specialist, Bessel van der Kolk observes a link between trauma and auto-immune disease.
[166] Deb Shapiro (2006), p. 181.

therapeutic relationship, in advocacy work or, of course, by needing care.

The first example of this relationship in most of our lives is with the parents, who are then superseded as we move out of infancy. Saturn and the Moon (indicators of past-life inheritance and the parents in this lifetime) are in Leo/fifth house and Gemini/third house respectively, suggesting a self-centred and rather parochial experience.

Case A might have inherited the feeling of being a big fish, but the pond is small; there is an urgent need for expansion, which she is seeking to effect through relationship and participating in the social world. What she is bringing to relationship is shown by her Scorpio Sun conjunct Uranus in the seventh: intensity, depth awareness and unconventionality. Her Sun–Uranus is in a wide dissociate trine with the Moon. Uranus is breaking up habitual patterns through disruptive and unpredictable impulses and circumstances.

Connective tissue in the body is Saturn-ruled. Saturn is the Father, the figure of authority, and it holds everything together as the structure and framework of life and of the body. Saturn expresses our 'mindset', the default settings of our assumptions about life: our perceived reality. Challenges to the Saturn conditioning can make a person fearful and insecure, as if a battering ram is being used against the citadel of the personality. It rocks the foundations. Case A's Saturn is in Leo. Saturn in Leo has the capacity to be autocratic and egotistical: I'm in charge so I'll do what I like and the devil take the hindmost! Its habit is to keep everyone else down with criticism or disregard in order to defend its position on top of the heap. With this position, vanity and poor self-regard grow alongside each other, actually malignantly nourishing each other. There can be a strong dislike of others that ironically and painfully shores up low self-esteem, intensifying a deep anxiety that one is disliked by others. It is a vicious circle. The kernel inside Saturn in Leo is joylessness. Case A's Inner Child (Sun/Leo), the eros of her uniqueness, is getting hammered by her authority figure, perhaps her personal father, and a deep old part of herself that is asking to be both feared and admired as the King of the Castle. Joy, eros and creativity are stifled.

Uranus is in an exact square to Saturn (and Saturn closely squares the Sun too). The revolutionaries are storming the citadel! Saturn in Leo is in its detriment and while this inhibits creativity and self-expression, it also encourages an evolution beyond merely repeating the pattern of the past (denoting potentially masterful creativity in maturity). The tendency to repeat is strong because Saturn feels like the Truth to us: it *is* our reality. Uranus is the Ambassador of the Soul,[167] breaking apart the cherished certainties of the Saturn placement in Case A's chart in order to release soul forces, urging her to orient towards authentic relationship. Uranus is overthrowing the established order of Saturn, the crowned king: a revolutionary lifetime.

---

[167] Suzanne Rough's turn of phrase (www.dkfoundation.co.uk).

Uranus will do whatever it takes to prevent Saturn's autocratic, self-obsessed rulership continuing. As Uranus is conjuncting the Sun, this is evidently part of the solar identity and soul purpose in this lifetime – and it is new ground for consciousness that is being broken. The north node is also in Scorpio in the seventh house (nearly in the eighth) underlining the importance of moving into the relational area of the chart and doing it with depth and intimacy. This is an injunction to open up to emotional and sexual relationship and to an awareness of what lies beneath surface appearances (that the Moon in Gemini is more than satisfied with). Scorpio/Pluto bring to light what has been repressed in this or previous lifetimes or in ancestral experience. This lifetime is one in which the disowned and exiled trauma within the family line or in past-life experience can be brought to light for the purpose of healing and regeneration. This seems to be vital for the reinvigoration of the line and for Case A's wellbeing in the present.

When major health issues hit hard, Case A was 26. She had to give up her home, career and friends and go back home to live with her parents. As I've said, it is our parents with whom most of us have our first relationship. In this chart, in which the issue of relating is so significant, it seems that really getting conscious about the relationship between herself and her parents, and understanding the family dynamics could be crucial for Case A. For all of us there is a dynamic tension between independence and dependency; this is especially observable in children and young people. It is a theme of crucial importance in this chart, reflected in the fraught first house, with Aries rising (sign and house of independence), and the condition of Saturn.

Both the Moon in Gemini and the sixth house of health (of which Virgo is on the cusp) are ruled by Mercury, which is in Libra in the sixth house, in a conjunction with Pluto. This conjunction (in Libra: relationship) suggests that Other, not-self, the partner carries a Pluto projection: overbearing, powerful, devouring. Mercury is the second-most sensitive planet in the chart, and Pluto, the slowest moving body, is the biggest hitter. Pluto rules Case A's Scorpio Sun and here it is bringing its insistent message of depth and renewal. Pluto operates often through drastic conditions, for instance, trauma. Mercury is being purged of the toxicity of obsolete ways of thinking and defunct interpretations of reality. Pluto drives out toxins. Mercury rules the nervous system, which is receiving Pluto's impact. Mercury–Pluto is attuned to threat and there may be a neurological over-reaction to perceived threats; this will be true at the psychological level too.

The transits in force when Case A nearly died were from Saturn, Uranus and Pluto – all of which, we have seen, are so important in the chart and in her expression of its dynamics through physical illness. Pluto was transiting over the midheaven and squaring the health axis (the Saturn/Neptune midpoint). Saturn was transiting the descendant by conjunction, bringing its message of bend or break, and the possibility of breakthrough in the fraught theme of partnership and relating. Uranus was making a quincunx by transit to natal Sun–Uranus. At the progressed level, the progressed Sun was conjuncting progressed Mercury, ruler of Case A's house of health.

There are real challenges in this chart: to come into relationship – and not only that, but to bring to light long-banished repressed trauma and to enter into deep intimacy, which is quite an ask when the default conditioning is 'I'm the King of the Castle and I operate at a superficial level' (to put it in very basic terms)! Further, the ascendant is in Aries, which is the antithesis of being relational. The first house contains Jupiter conjunct Chiron in Aries, showing the pain and wounding arising in this sign. Chiron in Aries feels stuck in Fortress Self, experiencing the intense pain of isolation. The challenge is to develop an authentic will: to find 'right action' and an appropriate use of will and initiative.

Aries, the will to be, is acting in a nuanced way in this chart (and nuance is not something associated with Aries). Its ruler, Mars, is in its fall in Cancer. This says it all. The desire is to come into emotion, to battle her way into a sense of belonging and to build a home. It feels like masculine Mars needs to be gentled and calmed by feminine Cancer, balancing the ability to act (Mars) with the capacity to hold and contain (Cancer). I think this placement gives energy for introspection at the feeling level rather than at the thinking level, which is highly purposeful in terms of overcoming the undertow of the Moon and to satisfy the Sun's path of development. There is a risk that energy is burnt up by being at war with her family and with her own human needs, and this risk intensifies the need to come home to her Self, the

Self that is whole and well and unharmed, beneath and beyond past trauma and personality strife. Case A is a powerful person with considerable creative and healing potential (Neptune in the eighth, trining both Jupiter and Saturn, shows psychic and healing abilities). I think this is a lifetime for deep healing and the clearing of ancestral and past-life trauma.

Client Comment
This is fascinating. I really feel you are accessing something with all this that I have been struggling with on a deep level lately.

Relationship with parents – complicated! There is a surface level which is fine/friendly and no one rocks the boat but both parents are formidable and set in their ways/quite controlling. There are some considerable issues from childhood where I believe they struggled to cope/connect with me and had mental health issues which led to some trauma and attachment issues. I have always loved them deeply although I have never truly connected with them and my relationship with them is emotionally distant. Particularly with my father who is a very unemotional, distant person; he is someone who doesn't like me to disagree with him or his views and will try and put me down/belittle me. I do stand up to him in an intellectual sense and we have had many heated debates, about politics mainly!

While in remission I felt actually able to engage with relationships for the first time in my life. Prior to this I had only had one half-hearted one, so that was a big difference for me. The fourth relationship I had in the remission period was with my partner that I am still with. He is the person I have connected with far more than any other in my life. We have had some issues but it is a very positive relationship. Neither of us is particularly close to family or friends and we have always spent all our time together (including working together in the past). Now he is my carer.

Just to say: there is nothing you have said that is inaccurate, but some things stood out to me as accurate straight away. Others didn't sink in properly for a while. All of it was accurate though and it's actually helped me on a deep level. I am having trauma therapy at the moment and this reading has helped me have a big breakthrough in terms of the relationship with my father and how it has affected my life so deeply. I had no idea that how I viewed the world and how I navigated life were related to that relationship but I now see they are.

His whole persona is about being feared and admired and that translates so much in my life. The way he is distant, uninvolved, punishes unfairly, belittles, disrespects, wants to control completely, wants me to believe and be everything he is – like a version of him. Being different equals rejection, and that is how I have viewed life, society and men. I have also behaved that way myself by being cool and distant and not wanting to show vulnerability or fear. That's so useful because I can now understand and address why I do things that are unhelpful.

The pattern seems to be that I avoided one on one relationships, including best friends and romantic partners, partly because in past lives (what I have learned through past life regression and readings) and on my mother's side there is a history of choosing an inappropriate partner and being catastrophically betrayed by them. This feeds into the other things you raise because what I did instead is latch myself on to groups, family, friends, and took responsibility for those people as if they were part of me. I would put their needs above mine because I saw us as one entity. That is how I was 'an enemy to myself'.

I see how my illness crises were connected to trying to avoid one to one relationships. During my second illness crisis I was in a healthy one to one relationship and the illness and what we went through showed me how a relationship can be positive and healing. This helps me make sense of where I am now and the path I'm on and helps to limit any anxiety that I am doing the wrong things.

It was really helpful for me to see what I bring to relationships. I have spent so much of my life influenced by others' needs that I really don't know who I am as a separate being, or what I have to offer just in myself. It has made me want to appreciate myself more and not dissociate from myself as much. In more recent times I have been able to become more vulnerable, and a healthy one to one relationship has been the catalyst for that.

Case B: Motherhood as Initiation

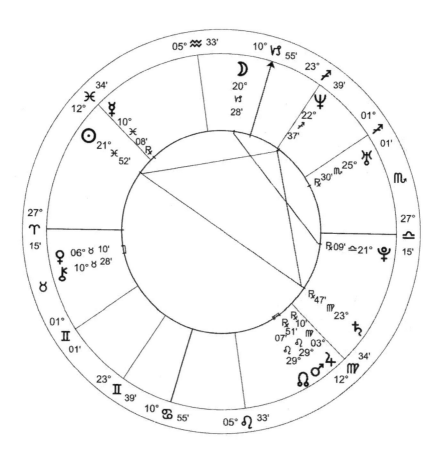

Symptom Picture

The symptoms Case B presents affect the lower back, right hip, leg and foot and are caused by sciatic pain. They initially started with lumbar pain during her first pregnancy. Sciatic pain was triggered earlier on with each of her three successive pregnancies. Six years on from her fourth and final pregnancy the pain is worse than ever, being constant in the right hip; pain radiates from the base of the spine to the outside of the hip to all areas of the leg, to the right foot and outside of the ankle. She can no longer flex her right foot. She has been prevented from picking up and carrying her children and is unable to have them sit on her lap for more than very short periods of time.

During the year following the birth of her last child she developed a lump in her neck, which led to the removal of part of her thyroid gland, compromising thyroid function. She says she 'ticks over, but is tired all the time', which anyone who has had small children will appreciate is a major impairment in managing the daily round.

Pregnancy	Moon
Hip	Sagittarius
Leg	Sagittarius/Capricorn/Aquarius
Foot	Pisces
Sciatic nerve/pain	Sagittarius, Mars, Jupiter
Inflexibility	Saturn
Lump in the neck/thyroid	Venus conjunct Chiron in Taurus

Purpose – the Path of the Sun
Sun in Pisces in the twelfth house. Awareness develops through opening to intuition; cultivating ideas of spirituality and service. There is a need to work on behalf of a vision that helps other people and gives something back to life in general.

Undertow – the Pull of the Past
Saturn in Virgo in the sixth house; Moon in Capricorn in the tenth. Tends to be dominated by the details of everyday life, and by the need to work hard. The unconscious assumption is that to have the right to be here one has to work really hard. There is a memory of acquiring status and achieving recognition for one's efforts: the belief that identity is conferred by material status.

Analysis
Pregnancy is an initiation from which there is no going back. Becoming a mother confronts a woman with her femininity, her early experience of being mothered herself and with a new level of dependency and of being depended upon (all of these issues are under the rulership of the Moon). As Case B's sciatic pain is crucially linked with her pregnancies, I took up her chart wondering what her experience of these issues might be. The sciatic nerve, hip and upper leg are under the rulership of Sagittarius, which in short is about having faith in life and a sense of expansion. Sagittarius likes a broad horizon and freedom to explore. Having a baby presents a radical shutdown of independent exploration: it necessitates surrender. People obviously respond differently to this self-

sacrifice, which is a thoroughgoing process in motherhood, as one aspect of life after another falls to the domination of the child's needs. The hip and upper leg provide the motive force in the body, reflecting how we uphold ourselves, our power to withstand circumstances, and how we move forward with strength and flexibility into the future.

A baby is an undeniable restriction on one's freedom to move forward; the partnership can mitigate or worsen this restriction depending on the level of support and understanding that is offered. Deb Shapiro notes that sciatica expresses 'fear about where you are going and your ability to cope with what lies ahead,'[168] both of which seem entirely understandable in the context of a first pregnancy.

Case B's Moon is in Capricorn in the tenth house making a close square to Pluto in the sixth house of health. This depicts Case B's mother as someone seeking status in the impersonal world, away from her family role; the Capricorn Moon shows she is a practical and responsible person but it is not a warm placement and can suggest someone who is emotionally controlled, even chilly. This situation with the Moon describes, of course, not only Case B's mother, but also her own emotional defaults and habits. It may be uncomfortable for many of us, but there is a sense in which we *are* our mothers (i.e. our experience of our mothers is the product of an internal pattern of our own emotional makeup) – and we need to resolve this. The square from Pluto suggests an

---

[168] Shapiro (2006), p. 162.

intense and potentially destructive emotional nature that will have impacted upon Case B during her infancy as unmet emotional needs. As Cancer is on the IC perhaps Case B's mother's sphere of operation was in the home and the worldly status she valued was sought through the partner: 'Aren't we a successful family?'

Case B's emotional conditioning (Moon) and internalised experience might lead her to swallow down unmet emotional needs and to feel that her success in the eyes of others depends upon her ability to reproduce the successful family along fairly traditional lines.

Pregnancy and early motherhood trigger the Moon–Pluto square. Pluto, the slowest-moving and therefore most powerful planet, has a massive impact on the sensitive Moon, which is very likely to be rather unconscious. The body has a role in presenting what is subliminal, in order that it can be raised into consciousness and addressed. Case B's body in pregnancy seems to be saying, 'This is intense, I don't know what comes next and I'm afraid.' Addressing these natural, difficult feelings may well help relieve symptoms, but Case B's Moon in Capricorn does not dispose her towards what might feel like emotional self-indulgence. She has been conditioned to have her emotional needs largely disregarded in favour of being practical and keeping the show on the road. This approach will inflame needs and fears that are not being given due recognition. Moving forward (Sagittarius) confidently into what is *always* an unknown future requires faith; when that faith is lacking or movement is unsupported emotionally or financially, the Sagittarian-ruled parts of the body speak up.

A strong and supportive relationship is the ideal basis for parenthood. Case B has Uranus in the seventh house of partnership, which suggests that she has a very freedom-seeking partner. Autonomy, that she may long to experience herself, is enacted by the Other, potentially making the partner unreliable. Case B may have been attracted to her partner for the very reason that she needs an unconventional relationship in which a sense of freedom can flourish. And this love of freedom can hit the bricks when pregnancy occurs and suddenly the future begins to look very circumscribed, however wanted the child might be. For mothers, there is no gainsaying the need to change and alter one's course and life expectations during pregnancy. The partner, irrespective of gender, has more latitude.

Case B has Aries rising, giving her an assertive and dynamic drive; Aries likes to be self-determining. Venus in the first house (house of Aries) shows a love of independence, which is likely to be reflected in the choice of partner being someone who loves their own independence too. The chart ruler, Mars, is exactly conjunct the Moon's north node on the 29th degree of Leo (the anaretic degree),[169] both of them conjunct Jupiter in early Virgo; all are in the fifth house. This shows

---

[169] The 29th degree of any sign is unstable, carrying the energy of the sign and its neighbour, as adjacent signs are antithetical in character. This instability will serve to bring the energies of both signs and especially of the planet involved to prominence in the life.

that it is purposeful for Case B to explore and express her abundant creativity. Establishing a strong sense of who she is as a distinct and unique person and expressing herself creatively are of major importance to her self-fulfilment. Children are, of course, associated with the fifth house and are a very significant aspect of her creativity, but the social and economic culture certainly does not value the raising of children, or regard parenting as the creative enterprise it most surely is. Case B herself may struggle to give it due regard, and she is likely to have creative gifts beyond parenting that she is longing to breathe life into.

Retrograde Mars on the anaretic degree alerts me to a difficulty with Case B's will and drive. Mars in Leo is disposited by her Pisces Sun in the twelfth house. Here it is acquainting itself with universal consciousness, seeking to come into alignment with a sense of the whole, attuned to subconscious attitudes and emotions. This gives her the potential to be highly intuitive, sensitive and inspired. She is learning how to serve, how to bring her unique gifts to contribute to others in the service of life itself. Motherhood can be an important element of this service, but it seems likely she may undervalue this, due to her early-life conditioning.

The leg is ruled by the final four signs of the zodiac: Sagittarius (upper), Capricorn (knee), Aquarius (lower) and Pisces (foot). The pain emanates from the sciatic nerve, ruled by Sagittarius. Neptune is in Sagittarius in the ninth house, the focal planet of a tight t-square[170] involving the Sun in Pisces (foot) opposing Saturn in Virgo, in the sixth house (ruling the Capricorn Moon and midheaven). Neptune is the voice of surrender and it is the Sun's ruler. In the ninth house Neptune denotes the sacrifice of the freedom to explore: the big horizon is swapped up for restriction to 'these four walls'. The t-square shows a tension (that will be largely registered by the Sun in Pisces, as the fastest-moving of the three planets involved) between the dream (Neptune) and the dreary reality (Saturn). Case B is susceptible to idealising and romanticising. She has a very real gift of imagination, which is an asset, but when it is not consciously employed it can be escapist and unrealistic. There is also a fear of inadequacy that comes with being highly idealistic, and a fear that reality is going to deliver disappointment – which it has to when our expectations are not realistic.

The fact that Case B can no longer flex the foot is reflected by Saturn (inflexibility) and its opposition to the Sun in Pisces (the feet). It is through the feet that we come into contact with the earth and all the beings that walk upon it: the One and All. The relationship between the self and the All is a fundamental aspect of developing consciousness through Pisces and the twelfth house – which is the solar path for Case B. The foot that cannot flex is perhaps a picture of fear and resistance about entering this watery consciousness, which is a considerable departure from the earthy past-life experience.

---

[170] A focal planet making squares (90°) to two planets that oppose each other (essentially, a right-angled triangle). A t-square is associated with struggle and motivation.

When Saturn is opposite the Sun there is usually an early experience of feeling disapproved of and chastened by the parents, which painfully cramps the child's sense of her own specialness. Neptune and Saturn mark the Sun with a sense of surrender and restriction that result in Case B feeling like a martyr – and one who should work very, very hard (Saturn in the sixth), and has had to forsake much for her family. The Sun in Pisces in the twelfth also carries a strong flavour of martyrdom, and it rules the fifth house of children.

The Sun–Saturn–Neptune t-square does not *have* to bring suffering and martyrish experiences (these may reflect conditioning she is trying to overcome). The chart suggests that there are gifts of imagination and spiritual inspiration that serve Case B's creative identity and confer power, beauty and meaning to what she is capable of creating. She is learning how to find appropriate forms for her gifts in order that she can share them and make a contribution to the wellbeing of other people too. As the opposite pole of the focal planet is in Gemini in the third house, perhaps she will find an outlet through teaching the young.

A year after giving birth to her fourth child, Case B discovered the lump in her neck, signified by Venus in Taurus in the first house of the chart in a conjunction with Chiron, the Wounded Healer. Venus is the ruler of Case B's seventh house of relationship. I've already said she may have experienced her partner as being very autonomous and perhaps unreliable (maybe through no fault of their own). Chiron brings a lot of pain to Case B's experience of relationship through feelings of rejection and inadequacy, that are actually common to all of us in differing ways – there is really deep learning for Case B in this (see the chapter dealing with Chiron). The neck reflects how we look at things, the points of view we take and whether we are rigid or supple in our viewpoints. The neck and throat link the head with the heart; this is where we speak up for ourselves and offer our truth.

Problems here suggest the head and the heart are not working together. The thyroid is the manifestation of the throat chakra: the energy of creative self-expression. A lump here shows that something was getting snarled up, withheld and stuck. This was probably the case for a very long time – who knows, for lifetimes perhaps? The health axis (midpoint of Saturn and Neptune) is 7-8° Taurus/Scorpio in Case B's chart. The midpoint of the Venus–Chiron conjunction is 8° Taurus/Scorpio, revealing the sensitivity of the neck, throat and thyroid. We have already seen the significance of Saturn and Neptune to Case B's Sun (her purpose and rightful identity in this lifetime). When Case B found the lump, transiting Chiron was conjuncting her Sun: she was seeking to integrate the pain she experiences in connection with relationship, and perhaps also in connection with her own drive for self-determination, which may disrupt partnership.

When Case B initially had sciatic symptoms during her first pregnancy, transiting Neptune was opposing her Mars and north node ('surrender your will and your self-seeking independence in order to find higher meaning'), and transiting Uranus was opposing Saturn ('the ground that supports you is breaking up under your feet; radical change is shattering the bonds of your old life to create more space for authenticity'). Both these transits will contribute to a sense of being out of control. The experience of *not knowing* is a challenging one that comes to us all periodically. If we can allow ourselves to bear with it, with a sense of openness and faith in life, just being with the way it is right now, we will find that life re-forms in a new pattern that allows for reinvigoration and new developments. However, let's face it: it is natural to fight disruption and disturbance. It is hard to lose our moorings, despite this being necessary to make the changes that we long for, so that we may become more truly ourselves.

Case C: The Path of the Moon

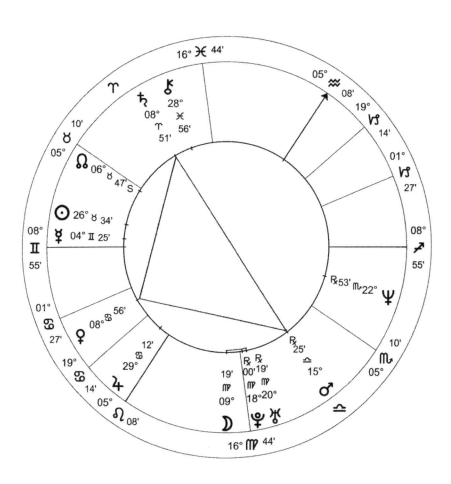

Symptom Picture

Case C has experienced endometriosis and fertility problems. She had one successful pregnancy, one ectopic pregnancy and four rounds of IVF resulting in five lost babies. She then had a hysterectomy at 35, also losing part of her bowel, and feels that she has never recovered her feminine power. Case C also carries deep regret retrospectively about having had IVF, feeling that she had flooded her body with drugs and 'gone against nature'. Her adult daughter is now experiencing issues just like hers, leaving Case C feeling devastated all over again. 'I know the lesson is children', she told me, 'but what does it mean?'

Fertility problems	Moon–Pluto, Uranus conjunct 5th-house cusp, Moon–Saturn
Endometriosis	Saturn (ruler of 8th)–Mars–Venus t-square
Ectopic pregnancy	T-square
Fallopian tubes	Mars in Libra in 5th

Purpose – the Path of the Sun

Sun in Taurus in the twelfth house. This is a lifetime for developing intuition and spiritual awareness through embodied, natural experience and sharing ideas, allowing her to come to a new understanding of the physical level of being.

Undertow – the Pull of the Past

Saturn in Aries in the eleventh house; Moon in Virgo in the fourth. There is an unconscious assumption that her energy is at the disposal of other people, with whom she shares common goals. Identity is conferred by the group. The emotional default leads her to diligently taking care of dependants, for example, as a mother, or to experience dependency. The need is to belong and be safe. An over-emphasis on physical and material wellbeing (Moon in earth) needs to be balanced or reoriented.

Analysis

Fertility and pregnancy are Moon issues. Endometriosis is an eighth house/Pluto problem where the cells of the womb migrate to other parts of the body; when menstruation occurs the bleeding from uterine cells external to the womb cannot leave the body. Endometriosis jeopardises fertility, causes extremely painful periods and has a big impact on health and wellbeing generally. I wonder if, underneath Case C's gynaecological problems, there was an unconscious fear of pregnancy, expressed by this pathology. Certainly the condition expresses an association of pain and woundedness with femininity. It also expresses something being suppressed and withheld from consciousness – the blood is not able to leave the body.

In Case C's birth chart the Moon is in the fourth house, indicating that she has a past-life memory of motherhood that is currently impressing her at the emotional level. The Moon creates a strong knee-jerk response: it is how we make ourselves feel safe and secure, responding through our habitual, emotional 'default settings'. The Moon provides emotional continuity from one life to another in order to orient and stabilise the personality, a bridge between lifetimes. The mother and early-life conditions represent what is being carried over energetically from past-life experience. Case C may have had the good fortune of having a warm, supportive, nurturing mother. Leo on the cusp of the fourth house suggests Case C consciously identifies with her mother. The Moon is strong in the fourth house, its 'natural' home; here the pull of the past is powerful. I can really understand why Case C has had such a significant maternal urge. The Moon is in Virgo and this sign is particularly associated with health, and has a tendency to express through the body.

The Moon reflects an area of life and a way of being that is already accomplished. Purposefulness, power and consciousness cannot be generated by repeating old accomplishments. For sure, our Moon placement, by sign and house, indicates resources, skills and experience that we can draw on as we orient towards our current identity, shown by the Sun's placement: it is here that the soul is trying to break new ground for consciousness and this is where we need to develop, this is the rightful centre of gravity for this lifetime. The Moon can, of course, support and reflect the Sun, but it cannot of itself provide vitality or energetic organisation and integration; only the Sun can provide these. The emotional body or the habit body, illustrated by the Moon, presents us with one path – and because it is the known and the familiar, it can seem very right for us. Case C's gynaecological problems have been, in a way, obstacles on her journey along this path of the Moon, helping to prevent her from merely repeating the lessons of a life already lived.

Her current identity is expressed by the Sun in Taurus (conjunct Mercury in Gemini) in the twelfth house. The twelfth house asks for sacrifice at the personality level. The personality being thus deprived of what it thinks is its heart's desire, prompts a great deal of seeking and really positive growth. Discontent is a great spur to our search for soul force and for meaning. The spiritual gifts of the twelfth house certainly have the potential to far exceed the losses suffered: what is taken from the personality here is compensated at the soul level of experience. The Sun is in opposition to Neptune in Scorpio in the sixth house, again this is a message of disappointment or sacrifice redeemed by spiritual compensation.

A Taurus Sun in the twelfth house suggests spiritual gifts arising through being in nature and having a strong, grounded experience of the body and the life of instinct and sensation. This embodied experience feeds a profound sense of the interconnectedness of all life. The north node's position in the same sign and house underscores the importance of this experience: the trajectory of the soul's journey over lifetimes is away from the drama and passion of a certain aspect of sexuality, towards the cultivation of real presence in the sensual experience of the body, which is the medium through which consciousness – and potentially enlightenment – can arise (Taurus is the sign associated with the Buddha).

To see what is causing the trouble with infertility and endometriosis we have to look at the condition of the Moon. Case C's Moon is conjunct Pluto (Moon–Pluto contacts are associated with fertility problems, endometriosis and hysterectomy). Pluto rules Case C's sixth house of health, bringing its influence into her somatic life. Case C is part of the mid-sixties generation born with the Uranus–Pluto conjunction; her conjunction is very close to the cusp of the fifth house. This is the house naturally ruled by the Sun, so is an important indicator of purpose. It is also the house of children, creativity, romance and the *eros* of the Inner Child. Uranus creates a strong impulse towards freedom and autonomy. As a transpersonal planet, it is conveying a soul directive through the fifth house: don't get tangled up with raising children, you need space to explore your own creativity. Pluto (also transpersonal) on the cusp of the fifth brings its message of transformation and regeneration, quite particularly to what I have called the '*eros* of the Inner Child': the playful, creative and expressive self – the joy of one's own uniqueness. Pluto often effects regeneration through experiences that are traumatic for the personality. Its placement on the fifth-house cusp can indicate abuse in childhood.

The condition of the eighth house, belonging naturally to Scorpio and Pluto, sheds some light on Case C's experience of Pluto. In her chart it is accidentally ruled by Capricorn; Capricorn's ruler, Saturn, is in Aries in the 11th house closely quincunx the Moon and exactly square Venus in Cancer. Saturn represents authority and the father, and I would guess that Case C experienced her father as oppressive to her mother, to herself and to the feminine generally. I would not be surprised to discover that he was in the Armed Forces, which aligns neatly with both sign and house placement. Venus in Cancer indicates love of the mother and of motherhood: it is very feminine and maternal. It is the focal planet of a cardinal t-square with Mars in Libra and Saturn in Aries. It is interesting to note that Libra rules the fallopian tubes, site of ectopic pregnancy.

Case C said that after her hysterectomy she never recovered her feminine power. I would suggest that it always felt severely under siege, Venus being embattled on one side by Mars and restricted on the other by Saturn. Feminine power may have gotten over-identified with biological motherhood, which although highly significant is only one aspect of the feminine. It is part of Case C's purpose in life to garner and articulate an embodied understanding of feminine power. The midpoint of Mars/Saturn is associated with glandular dysfunction; Case C's Venus in Cancer is three degrees away from this midpoint, suggesting that physiologically a glandular dysfunction may have been involved in her endometriosis and fertility issues.

But beneath these issues might be childhood experiences of an abusive authority figure, perhaps her father himself, and a mother who seems under his thumb. And these are childhood echoes of past-life experiences over many lifetimes where repressive attitudes towards the feminine were held (Saturn represents what has conditioned the mindset over

240

many lifetimes) and the more recent past-life experience of motherhood that is active in the memory (the Moon representing the conditioning of the memory/emotional body).

Case C *has* become a mother in this lifetime *and* she has had a deep experience of the impulse towards motherhood, and of femaleness in general. Potentially her life is teaching her that there is much more to femaleness and feminine power than having children. Her Venus in Cancer is the esoteric ruler of the chart (Gemini is rising) and the ruler of her Taurus Sun: it gives us a strong sense of how she can acquire power and purpose. There it is, in the second house, suggesting that key values and resources are the cultivation of a sense of connection, of belonging, of unconditional love for what is vulnerable. It suggests that she finds purpose through her ability to love children but also, and perhaps more significantly, to love the feminine. She has the capacity for considerable emotional intelligence and the ability to offer care and to serve physical life from her understanding of sacred imperatives acquired by her twelfth-house Sun in Taurus.

There is a need to heal early childhood experiences and to value herself as a creative, even visionary, individual. As adults we are both mother and father to our own Inner Child who potentially brings much creativity, healing and wisdom into our lives. Case C is learning to value and nurture her femininity and that which is vulnerable *within* herself – her own joy, her own desire and drive to create: the Inner Child.

Motherhood has been a very difficult and painful path, but it is also her path towards the Sun and acquiring consciousness and power.

Client Comment

This was extremely accurate. My father was very strict and I was very frightened of him as a child. He was 40 when I was born and I don't think he was particularly pleased. My mother was very loving but very controlling too – even to this day. My intuitive skills are indeed developing nicely now and that has happened over the last ten years or so but recently I have begun to believe in myself a lot more and am now doing much better as a result.

Case D: Unorthodox by Design

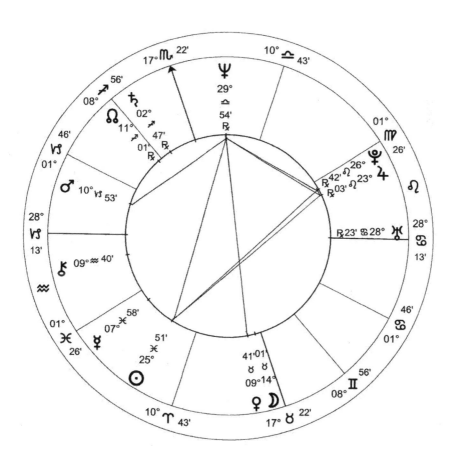

Symptom Picture

Case D presented me with a health picture that included four seemingly discrete conditions. The first is of frequent migraine and nausea that led to a diagnosis of multiple allergies and chemical sensitivities sufficiently serious to render her disabled for five years. At both the beginning and end of this period she was hospitalised for unrelated pneumonia. She has the auto-immune condition, rheumatoid arthritis, and also experienced endometriosis necessitating a complete hysterectomy that took place in the middle of her years of disability. Case D told me that her health problems began to improve as soon as she decided to leave her marriage.

Immune system	Pisces, Neptune
Allergies and sensitivities	Neptune
Rheumatoid arthritis	Saturn, Mars, Jupiter, Neptune
Joints	Saturn
Inflammation	Mars
Pneumonia	Mercury, Moon in 3rd house
Endometriosis	Venus/Pluto = cusp of 6th
Hysterectomy	Cancer, Moon, Pluto

Purpose – the Path of the Sun

Sun in Pisces in the second house. The current identity is developing awareness by unfolding a practical, down-to-earth experience of spiritual matters, intuition and service. She serves by showing up in her body and helping spiritual forces flow through human-made physical arrangements.

Undertow – the Pull of the Past
Saturn in Sagittarius in the tenth house; Moon in Taurus in the third. An unconscious assumption is that one should be ambitious and acquire status, bolstered by relationship or hitching a ride to status on the back of relationship (Jupiter in the seventh disposits Saturn). Patterns are about assuming authority and responsibility in the impersonal world, perhaps in a religious setting.

There is a preoccupation with material resources and security. Identity is conferred by membership of the clan: a parochial, inward focus. The concern is with the immediate surroundings and the physical appetites. There is a developmental need to balance this preoccupation.

Analysis
Neptune is the significator of the immune system, which pertains to allergies and sensitivities, and to the rheumatoid arthritis, an auto-immune disorder. It is the ruler of Case D's Sun in Pisces and it is relevant to note that Neptune is retrograde on the 29th degree of Libra, the anaretic degree. The anaretic degree is where the energy of one sign transforms into the next, which is antithetical in character. A placement here will sensitise a person to both signs, bringing the character of both – in this case, Libra and Scorpio – into conscious awareness by virtue of the difficulty presented. And the difficulty with the anaretic degree is significant, such

that it frequently manifests as a bodily symptom, prompting the personality to greater consciousness and integration. Saturn, Mars and Jupiter are implicated in the arthritis: Saturn's sign, Capricorn, ruling the joints, inflammation being a process of Mars, and Jupiter ruling blood (which in rheumatoid arthritis carries an abnormal factor impelling the immune system to attack the membrane around the joints). Mars is also involved in migraine. Pneumonia is a lung disease, ruled by Mercury. Endometriosis is signified by Venus and Pluto, hysterectomy by Cancer/the Moon (womb) and Pluto (surgery).

The first thing I notice about the chart is an exact conjunction of retrograde Uranus and the descendant, the relationship angle. Case D has a powerful impulse to be free, either *of* committed relationship but certainly *in* it. Uranus and the descendant are in Cancer, sign of motherhood and femininity, ruled by the Moon – as is the sixth house of Case D's chart. Case D is part of the post-war generation of people for whom the experience of home/mother/women was significantly disrupted, allowing for more freedom in how women's roles were perceived. Uranus' sign, Aquarius, is in the first house of Case D's chart, showing that unorthodox, freedom-seeking Uranian behaviour is how Case D presents and asserts herself. She's designed to be unorthodox – underscored by the presence of the Moon's north node in the eleventh house (naturally ruled by Uranus/Aquarius).

Chiron is in Aquarius in the first house indicating that this maverick quality is experienced as a painful problem that makes her feel a bit like an alien, disconnected from others. Capricorn is on the ascendant: it likes to adhere to convention, to gain the endorsement and acknowledgement of the world in general. But Case D's strong angular Uranus throws a spanner in the works, wrecking her conventional façade. She has likely disowned her eccentric, disruptive and unpredictable elements and projected them on to the Other, importing her Uranian impulse towards freedom via the partner (this is typically what can happen with the descendant and the seventh house). The marriage would then be experienced as turbulent and problematic enough for her to justify walking out, thereby claiming her (perfectly legitimate) requirement for personal freedom and self-determination.

There is a strong picture in the chart of breaking out of conditioned ideas of self and other, and of the conventions of relationship generally. The Moon is conjunct Venus and the IC (all in Taurus), showing that her early-life conditioning is about material stability being acquired by making accommodations to partnership and motherhood, to the extent that one is mothering the partner (this interpretation was later confirmed by the client). This is the experience of Case D's motherline back through the generations. The Moon, of course, reflects a past life that currently conditions memory and emotional reactions. Case D both believes that safety and emotional security reside in relationship, *and* at the same time, that she needs to break away from restrictive relationship in order to fulfil the requirements of her current identity. Quite a tension to hold.

Uranus on the descendant indicates how urgently this break with the past is needed. Venus describes the lover and the impulse towards relationship while Mars describes self in terms of self-assertion and the desire nature (so they are both key considerations in understanding the experience of relationship). Case D may well have chosen a husband who wanted her to be a very traditional wife (Venus/Moon in Taurus).

Case D's Mars is exalted in Capricorn but tenants the twelfth house, a very difficult placement for Mars, thwarting the personal will and disallowing a straightforward assertion of self. In the twelfth house the drive of Mars must be used on behalf of others. Service is key here: shown by a close quintile between Mars and Neptune;[171] a wide opposition (the only one) of Venus and Neptune; and the Sun in Pisces, indicating that new ground for consciousness is being broken in this sign. The Mars-ruled first house is tenanted by Chiron, indicating the will feels wounded and that there is a great capacity for healing, compassion and wisdom through the undoubtedly tricky dilemma of authentic self-actualisation and appropriate use of personal will.

Problems with expressing the will can manifest in inflammation, which features in Case D's migraine and arthritis, as anger and irritation are controlled and internalised. The seventh house of relationship is tenanted by a conjunction of Jupiter and Pluto (quincunx the Sun),

---

[171] I have found that quintiles (72°) and septiles (51/2°) refer to themes within the chart that serve the spiritual unfolding of the individual lifetime.

suggesting that the partner is experienced as powerful, compelling and perhaps controlling. Case D's experience of relationship is deeply transformative (Pluto's principle) and great healing can be accessed as she withdraws projections made on to the other, thus reclaiming her own instinctual power and energy.

The dynamics around self and other and the issue of relationship are obviously complex and difficult, and as such, a challenge to integrate consciously. The auto-immune health issues offer Case D a poetic expression of the tensions she is enmeshed in, as the body has sought to communicate the dilemma to the conscious personality. Migraine and nausea necessitate withdrawal and thus create space from others – there's nothing like throwing up to carve out a bit of personal space! Allergies and sensitivities show chronic aggravation caused by the experience of the invasive, restricting Other. The painful joints seem to reflect the strain between the superficial desire to appear conventional and the maverick identity that lurks beneath. Having said this, the health issues do not shout loudly from the chart, as is the case with some people, but are subtle and multi-layered.

I could not initially see significators for pneumonia in the chart. Sure, the Moon/Venus conjunction is in the third house, which governs lungs, but other than receiving a square from Chiron appears to be unafflicted. Gemini (ruler of respiration) rules the fifth house, which is empty apart from the south node of the Moon. Mercury (respiration) squares the north node and Saturn, but is otherwise unchallenged, in

Pisces in the second house. Midpoints are useful when there is a need to drill down.

The midpoint of Venus/Mars (important because of the huge relationship theme of this person's lifetime) is Mercury, which, like a lynchpin, sextiles both of them, perhaps bringing the challenge of relationship into the physiological functioning of the lungs. Grief in TCM is the emotion associated with the lungs, and, as her second hospitalisation with pneumonia was in the same year that she left her husband, maybe the lungs were expressing grief about her marriage experience and for the perceived loss of love, which after all is a fundamental human need. However, this still feels rather tenuous. The health axis is the midpoint of Saturn and Neptune. In Case D's chart the Moon is one degree off the far Saturn/Neptune midpoint. The Moon is the most sensitive point in the chart; as noted it is in the third house (lungs); it occupies Taurus (relating to embodiment and sensation); and it rules the sixth house. The experience of hospitalisation is itself a twelfth-house matter, bringing us back to Mars and the use of the personal will and the desire for self-actualisation.

The endometriosis and hysterectomy are also only subtly indicated in the chart. The womb is ruled by the Moon, sensitised at the midpoint of Saturn/Neptune, and as ruler of the sixth house. Endometriosis is related to the eighth house and Pluto and therefore to the experience of sexuality and intimacy – the deepest and most hidden aspects of human relating. Pluto, as we have seen, is in the seventh house, pertaining to Case D's experience of her partner, who is likely to have worn the compelling mask of Pluto. It is conjunct Jupiter, which rules the blood (these planets together signify menstruation). Jupiter–Pluto are quincunx the Sun, as is Neptune, forming a yod[172] with the Sun at its apex, suggesting that this health issue will create a turning point in the life resulting in greater consciousness of authentic identity. Menstruation is terribly painful with this condition, amplifying perhaps a person's sense of the pain of femininity. Remember, Case D is part of the Uranus in Cancer generation that is breaking out of traditional notions of womanhood, home and motherhood. There is an inward revolution against the feminine being seen as contingent, being subsumed and relegated to an inferior status as soon as she enters relationship; this is a really painful fate to endure – it could feel psychically annihilating to someone like Case D whose seventh house shows us that she projects such control and power on to her partner.

To find evidence of this condition coming into the body, as well as looking at the Moon and Pluto, I look at Mercury, ruler of Case D's untenanted eighth house (reproduction, mysteries, sexuality, depth encounter) and Venus (as the feminine principle), which is notably the sole dispositor of the chart. The midpoints of Venus/Pluto and Mercury/Pluto are interesting: Venus/Pluto equals the very degree on the cusp of the sixth house; Mercury/Pluto equals Saturn in Sagittarius. Saturn is the chart ruler, strong in the tenth, squaring both

---

[172] A triangular configuration in which the apex planet is quincunx (150°) the other two planets, which sextile (60°) each other. It signifies that an important mental or emotional readjustment is potentially to be made.

Mercury and Pluto, suggesting a painful encounter (stifling her voice) with the father or a father figure, and with authority and convention in general. Case D has a Capricorn ascendant, she works with this constructive, practical, pragmatic and authoritative energy, but she is far from being a conventional personality. Her health struggles and her experience of relationship will have served, I suspect, to liberate her unusual, maverick energy through which she is designed to come into contact with 'the group': communities of alternative types with whom she is able to find meaning by creating shared projects (north node in Sagittarius in the eleventh house), thus performing the service to others and to life that her Sun in Pisces requires and enjoys.

Client Comment

I've known for some time now that my relationships are never casual. Even short-lived ones seem somehow fated, often as a learning or transformative experience. The trouble is I've never had a relationship, be it friendship or intimate, that didn't make me feel chained or caged at some point. When I'm in a relationship ... life becomes a drudge. I've always been happiest when I'm alone.

I did not realise that freedom was so important to me until about ten years ago when I was working with a life coach. It is also correct that beauty is very important to me. Everywhere I go, I do my best to bring order and beauty to my surroundings. You are also correct that service to others is the thing that drives me. I worked for a non-profit religious organisation for nearly 30 years and I now serve as a teacher's aide at an elementary school.

I have been described as weird for as long as I can remember. I have always vacillated between creative/unorthodox and staid/conservative. Still, I'm also the person who is so dependable and discreet that people and organisations give me the keys to all their important things.

I have often thought that many of my illnesses were brought about by my own thoughts of 'I can't, won't or don't want to do this or that.'

Case E: Rocked at the Roots

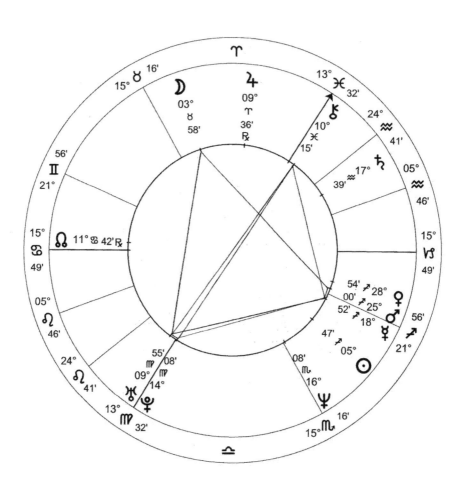

Symptom Picture

Historically, Case E suffered with Crohn's Disease. She had symptoms (frequent tummy bugs, digestive irregularity, bloating and abdominal discomfort) from when she was around twenty. Diagnosis came when, at twenty-three, she was hospitalised with cramps and vomiting. She had a massive allergic reaction to drugs administered in hospital that led to high fever and hallucinations. She was treated with antibiotics which deepened her unwellness.

A positive outcome of this acute episode in hospital was that she became aware that her mental attitude had an effect on her symptoms; she intuitively used visualisation and breathing techniques to calm symptoms. She felt she was being guided in this way, for no one had ever taught her these things.

Crohn's Disease (digestive tract inflammation)	IC–Uranus–Pluto in Virgo, Mercury–Mars in 6th, t-square of Mercury, Chiron, Uranus–Pluto
Cramps and vomiting	Moon, Mars, Uranus
Allergic reaction	Mars/Neptune = Sun
Fever	Mars
Digestion	Virgo, Mercury, 6th house

Purpose – the Path of the Sun

Sun in Sagittarius in the fifth house. In this lifetime power and purpose come through an exploration of creative individuality, of other cultures and wisdom-knowledge to bring joy and meaning into Case E's sense of her own uniqueness.

Undertow – the Pull of the Past

Saturn in Aquarius in the eighth house; Moon in Taurus in the tenth. The developmental context of the chart is that Case E is, in this lifetime, fearful and mistrustful of intimate relationship (Saturn in Aquarius in the eighth house) due to the conditioning over many lifetimes of merging in intimate relationships and cleaving to them as a source of identity, feeling beholden and contingent; relationship thus providing her uncomfortable *raison d'être.* This placement provokes considerable fear of rejection and feelings of contingency; also a fear of one's own hidden depths and issues around control. The emotional body is conditioned by the memory of acquiring status; identity has been oriented in the past towards security and acquisition.

Analysis

Crohn's Disease is an inflammatory bowel disease that can affect any part of the digestive tract. Digestive processes are ruled by Mercury, inflammation by Mars. In Case E's chart they are conjunct, with the cusp of the sixth house at their exact midpoint, all in Sagittarius, like Case E's Sun (in the fifth house). So Jupiter rules both the sixth house and this significant Mercury–Mars conjunction, and, located in Aries, is in mutual reception with Mars, bringing increased heat, fire and energy into the sixth house. There is great energy for activity here and, as the sixth house is about vocation as well as health, there is the suggestion that if the drive of Mars can

256

be expressed outwardly through work and physical activity, its disruptive internal expression might be relieved. The time of life when Case E was diagnosed with Crohn's is the time when the question, 'What the heck am I going to do with my life?' becomes particularly pressing, in the wake of transiting Saturn's closing square to its natal position.

The entire digestive tract involves Taurus (oesophagus), Cancer (stomach), Virgo (small intestine) and Scorpio (large intestine). Case E's Moon is in Taurus; her ascendant in Cancer; her IC, straddled by Uranus conjunct Pluto (Scorpio's ruler) in Virgo; and Neptune is on the fifth-house cusp in Scorpio (Saturn is in the eighth house, naturally ruled by Scorpio). I am particularly interested in the Uranus–Pluto conjunction in Virgo on the IC. The angles of the chart are places of great sensitivity and the IC is the lowest, most northerly point in the chart: the most secret, private, nocturnal area, which points to the deep roots of a person's life. You could call the IC the taproot. It is where we plug into the family lineage, particularly (though not exclusively) the ancestral motherline.

The Uranus–Pluto conjunction marks the generation born in the mid-sixties, charging it with revolutionising and technologising modes of work and attitudes towards health, the results of which are so evident now in computerisation and online, remote working. When the generational planets (Saturn, Chiron, Uranus, Neptune, Pluto: the slow-moving ones) touch a personal point in the chart, as they do here, the individual receives the impact strongly in their personal experience. Case E's IC , the roots of her being, are receiving the depth-charge of Uranus–Pluto, which I would imagine would bring disruption, unpredictability and deep emotional upset (and probably trauma) into her experience of her mother, home and early life. This is likely to be well hidden, perhaps even subconscious to Case E herself; those of her motherline may well have had their own versions of this experience. With Pluto in the fourth house only one degree from the IC, I would suspect the presence or feeling of danger or threat in the home. Pluto rules the fifth house of love, creativity and children; Neptune is on the cusp of the fifth and rules the MC (indicator of the father): was the father or an authority figure a threat to Case E, as a child?

Case E later confirmed that her father was authoritarian, requiring his children to be seen and not heard. He would 'bellow' at any protest or dissent. Growing up in Holland during the World War Two, he had had harsh experiences at the hands of the Dutch authorities and was imprisoned in a camp after the war, as his own father was outspoken about having witnessed Dutch police collaboration with the transportation of Jews to Auschwitz. He became suicidal when Case E was twelve, which 'kept the family on eggshells' and must have cast a huge and ominous Plutonic shadow over them all.

Problems with digestion suggest that the system is overwhelmed by an influx of impressions that is hard to assimilate. Just as we digest our food, we digest our experience. In cases of people with great sensitivity

258

(Neptunians, particularly), the energy body can be 'leaky' and they will find themselves much affected by whatever and whomever is in their environment. Case E used to feel that her tummy was 'falling out', as if she had to keep a hand on it, to prevent it from falling.

Sensitive people need to be well grounded and maintain good personal and energetic boundaries, so as to cope better. While this chart is not exceptionally sensitive (though it has a Cancer ascendant, Pisces MC and Chiron in Pisces), it is rocked at its roots, as I have described. Mercury–Mars and Mars–Venus in the sixth house create the tendency to somatise – to express energies through the physical vehicle. Uranus (precisely inconjunct the sixth-house ruler, Jupiter) has spasmodic and de-regulating effects in the body; Pluto, significator of the bowel, deals with elimination at the physical and emotional levels.

Mercury, in its fall and squared by both Uranus and Pluto, is trying to assimilate the disruptive and threatening experiences these planets describe; Mercury's job is to discern and analyse incoming content (whether rational, sensory or digestive). It is the apex of a mutable t-square with Uranus–Pluto on one side, Chiron on the other: stressful, seemingly traumatic and wounding content, erupting from the subliminal level into conscious cognition. Sensitive Mercury, much stressed by its condition, is additionally agitated by Mars. Mars defends planets it touches. It goes to war on Mercury's behalf in a bodily overdrive that is reflected in inflammation. Mars is the dispositor of Jupiter in Aries (ruler of the sixth house). Aries is intercepted in the tenth house (house of father and authority), so Mars does not have an easy outlet in the external world.

It might be pertinent to note that Mars is the planet of sexual desire. As the symptoms began in early adulthood, around age nineteen/twenty, there may be an element of suppressed and problematic sexuality at work in the pathology. Perhaps an experience has triggered early-life content causing an allergic response in the energy body: Mars is not only the bringer of war, but the bringer of adrenalin and fever. It conjuncts Venus (love, attraction, relationship), suggesting a fiery intense response to the matter of relationship.

Both Uranus (cramps) and Mars (anger) trine the Moon (vomiting): a disruptive, threatening memory is forcibly ejected and thus brought into the light and into Case E's emotional lexicon. Is this process bringing into the awareness the squashed and repressed feelings and sensations of the child – and of the ancestors also? Purging is Plutonic too, in that it brings unconscious material that has become 'toxic' into consciousness, in order that it can be addressed and so as to purify the body, allowing for healing and transformation.

Case E also shared some recent symptoms (gallbladder polyps), which she thinks relate to solar plexus chakra issues. She defines these as 'feeling everything from other people, having difficulty being heard and fear of exposure.' Her habit is to hide and keep quiet (which relates, to some extent in this lifetime, to her experience of her father). To my ears, these issues sound very like the ones relating to the parts of her chart discussed in relation to Crohn's Disease. An explosive force is buried at the root of the chart (Uranus–Pluto), the cognitive function is overwhelmed and Mars has gone into hyper-drive.

Looking at the health midpoints in Case E's chart was interesting. The Mars/Neptune midpoint (susceptibility to toxicity and allergic conditions, drug sensitivity) is 5° Sagittarius occupied by the Sun. Is this perhaps an indicator for the massive allergic response in hospital (which was notably productive of insight and consciousness at the time), as well as to the condition generally? Mars/Pluto (destruction of cells, heavy accidents) is 4-5° Scorpio, opposite the Moon, suggestive, in Marcia Starck's view, of 'problems with female reproductive cycle; emotional upheavals; powerful and deep emotional encounters.'[173] Case E later confirmed experiencing such difficulties, saying 'somehow I never had children', though no physiological cause was ever identified. Obviously, sexuality is significant to these two planets, which prods the Saturn fear of intimacy in this chart. Finally, the Mars/Uranus midpoint (nervous system) is 2° Scorpio (opposite the Moon within 2°), denoting a highly sensitive nervous system and intuitive abilities. Working consciously and 'hygienically' with this capacity might mitigate somatic responses.

---

[173] Starck (1982), p. 30.

At the time of hospitalisation transiting Uranus was conjunct natal Mars in the sixth house; transiting Pluto was inconjunct natal Jupiter (ruler of the sixth) and sextile to natal Uranus; transiting Saturn was squaring the crucial MC/IC axis, including a square to Uranus–Pluto, moving towards a conjunction with natal Mercury; and transiting Chiron was opposite natal Mercury occupying the 'empty degree'[174] of the highly significant t-square (as noted) in which it is involved.

Mercury and the sixth-house Mars–Venus give the strong suggestion that finding a vocation that includes health, healing and understanding the wisdom of the body will fuel her creative purpose (Case E now works as a homoeopath). Her creative capacity brings emotional healing (Scorpio rules the fifth) and she is urged to use it in service to others, to her ancestors and to all life (Neptune conjunct fifth-house cusp).

---

[174] The 'empty degree' of a t-square is opposite the focal planet, likely to be both a place of balance and of challenge to the functioning of the t-square.

Case F: Freeing the Creative Will

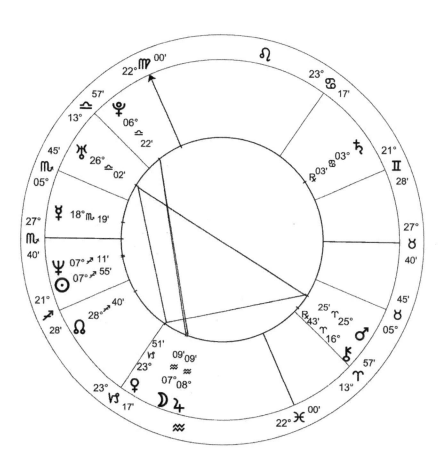

Symptom Picture

An extremely painful relationship breakdown, during which Case F felt his heart was 'broken open', gave rise to him urgently questioning many aspects of his life and losing the will to continue his regular work. He spent some months travelling and making music, for which he has an unusual gift. He returned and tried to resume work, but experienced intense resistance and pain on the right side of his lower abdomen. The intensity of this pain led to hospitalisation and yet there was no positive diagnosis except inguinal hernia, fatigue and low-level anaemia.

Pain	Mars, Aries, 1st house
Abdomen	Cancer
Right side	Mercury in Scorpio in 12th
Inguinal hernia	Mars, Aries, Scorpio, 8th
Fatigue	Mars, Aries, 1st house, Neptune
Anaemia	Mars, Aries, 1st house, Neptune in 1st

Purpose – the Path of the Sun

Sun conjunct Neptune in Sagittarius in the first house. Awareness is developed by becoming effective, cultivating the will forces. This person is intuitive, artistic, open and optimistic. He needs to learn to be able to assert himself on behalf of an artistic vision that is sustaining to himself and others.

Undertow – the Pull of the Past

Saturn in Cancer in the eighth house; Moon in Aquarius in the third. There is fear of intimacy and rejection. Feminine energy is perceived as devouring or over-powering. There is anxiety about rejection, emotion and sexuality. Identity is assumed to be conferred by relationship. The emotional response to this is to be as detached as possible, to take an intellectual position, to live in the head and to try and get as free as possible.

Analysis

This crisis was precipitated by transiting Pluto (the chart ruler) making a conjunction with natal Venus, the lover. Pluto transits are the most powerful we experience. They tend to clear from our lives, situations and relationships that no longer serve, often in dramatic – even traumatic – ways. Pluto transits are marked by emotional pain, intensity and the need to learn to roll with the punches. Pluto represents what is unconscious, and so is often expressed through the agency of another person, because it signifies content and force that have been disowned. When it makes contact with a personal planet, like Venus, it finds a fracture line through which its energy can flow into conscious experience, where it makes a transformative impact, putting a person in touch with potent unconscious material which is asking to be resolved and assimilated.

Venus is the focal planet of one of the principle features of Case F's chart: a cardinal t-square, including Mars and Uranus. This indicates Case F is a person who has a driving desire

(Mars) towards freedom (Uranus), which is naturally compromised by relationship (Venus). Venus is in Capricorn suggesting that feelings of safety and security, even status, are delivered by the partner. Tensions can develop within relationships that push the partner to say, 'Enough!', thus granting the wished-for freedom, though it has not consciously been sought. It is not wrong to need plenty of room for manoeuvre. Not everyone is designed for the compromises of conventional partnership or family life. That does not mean they are barred from these things, just that they need to find ways of doing them differently. Venus is also the ruler of Case F's sixth (work and health) and seventh (committed partnership) houses; it is no surprise that Pluto's transit of Venus triggered problems in these areas of life. Pluto's action is to purge and to purify of inauthenticity the planetary principles it contacts by transit, by bringing repressed material into the light of consciousness. This transit was happening in the third house of the chart, relating to Case F's immediate environment, his siblings, and to how he thinks, perceives and thus constructs his personal reality. No wonder he felt he had to 'question everything'. We need to see the context of the chart to understand the requirements of this man's lifetime, for it is going against the grain of ourselves that lands us in trouble.

Case F has the Sun in Sagittarius *exactly* conjunct Neptune in the first house. This shows he is wide open to intuition and influences of a very subtle nature, including guidance and inspiration from spirit. His musical gift is an outward sign of this. The Sun has to organise and integrate the rest of the chart, and here it is in the first house, declaring that he needs to assert himself, to honour his own will, which is described by the Sun/Neptune conjunction: creatively inspired, consciously questing for meaning that is able to encompass pretty cosmic dimensions – also that it is his will to serve a higher vision of life. This need, when it is not part of Case F's conscious reckoning, gets subjugated by the compromises of relationship. He has experiences of transcendence, beauty and Love with a capital 'L'; and the longing for more of these makes him idealistic, but also perhaps escapist and despairing of the possibility of actualising such beauty in the rather grim and grotty world we find around us. A human partner cannot satisfy this longing.

Sagittarius seeks expansion; there is a journey that needs to be made and so Case F needs to leave the known and the safe. He has to be aware that he is susceptible to delusions about his own importance and to losing touch with reality, such is the power of his Neptune. It makes him highly sensitive, both psychically and physically, and is associated with nebulous conditions that evade diagnosis. Neptune rules the IC of the chart: the lowest angle, where we root down into our personal history, early childhood and our ancestral lineage. The direction of the journey is inward and downward, and is to be made as an act of service to his ancestors and predecessors. Case F is not the kind of Sagittarian to be satisfied by foreign travel or by outward adventures alone, although these may play a part. This is borne out by the Sun's ruler, Jupiter, being conjunct the Moon (natural ruler of the IC), and the Sagittarian ninth house being

267

under the accidental rulership of the Moon. The Moon complex, of course, refers to a former mode of being, which needs to be moderated and overcome if the potential of the current lifetime is to be fulfilled.

Case F's Neptune is really powerful. It inclines him towards things mystical and things narcotic. He needs trusted friends to help him 'reality check'. He is open to psychic influences, so he has to be able to choose when to be open and when to be closed, to have strong boundaries and good habits of psychic hygiene. Without these things he readily becomes subject to psychic swamping and overwhelm. Case F may have been emotionally invaded by his mother, leading to great difficulties in growing away from her influence and adequately separating. He may not have effectively distinguished between himself and his mother; this intrusion will likely be projected on to women in general, and he readily feels dominated and manipulated (Pluto trines the Moon–Jupiter conjunction).

As Scorpio is on the ascendant he seeks emotional intensity, power and transformation. There is a capacity for depth awareness that needs to be conscious to be useful; if and when Scorpionic folk tire of personal drama, they are capable of great depth and emotional penetration. An awareness of what lies beneath appearances is a potential source of wisdom and healing for this man. People with Scorpio rising are known for their ability to transform themselves and for taking drastic action and having intense experiences, because there is a lot of power coursing through this sign.

The north node – indicating the trajectory of the soul's journey over lifetimes – is in Sagittarius in the second house. This is about finding wisdom, freedom and meaning through the body and within nature. He cannot rely on logic to find the truth he needs. He needs to give up seeking information or the opinions of others, instead to seek understanding, wisdom and the guidance of his own inner truth. The more embodied his experience is, the more satisfying it will be; this is not a lifetime for developing theory.

The inguinal hernia expresses the problem that the old container is no longer holding: the inside is getting pushed towards the outside. This may reflect an early-life pattern of feeling unheld, uncontained and therefore unsafe. The hernia and anaemia (iron deficiency) both suggest a malfunctioning Mars (it rules the sacral area and its metal is iron), which is of course being squared by transiting Pluto. Mars is the will and if we do not know what we are doing, then its normally direct, outward energy can get snarled up in inward, potentially pathological, processes. Natal Mars is in the fifth house, suggesting it will function better if there is a creative outlet and, as it is in Aries, it needs to take action and acquire autonomy. Depression, anger and lethargy result from a poorly directed Mars in Aries.

As well as Mars, we could look at Scorpio/Pluto energy in the chart to refer to the hernia. Saturn in the eighth house expresses blocked or troubled sexuality; Mercury in Scorpio all at sea in the twelfth, making an exact sesquiquadrate (135°

angle) to Saturn, is a fracture line for this Plutonic energy, which, as noted, is active through transit.

There is a need for Case F to find a point of union between his inner experience of the masculine and the feminine (Venus square Mars). His creative gift is a way for him to do this and when he works with this he does it on behalf of 'all his relations' (his ancestral line), which is a necessary part of his becoming himself and acquiring power (Pisces on IC, Sun conjunct Neptune).

Mars and Uranus (both part of the natal t-square that is being triggered by Pluto) pertain to sensitivities and diseases of the nervous system. Their midpoint in any chart will point to this theme. In Case F's chart the midpoint of Mars and Uranus is just two degrees from natal Venus, suggesting that the pain Case F experiences could, at the physiological level, be nervous in origin. It is, I would offer, a reflection of the will to freedom – freedom in relationships, creative freedom, artistic will, the desire to break out of conventions and to vent masculine strength (whilst being rather allergic to the masculine influence in his early life) and to find its relationship with his own inner feminine force. There is also very likely leftover emotional pain from the invasion/separation dynamic with the mother that is announcing itself as urgent work to be dealt with – on behalf of his own Inner Child and for the ancestral line.

Pluto's transits are famously deep and transformative. They feel 'fated'. It is time for Case F to befriend his own Shadow –

he will find there, along with shame and pain, some glorious qualities and treasures that have been stifled or secreted away. Moving towards work which uses his creativity (Mars in the fifth house) and his independent spirit (Aries rules the fifth), and includes an element of communication or teaching (Venus in the third house rules the sixth house) would serve his sense of purpose and authenticity. Finding ways to integrate the powerful content being released by Pluto will bring healing – shamanic, psychotherapeutic and creative paths would all be appropriate. This is an initiation into a deeper level of self-knowledge and understanding of life, which will allow him to *become himself*, to do what he must to serve his ancestors, and to enter relationships authentically, with an honest and right regard for his legitimate needs for freedom and creative self-expression.

Case G: All in the Mind

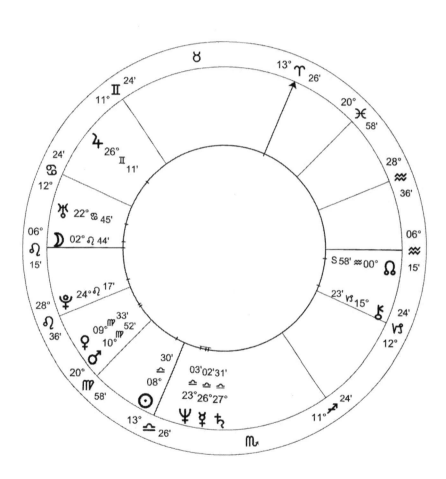

Symptom Picture

Case G had a difficult childhood and has experienced anxiety and depression throughout her life, though it is lessening as she gets older and works with her issues. When she hit the classic age of the midlife crisis (41/42), as transiting Uranus opposes its natal position, she was totally burnt out from teaching; it was time to deal with her issues. Case G has, since then, been on a healing journey.

Anxiety	Mercury square Uranus
Depression	Mercury conjunct Saturn and Neptune
Burn-out	Mercury square Uranus, Aquarius on DES

Purpose – the Path of the Sun

Sun in Libra in the third house. The conscious identity in this lifetime is constellated around developing mind: thinking, learning, communication and social awareness. This is a time for becoming relational, developing awareness by experiencing 'Other' in relationship, and through interpersonal dynamics. Self-understanding arises through detachment and mental reflection.

Undertow – the Pull of the Past

Saturn in Libra in the fourth house; Moon in Leo in the twelfth. Unconscious patterns are around dependency and belonging: cultivating dependency as a way of feeling safe. Patterns in relation to 'mother' and mothering; mother looms large and feels powerful and assertive, devouring even. Case G makes the assumption that safety is derived through being dependent or depended upon.

She has a sense of herself as a special individual, which is facilitated by retreat or by self-sacrifice: there is a need to withdraw from the general commerce of the world in order to feel emotionally comfortable. The use of the will and impulsiveness need to be balanced and brought under control (Moon in fire).

Analysis

Case G's natal Uranus is in the twelfth house of the chart, so transiting Uranus was opposing it from the sixth house of work and health when she reached the point of burn-out at work. At the same time transiting Saturn was opposing her natal Venus–Mars conjunction (Mars rules the MC – career, Venus rules the IC – home, inner life); and transiting Pluto was squaring natal Pluto (another midlife transit). All in all, she was up against it. To paraphrase Matthew Sanford, seeking begins when our options run out.[175]

Case G is part of the generation of people born in the early 1950s with Saturn conjunct Neptune (the planets whose midpoint is the health axis). This is the meeting of form and

---

[175] *Waking* is an account of Matthew Sanford's experience of being rendered paraplegic at thirteen in a car crash that killed his father and sister. He describes his journey towards finding healing, meaning and purpose, becoming in adulthood a yoga teacher, sharing inspiration about the body–mind relationship.

formlessness, practicality and inspiration, and these people can have great spiritual capacities and aspirations. Case G's conjunction is four degrees apart, with Mercury (cognition, perception, communication) sitting in the middle. Case G's mind is subject to the strong influence of the Saturn–Neptune conjunction. Because the conjunction planets are generational, the cohort with whom she grew up would also have their Saturn–Neptunes conjunct her highly impressible Mercury. People who have personal planets in aspect to transpersonal planets are like fracture lines through which the collective finds its expression.

No doubt Case G has significant spiritual insight to impart and share. As her Mercury rules the third house of teaching and communicating, and the eleventh house of groups, the suggestion is that she can potentially teach others, especially in group situations, bringing to them her experience of the gifts and challenges of this conjunction. Her communication, verbal and written, could be inspired!

Another manifestation of the conjunction is depression and anxiety, which is being brought directly into the cognitive function due to Mercury's placement. Neptune has the effect of opening the mind to high-vibration influences, making Case G very intuitive and potentially psychic (certainly sensitive). This might make her spaced out and feel quite disconnected. Neptune erodes boundaries and the sense of separation (which is vital to functioning at the personality level of consciousness). It famously imparts 'divine discontent': deep longings that can only be satisfied by meaningful spiritual engagement. When we try to satisfy Neptune's yearning at the personality level it makes us escapist, unrealistic and readily deluded. Neptune lifts us out of the personality perspective towards glimpses of transcendence; it provides invaluable inspiration for the artist and the spiritual seeker. Its influence needs to be applied for non-selfish ends; it is hard to handle if one has no appreciation of spiritual life, tending to make us self-sacrificing to a martyrish extent. Saturn, meanwhile has a grounded and limiting effect (which acts productively on illimitable, dreamy Neptune) but stamps pretty heavily on sensitive Mercury. It is productive of melancholy and a serious turn of mind.

This can result in depression and pessimism. But melancholy is a rich territory, tempering Case G's mind with a taste for solitary inward exploration, which I imagine could be very nourishing and interesting. Saturn also gives the gift of form to Case G's Neptune-infused Mercury, allowing her to think and express herself constructively and intelligently. It is important to see that although anxiety and depression feel like a curse, they are also accompanied by a blessing. The blessing and the curse are both signified by Saturn–Neptune; Case G can choose to see this differently, which it sounds like she has increasingly been doing.

As the Saturn–Neptune–Mercury conjunction is in the fourth house, it is part of the description of her early life, which was troubled. This is also shown by the Moon conjunct Uranus in the twelfth house, which can signify separation from the mother in the first two hours of life, and certainly brings feelings of abandonment and issues, again, with personal boundaries. In the fourth house Neptune can also express abandonment, while Saturn can bring harshness and punitiveness into the context of home and childhood. The early-life conditioning is a reiteration of past-life experience, providing some orientation in the current life circumstances, but also needing to be outgrown. It can take a very long time to overcome conditioning: it requires significant maturity to take this level of responsibility for our experience. Difficulty – like, for example, physical or mental ill-health – is a great spur, whereas ease can be an enemy to growth and development.

Case G's Sun is in Libra in the third house (ruled naturally and accidentally by Mercury). Libra is the sign of ease and harmony and can produce lifetimes disconcerting for their lack of challenge; the Libra Sun often has an expectation of ease and can readily feel that challenge is a sure sign that something is seriously out of whack. It is not. It is a signal to the personality that growth and change are on the agenda. Her Sun indicates that Case G is gaining awareness crucial to her development through using her mental faculties in this lifetime. Intelligent reflection and a reasoned interrogation of the nature of perception and of the way in which it gives rise to her experience of reality are significant and purposeful activities. Exploring the nature of mind and sharing her explorations, as a teacher, or a writer, for the purposes of healing would be a useful expression of her Sun, mitigating her depressive tendencies. Harvesting the significant rewards of her Saturn–Neptune–Mercury conjunction do much to alleviate its negative influence.

The chart has a very low water count (and, interestingly a wilful, fiery ascendant and midheaven), signalling that the emotional life is out of balance. Emotional difficulties can turn people towards seeking help at a higher level, which this chart suggests is part of Case G's design. The water imbalance creates difficulties, such that Case G will have had to learn about the feeling life of herself and others, to cultivate emotional connections *consciously* and to learn the value of feeling, which in part is to warm and humanise the intellect, while the intellect tempers the excesses and subjectivity of feeling so that our actions may be aligned with, and guided by both.

Client Comment
Your case study definitely resonates. It has been essential for me to have a spiritual practice, which I have had for the past forty years. I started searching as a child. It has been much needed and has also led to growth. I have also done in-depth psychotherapy, which again was much needed and has helped me understand something of how the mind works. I have also had times of self-sacrifice, which was one reason for burn-out and have struggled generally with boundaries.

I too think that illness has a higher purpose.

Case H: To See and Be Seen

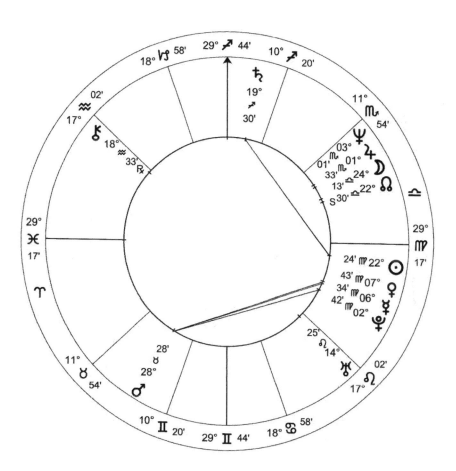

279

Symptom Picture

Case H has experienced problems with her vision for most of her life. When she was six, a measles infection left her with poor eyesight. She now has progressive myopia. At 40 she received a diagnosis of a blood condition called paraproteinemia. This causes crystalline formations in the blood, which accumulate in Case H's corneas, giving her night blindness; direct light creates glare, obviously debilitating her daytime vision too. This, she informed me, is a very unusual medical condition. On the cusp of the sixth house (health, body) is Uranus (unusualness) in Leo (the eyes). Case H added that her 'condition has a 25 per cent chance of developing into multiple myeloma which has no known cure'.

Myopia	Sun square Saturn
Paraproteinemia	Sun square Saturn
Crystallisation in blood	Saturn in Sagittarius
Blood	Jupiter conjunct Moon and Neptune
Vision	Leo rules 6th, Uranus in Leo in 6th, Sun in 6th
Multiple myeloma	Mars square Mercury–Venus–Pluto, Mars quincunx Moon–Jupiter–Neptune
Bone Marrow	Cancer, Moon
Infection	Mars
Hidden cell proliferation	Neptune, Pluto, Jupiter

Purpose – the Path of the Sun

Sun in Virgo in the sixth house. This lifetime is for developing awareness through an intelligent use of physical energy and learning to understand health and healing, cultivating good habits and identifying a vocation.

Undertow – the Pull of the Past

Saturn in Sagittarius in the ninth house; Moon in Libra in the seventh. There is unconscious domination by religious ideology and the belief that faith and learning need to look a certain way in order to be valid. This feels impersonal and highly restrictive.

Emotionally, the conditioning pushes the notion that relationship is the be-all and end-all. There is a tendency to live in the head and to believe everything she thinks, which needs to be overcome to free up energy for the legitimate identity.

Analysis

The first thing that draws my attention about this chart is that the angles are on the anaretic degrees of the mutable signs, suggesting a lifetime of reorientation that is forcing its way into consciousness.

The Sun (vision) is in Virgo in the sixth along with Mercury, which is flanked on either side by Venus and Pluto. Mercury is the sole dispositor. The emphasis in Virgo and in the sixth house create strong somatic tendencies: the physical health of the body is very much the medium for consciousness to arise. There is only one opposition (Chiron–Uranus) which suggests that Case H could be very subjective. Mercury is the indicator of her rational processes and sensory perceptions (how she makes sense of things and her sensory processing). Its conjunction with Pluto tells us that her perception is being intensified and driven deep: she is developing depth awareness. Case H is potentially capable of considerable insight, especially in the areas of occult information and sexuality (Pluto rules her eighth house), and deep thought. Her communication is probably intense, powerful and insightful. There is a capacity for truthfulness that could have a drastic impact. Mercury, Venus and Pluto receive a square from Mars that both motivates and inflames Case H's communication and thinking.

Mars trines the Sun, giving Case H energy and drive. It is the Sun (vision) and Leo (the eyes) that we need to look to, to try and understand Case H's health problem. As I have said, Uranus in Leo sits on the cusp of the sixth house. Uranus always indicates the area and manner in which liberation and authenticity are being sought. For Case H, it is her experience of health and the body that insists on her not fitting in, not towing the line; she has to approach the daily life of health, work and habit in very different ways. The impact of pathology on her vision has been one way of achieving this. That this area of life (ruled by the sixth house) has been subject to unusual influence serves Case H's Sun, by generating consciousness. The crystallisation process is ruled by Saturn.

Case H's Saturn is in Sagittarius in the ninth house making a stressful square aspect to the Sun, creating obstacles to confidence, self-esteem and a clear sense of identity. It may be that strong religious beliefs were held by her family, making her feel judged, guilty and not good enough. Dogmatic Christian views propound bodily shame and shame around sexual expression, which warp our culture generally. Case H's Mercury–Pluto conjunction charges her thinking and communication with powerful and passionate emotion, so she may be particularly prone to suffer by imbibing religious and cultural prohibitions.

When generational planets (Pluto, Neptune, Uranus, Chiron and Saturn) aspect personal planets (Moon, Mercury, Venus, Sun, Mars, Jupiter) in an individual's chart, that individual is carrying the charge of the general collective experience very strongly. In Case H's example, all her peers at school and friends in her age group have their Pluto conjuncting her Mercury and Venus; all their Neptune placements emphasise her conjunction between the Moon, Jupiter and Neptune. These individuals are like the messengers to their generational cohorts.

The Sun being squared by Saturn is, in a literal astrological interpretation, crystals in the eyes. That the crystals are formed in the blood brings in Jupiter, ruler of blood. Jupiter, conjunct both Moon and Neptune in Case H's chart, disposits her Saturn in Sagittarius. I think it is the strong Virgo/sixth house emphasis that brings these energies into the body. But it is more than this. Anyone with this emphasis would be predisposed to somatising energies (expressing forces through the body as symptoms or sensations), but it is not an inevitability. Our vision is an expression of our willingness to see and to be seen. Eyesight and the health of the eyes may show our rejection of the world in our immediate environment or/and our fear of rejection by those around us. When we are uncomfortable with what we are seeing, and this discomfort is not resolved, it can manifest as a distortion in vision. That Case H's paraproteinemia is a problem of the blood suggests that there is a familial or ancestral context to her health problem.

Myopia is caused by contraction of the eye muscles. Like crystallisation, contraction is a byword for Saturn. Myopia might be an expression of the desire to retreat, to blur out what lies ahead, a fear of the future, or obsessing over details (a tendency to which this emphasis in Virgo is highly susceptible).

The midpoint of Mars/Saturn (the axis showing functional inhibition) is 8° Virgo (conjuncting Case H's natal Mercury–Venus–Pluto conjunction); Mercury rules sensory processes, while Venus rules relational energy. The axis of toxicity, shown by the midpoint of Mars/Neptune is 15° Leo, conjunct Uranus and the sixth-house cusp, suggesting that physiologically the problem could be a toxic condition. While these may be important diagnostic pointers, they do not deal with the underlying difficulty, which is the retreat from seeing clearly and from wanting thus to be seen. This I suggest arises from early-life conditions (which are in turn echoes of past-life energies) that combine to drive her towards her Sun in Virgo in the sixth house, which as I have said rules vision but also lights the route to purpose, identity and power. Case H's health issues may contribute to moving her towards her Sun as she will have had to develop insight and understanding around physical processes. She can use this awareness to orient *away* from intrusive parental voices and her family identity, and towards finding a vocation that allows her to help other people. Meanwhile her problems with vision guide her towards addressing her issue around seeing and being seen, which potentially serves her to develop increasingly her authenticity and independence.

Finally, to address Case H's comment that her condition has a 25 per cent chance to develop into multiple myeloma, an incurable cancerous condition. This is where plasma cells proliferate uncontrollably in the bone marrow and malfunction in such a way as to make infection more likely. Mars occupies the Saturn/Neptune midpoint (the health axis) suggesting susceptibility to infection and compromised adrenal function. Galvanising the will and positively fostering clear intent is possibly a way to mitigate ill effects. This person has the 29th degree of Pisces on the ascendant, showing that she is generating consciousness around the issue of willpower and self-assertion (Aries/Mars). Mars receives a square from Pluto and a quincunx from Neptune: it is significantly beleaguered in the second house of the chart (the body as a resource). The will is being tempered by the forces of these outer planets, to become empowered (Pluto) in order to serve and to make a significant contribution

(Neptune). Over-identification with diagnoses and physical conditions tends to be a shortcoming of Virgo. Programming the psyche with phrases such as 'a 25 per cent chance to get incurable cancer', although a totally understandable anxiety, is not a prescription for good health.

Client Comment
I do try to stay out of the limelight. My parents weren't especially religious but my dad never showed much in the way of encouragement, despite my being the first in my family to pass the Eleven Plus, to go to grammar school and then university. I graduated with a good honours degree in English and spent twenty years as head of the English department at a large secondary school. I am also an extremely talented artist.

[From this comment, it seems to me that there is a live issue about *being seen* and acknowledged.]

Case J: The Pressure to Overcome the Past

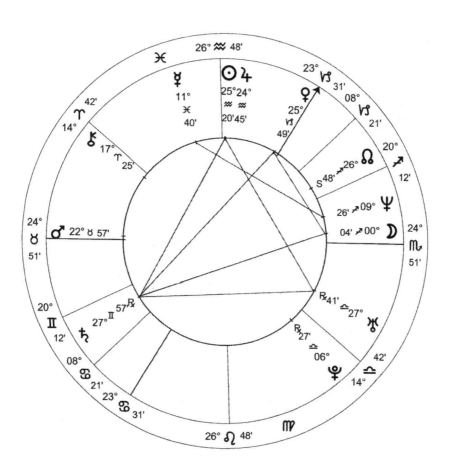

Symptom Picture

Case J has multiple sclerosis, which is an auto-immune disease where the immune system attacks the myelin sheath surrounding nerve fibres causing neurological impairment. The myelin sheath is a bit like insulation around electrical wires; when it is damaged nervous impulses are not 'conducted' efficiently, resulting in highly various presentations. The key symptoms Case J experiences on a regular basis are chronic fatigue, migraine with aura, heaviness in the limbs, 'vibrating legs', memory problems, struggling to find words and getting them jumbled up, and random burning sensations. During relapses she experiences facial paralysis, numb legs, optic neuritis (inflammation of the optic nerve, leading to blindness), and paralysis in one foot. Case J describes the main challenge arising from her condition as cognitive: just having a conversation zaps her energy, leading her to avoid social situations. She has had to give up work.

Auto-immune disease	Neptune
Nerve issues	Mercury
Cognitive issues	Mercury
Chronic fatigue	Neptune
Migraine with aura	Mars (migraine), Neptune (aura)
Heavy limbs	Saturn
Vibrating legs	Uranus
Facial paralysis	Mars
Optic neuritis	Mars (inflammation), Mercury (nerves)

| Paralysis of foot | Neptune, 12th house, Pisces |

Purpose – the Path of the Sun
Sun in Aquarius in tenth/eleventh houses. Awareness is being developed through engaging in communal endeavour and group activity. There is a capacity for brilliant innovations and learning to do things differently, challenging orthodoxies by engaging creative individuality.

Undertow – the Pull of the Past
Saturn in Gemini in the second house; Moon in Sagittarius in the seventh. The conditioned unconscious belief is that there is 'not enough'; this fear of lack and poverty, it is assumed can be overcome by schooling and acquiring education. The body, as a resource, cannot be relied upon.

The emotional conditioning makes this person believe that freedom can be found through relationship; there is an excessive focus on 'other' – the need to make everything OK for the partner; in some way the parent is experienced as the partner. There is a need to bring balance to wilfulness (Moon in fire).

Analysis
Work and health belong to the sixth house, which describes our use of functional energy, our mode of operation. Naturally, any health issue, acute or chronic, will affect how we operate and whether or not we can show up for work. Uranus, planet of disruption, is retrograde in the sixth house of Case J's chart. Its retrograde motion signals that it will

make its presence felt in a way that really requires conscious processing; a retrograde natal planet becomes a strong feature of one's internal landscape. The principle of Uranus is liberation. It is breaking up and breaking through personality conditioning in order to make room for the soul's perspective. Case J is trying to break free of conditioning that restricts her understanding of physical energy, bodily health and what constitutes worthwhile activity. Uranus is associated with spasmodic activity and the 'electrical' forces that flow through nerve channels, including the neurological activity in the corticospinal tract. As the ruler of Case J's Sun in Aquarius its activity will be related to Case J moving towards her solar purpose (conscious identity, power potential, fulfilment), which is about breaking out of conventions and rethinking social systems and involving herself with community projects along shared humanitarian lines. Aquarians want to find ways of doing things differently, such that they benefit all: 'for the many, not the few.'

It is crucial for Case J to affiliate with 'the group' as a vehicle for activity, particularly so as her Sun is active in the eleventh house (naturally ruled by Aquarius). Aligning with others is key to moving beyond the conditioning of the past as signified by Saturn and the Moon. The influence of Uranus, which can bring flashes of brilliance and intuition, needs to be grounded, just as lightning needs to be conducted – otherwise it can be destructive.

Saturn is in Gemini in the second house. Mercury-ruled Gemini governs the nervous system, cognitive function, communication and the arms, all associated with key symptoms (see table). The second house rules resources and values; the theme of embodiment arises through Taurus and the second house, reflecting how the bodily health is experienced as a resource. Saturn is always the indicator of chronic blockage and difficulty. Here, the body is experienced as the problem, which may be due to lifetimes of acquiring security through cornering resources, identifying possessions and material satisfaction with wellbeing: over-identification with the physical plane. We can hoard all we like, our mountains of stuff cannot make us happy and will not heal our bodies.[176]

Being in Gemini, Saturn also suggests being stuck in ideas and concepts that are obsolete in terms of the situation that one currently occupies. Case J's Saturn makes an exact trine with Uranus, indicating that the impulse to overcome the Saturn mindset is ripe: there is an opportunity here to break through lifetimes of conditioning, and a pressure to do so. The Moon shows emotional conditioning carried over from a past life that is impressing the memory, creating emotional defaults in this lifetime. Case J's Moon is in Sagittarius in the seventh house of partnership. Sagittarius signifies the upper leg (Aquarius, the lower leg); the legs are strongly affected in the

---

[176] The client later informed me that hoarding was not an issue for her; the tendency would certainly be stronger if Saturn occupied an earth sign in the second house, if the chart's earth count was high (it's low) and if the Saturn–Pluto square were tighter (Pluto lending obsessive–compulsive tendencies). Hoarding can, of course, happen at the mental level too, cramming our minds with input to allay fear.

symptom picture (and, notably, the signs representing the legs are tenanted by both Sun and Moon). The Moon in the seventh indicates a tendency towards the appeasement of others and subjugation of one's own needs to those of the other (in early life the other is a parent). Case J may be a person caught up in meeting the needs of others, failing to give due regard to her own requirements.

Significantly, there is a quincunx (strain) between the Moon and Saturn that is part of a yod, with Saturn at the apex. The Moon sextiles Venus, which happens to be ruler of the chart and of the sixth house. This sextile points to the need to work with emotional reactions that arise in relationship, especially in terms of responding appropriately to infantile needs. There seems to be an issue associated with femininity and motherhood that Case J is experiencing on behalf of her motherline (the Moon rules the IC). Perhaps she comes from a long line of women who have sacrificed themselves on the altar of relationship. Case J is certainly part of the Pluto in Libra generation, seeking new ways of handling one to one relationship. Her yod suggests that dealing with such issues helps Case J cast out the negative aspects of Saturn (acquisitiveness and hoarding – in intellectual and material terms, intellectual pedantry, stuck thinking) in order to benefit from a mature Saturn expression, which is pragmatic, self-disciplined, capable of self-responsibility and self-enabling.

Obviously this is a very complex picture so it is especially helpful to break it down into astrological significators, presented in the table.

As Neptune rules auto-immune disease, it makes sense to look at the condition of Neptune in the chart. It is in the seventh house squaring Mercury (underscoring the need to dissolve obsolete mental conditioning) and conjunct the Moon (bringing its influence strongly into the emotional body), exacerbating the over-regard for other by infusing it with projections of idealism, unrealistic expectation, longing, self-sacrifice and even martyrishness. Neptune erodes boundaries, so in contact with the Moon it dissolves one's sense of emotional containment. I would expect Case J to be extremely open and unboundaried at a psychic level.

This was probably her experience in babyhood, suggesting that for some reason containment and secure attachment was not reliably available from the mother. This aspect can indicate a deep feeling of abandonment, but by way of compensation it also brings great spiritual gifts of sensitivity, inspiration, imagination and compassion, but Case J has to develop a regime of psychic hygiene, otherwise she is flooded with the psychic and emotional content floating around in the atmosphere, which she is quite likely to experience as originating with her. Being overwhelmed by this content could well be an element of Case J's chronic fatigue, another Neptunian condition. There is a need to withdraw idealised projections that are made on to others, including perhaps her mother. Neptune is about transcendence, it inspires us towards Oneness, interconnection and seeking the divine; it cannot be satisfied by human beings, especially not by just one human being. It is about divine love and is fulfilled at the spiritual level of our experience.

Neptune, as noted, squares Mercury (in its fall in Neptune's sign, Pisces): Mercury rules the nervous system, cognition and communication; Neptune is eroding all these processes, in an attempt to raise their vibration. This aspect creates a tendency to woolliness and overwhelm; again, it asks for psychic boundaries, to choose when to be wide open and when to be contained. Case J has a talent to express insights and wisdom that arise through her ability to connect with *spirit*. It needs to be safeguarded and treasured. Her symptoms suggest that she is not consciously dealing with this ability. The Neptune-ruled feet reflect our relationship with its planetary influence; paralysis here suggests stuckness and withdrawal. Neptune's activity of erosion and dissolution is always trying to eliminate our sense of separation: we are not separate, but part of the One Life, the Web of Being.

The inspiration Neptune brings is to move us out of separative consciousness, affording us magnificent glimpses of non-dual reality. We need to be really grounded and practical to be usefully in touch with that energy; when we are, we are open to profound inspiration that redeems the sufferings of the personality perspective. It is not helpful to be blown apart and incapable of activity in the physical world. At its worst Neptune manifests as psychosis, delusion and substance abuse – testament to the torments of highly sensitive and gifted people in a society that fails to acknowledge a spiritual dimension (and places little value on spiritual seekers and artists, who are the conveyors of Neptune's beauty and inspiration into the world).

The final planet specifically associated with Case J's symptoms is Mars, which is rising, two degrees above the ascendant, in Taurus, making its presence strongly felt. As I mentioned in reference to Saturn in the second house, Taurus and the second house both deal with embodiment at the level of sensation. Mars brings a desire for sensation (it could also fall under Saturn's spell and make having lots of nice things very desirable). It brings drive, vigour and a bit of push and shove, and is the natural ruler of the ascendant. It rules conditions of heat and redness, inflammation and headache. Mars is, of course, the will to be; it needs to be channelled into activity. When it is not, perhaps because there is confusion about how to move forward in life or a lack of self-assertiveness, it spills out into pathological expressions, like the eruption of anger, a headache, a physical or emotional flare-up: in Case J's case, neuritis and 'random burning sensations'. If chronically suppressed, Mars also manifests in lethargy and depression.

I have been at pains to point out Case J's conditioning with regard to relationship. It feels like Mars on the ascendant is providing her with a sword and shield, to put her own needs on the map. Aries, Mars and the first house pertain to the head and face. Facial paralysis is a picture of the failure to advocate on behalf of self. Case J needs to become assertive and effective. No more lifetimes of being a pushover for the other. Chiron in Aries underscores this need to become self-actualising and initiating; it also points to the pain and shame that are felt in connection with this issue. There is much healing potential here. Venus, the relationship principle, rules the sixth house, is part of the yod and conjunct the midheaven, showing that exploring this principle is part of Case J's lifepath.

Client Comment
I'm completely blown away with how accurate this reading is!

You touched on my childhood and relationship with my Mother. It was a tough childhood: my Mother was pregnant with me at the age of 16, she married my biological father and had me at 17 and he committed suicide when I was five. My Mother fell apart, she leaned on me for support and turned to alcohol; what I can remember of my childhood was an emotional rollercoaster. I had to be the one that held it together.

I do believe that I have a spiritual gift. I recently came out of a 16-year emotionally abusive relationship. Since it ended I've started my spiritual journey and I see the bigger picture. It's as if I've awakened! I do need to find a regime of psychic hygiene as you put it, as feeling overwhelmed happens daily. It's hard to know how to start, but I'm guessing mindfulness and meditation is a good place.

There have been issues of substance and alcohol abuse but thankfully those days have gone. Regarding MS, I'm blown away with the accuracy! I see that it could have come from suppressing my own feelings and needs in early childhood, trying to comfort my Mother, and because of all the suppression throughout my life, now manifesting through MS.

Case K: The Digestion of Experience

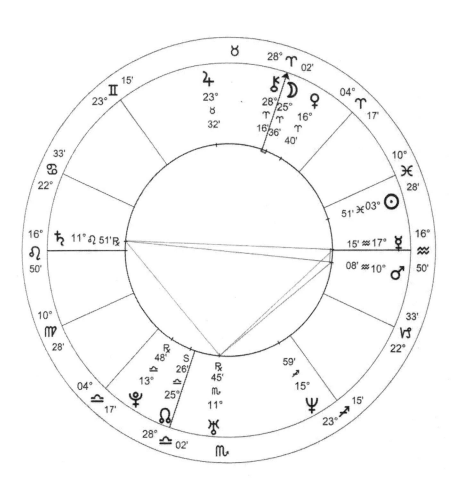

Symptom Picture

Some of Case K's health challenges relate to chronic digestive pain, ongoing for fourteen years, which wakes her at 5am and prevents her from going back to sleep. The pain is sometimes in the stomach, sometimes in the bowel. She also has weak liver function:- sluggishness, tiredness, acute frontal headache, aching eyes, nausea and general debility. She thinks this is probably caused by the hormonal disturbances of perimenopause. Emotionally she can feel angry and frustrated. Case K gets exhausted and has a tendency to burn out. All of these issues necessitate rest, making her feel unreliable when she has to cancel appointments and arrangements. She finds it hard having to stay in bed doing nothing when she would rather be active. She has however, as a result of her symptoms, become knowledgeable about diet and nutrition.

Digestion	Mercury, 6th house
Digestive pain	Mercury–Mars
Burn-out	Aquarius, Mars–Saturn–Uranus t-square, fire
Large intestine	Pluto
Stomach	Moon, 4th house
Nausea	Uranus in 4th house (apex of t-square)
Liver	9th house
Liver function	Jupiter
Headache	Mars (t-square), Aries
General debility	Saturn (t-square)

Anger, frustration	Aries Moon, Mars (t-square)

Purpose – the Path of the Sun

Sun in Pisces in the seventh house. The solar purpose is to develop awareness through the experience of committed relationship and one-to-one working. The current identity is highly intuitive. The need is to open consciousness to the feeling life, developing emotional self-awareness in the context of relating.

Undertow – the Pull of the Past

Saturn in Leo in the twelfth house, Moon in Aries in the ninth. The conditioned consciousness has an ardently 'religious', even zealous, sensibility. The fire gives passion, drive and strong impulses towards activity. The fiery will needs to be balanced; fire dominates the whole chart. Identity has been conferred by the group and is not 'individual' as such. The structuring principle is all at sea in the twelfth house and there may be a sense in which the father, that which bestows authority, is experienced as lost, and a sense of impermanence overwhelms the psyche. In Leo, Saturn can produce autocratic tendencies, which may increase in proportion to the fear of loss. There is a memory (Moon) of leadership and status gained through self-assertion on behalf of the group. The emotional script tells this person that independence and freedom confer safety.

Analysis

The impulse towards activity and the powerful yang charge in this chart, loaded with fire, are driving the energy upwards and outwards. The other elements are low: they need to be brought in consciously to moderate the will, which can readily domineer over the whole personality. Looking at the chart it is immediately noticeable that Chiron in Aries is *exactly* conjunct the midheaven, and Mercury in Aquarius is just one degree off the descendant. The angles of the chart are highly sensitive. They are like breaches in a dam, allowing planetary energy to flood into experience. The midheaven anchors us into the impersonal world, describing who we are 'in the world', our status and our station in life, including career. These things for Case K are flooded with the energy of the Wounded Healer, suggesting that there is significant pain and shame in relation to her experience of 'the world' and her place in it. Equally, there is a great capacity for empathy and compassion, operating as a healer, guide and mentor. The midheaven also pertains to experience of the father (which Chiron's placement here and the condition of Saturn suggest is troubled), so there will be a strongly personal dimension to this midheaven predicament.

Mercury on the descendant is also conjunct Mars (in the sixth house of health – and, pertinently, digestion), bringing fire and drive to mental processes, which are speedy and cerebral in Aquarius. Case K is driven towards stimulating exchanges with others that feel energising and insightful. Because Mercury sits on the angle it feels like it is always switched on, always being stimulated with Aquarius' high-frequency

301

energy. Mars fires up Case K's mental processes; she really *wants* to engage with people and ideas, making theoretical connections and enjoying the fizzes and flashes of insight. Mind: such a brilliant tool, and so terrible a master. It does not know when to stop! Digestive debility is signified by Mercury and Mars, and here they are in a conjunction that is part of a fixed t-square with Saturn and Uranus. *All incoming impressions need to be digested.*

This t-square features in most elements of the symptom picture, as you can see looking at the table belonging to this case study. It is significant as it expresses a dynamic between past-life consciousness (signified by Saturn and Mars – as the ruler of the Moon) and the path of innovation in this lifetime (Uranus).

Just as Case K's mental processes are fired up, her digestive processes can readily become inflamed. Aquarian energy is like lightning, it needs to be earthed. Digestion describes how we cope with the physical, earthy impress the world makes upon us. People who are sensitive and open (like Case K, who is a Pisces Sun) are prone to taking in a great many influences from all that is around them, physically, mentally and emotionally. Case K's Mercury is an open door, unwittingly welcoming these influences into her mental and digestive processes. She may be trying to digest very much more than rightfully belongs to her. This raises questions of being grounded, of psychic hygiene and of developing excellent boundaries.

Digestion involves taking in 'food' (physical and immaterial), discriminating between what is beneficial and what is not, assimilating the beneficial and excreting the non-beneficial. In TCM the large intestine relates to grief and its special time is 5am to 7am; waking at 5am suggests an imbalance here. The large intestine is our underworld. Ruled by Scorpio, it transforms the products of the small intestine by absorbing water (emotional processing), and eliminates waste. Dethlefsen and Dahlke refer to the link between defecation and generosity, shit and money.[177] There may be anxiety about resources (which we will see is reflected in the lack of earth in the chart and the condition of Jupiter in Taurus, sign of consolidation and abundance). At the exact midpoint of Mercury (digestive processes) and Pluto (elimination) is Neptune, ruler of Case K's Sun.

Neptune sensitises the two other planets and contributes to the sense of dispersal, ungroundedness and needing to 'earth' the system. There may well be grief (personal or collective) to be released. Perhaps there is a decision to be made and clear intent formulated about whether Case K wishes to serve the collective by processing its repressed emotions; it would be good to dedicate the body for personal use until it is strong enough to serve. As Saturn is in the twelfth house, there may be a karmic dimension to this dilemma – there may be a subconscious undertaking to serve in this capacity. There is an extreme lack of earth in Case K's chart: only Jupiter (ruling liver function) in Taurus, which is almost

---

[177] Dethlefsen and Dahlke (1990), p. 135.

entirely unaspected (and therefore unintegrated). This is part of the 'design' of Case K's life; it is not wrong. Imbalance (we all have some) is a great teacher, helping us to become conscious of what it is we lack. It enables us to grow and develop, which is vital to our physical, mental and spiritual wellbeing. Case K needs to bring earth consciously into her life: mundane tasks, cooking, gardening, caring for the body, physical contact and rest. Being in nature is a way of earthing ourselves, but Case K is so open to stimulation and ideation that I think she would benefit more from things that are useful but boring!

Exhaustion and burn-out are generally associated with Aquarius, and seem to be another aspect of the Mercury–Mars situation. Aquarius can be a zealous crusader and often thinks that it is helping others by working itself into the ground in the name of service. Over-doing helps no one. It is interesting that all her complaints cause Case K to rest. Fire dominates the chart heavily; she is motivated, active, enthusiastic, trail-blazing, ardent and intense: not given to resting. Ill health plays a part in restoring this balance, providing a space in which to feel and reflect and come all the way back down to the ground, which is the basis for any kind of stability. A fixed t-square with Uranus in Scorpio as the focal planet squaring Mars and Saturn is a picture of the energetic pattern: over-stimulation and the personal will being blocked. The balance is found opposite the focal planet in lovely lazy, earthy Taurus: fixed earth, consolidation, resilience, abundance.

A hard aspect between Saturn and Uranus indicates an attempt to break through mental conditioning (Saturn) by emotional upheaval and disruption (Uranus) in order to open up some space for authenticity. There is something egocentric and autocratic about past-life experience when Saturn is in Leo. Case K's Saturn is in the twelfth house, suggesting, as noted, that she could be undertaking to transmute more than merely individual karma. Responsibility and commitment in this direction need to be assumed with great clarity.

As Jupiter is almost unaspected, it may be seeking to become more conscious through the liver function. The liver is associated with energy storage (putting down fat) and energy generation, the processing of proteins and detoxification. Its processes are ruled by Jupiter whose principle is *expansion*, freedom and faith in life. The liver is the dumping ground for toxic emotions; its malfunction often relates to conditions of excess, because Jupiter has expansive effects. Dethlefsen and Dahlke write:

> A sick liver shows us that we are taking in more of something than we can possibly cope with: it is an index of immoderation, exaggerated ideas of expansion and over-lofty ideals.[178]

We have already seen that there is a theme of taking in more than can be comfortably processed; I wonder if a similar thing

---

[178] Dethlefsen and Dahlke (1990), p. 138.

is happening with the liver. Perhaps there is perpetual studying, which disallows integration. There may be a tendency to go beyond her limits and expect too much of herself, exacerbated by self-criticism (headache?), a resistance to offer herself approval and habitual striving to achieve and *be someone* (Moon in Aries conjunct Chiron and midheaven: conditioning that needs to be adapted to the solar purpose in this lifetime). The emotion associated with the liver in TCM is anger, which in astrology is signified by Mars and Aries; the t-square with Mars, Saturn and Uranus is the very picture of frustration, irritation and thwartedness – I see this pattern contributing to headache, tiredness and debility too. Moon, Venus, Chiron and the midheaven are all in Aries, sign of the will to be and to do. The Moon here shows that this wilfulness is an imprint made in early life (the mother) and in a past life that is active in the memory: it is a feature of the 'pain body' – conditioning that needs to be overcome. The potential here is for Case K to develop a highly disciplined will that is effective in breaking new ground for freedom and authenticity, facilitating the flow of soul forces through personal activity that allows her to explore relationships and develop the emotional level.

Aries is assertive and competitive, restless in its striving. It is also uncompromisingly independent and unilateral. This is the emotional default operating in Case K's chart. The Sun is in the house of relationship and the Moon's north node is in Libra. These indications clearly show that this lifetime is one in which there is to be a radical change of direction, from fire to water, from activity to feeling, from 'me, me, me!' to 'you, we, us!' Case K is undertaking a journey from exclusive self-reliance and independence towards the necessary acknowledgement of mutuality and interdependence. This is the way in which consciousness and fulfilment can arise.

The Moon conjunct Chiron speaks of wounding associated with the mother and the feminine energy, which is reflected in the stomach: the ability to receive, to hold and contain. Nausea represents the rejection of some element or idea, which may pertain to this mother-wound and to disturbances imbibed in early life that need now to be expelled, denoted here by Uranus (upset) in the fourth house (stomach). With regard to aching eyes: eyes are ruled by the Sun and Moon, which also figure as the parents in the chart; aches are ruled by Saturn – chronic patterns of mental conditioning informing the pain body. There may be parental attitudes that need to be left behind, maybe some childhood experiences that want to be mourned and released. Perhaps something in the current environment is stimulating early memories that can now safely surface.

Digestive symptoms began fourteen years ago, when transiting Neptune moved over the descendant and Mercury (signifier of digestion), and transiting Saturn moved over the ascendant, opposing Mercury. The midpoint of these two planets in the chart, Saturn and Neptune, is the health axis. For Case K, the Saturn/Neptune midpoint is occupied by Pluto (signifier of the large intestine), which can indicate a chronic condition in that organ. The Virgo–Pisces polarity is susceptible to somatic expression, and Case K, as noted, has a

Pisces Sun (and Virgo rules the second house of 'the body as a resource'). The value of this somatic tendency is that it brings refined cosmic energies into the most personal earthly expression: through the body. The body is our own interface between the Seen and the Unseen. Life on Planet Earth is characterised by physical manifestation: this is where refined energies are clothed in form and made visible and tangible – we show up in bodies! Embodiment and physical presence are where it is at for us earthlings. There is a strong injunction expressed through Virgo–Pisces to digest fully the earth experience. Virgo digs and Pisces dreams; digging without dreaming is drudgery; dreaming without digging is pie in the sky.

Case L: Transforming Individuality

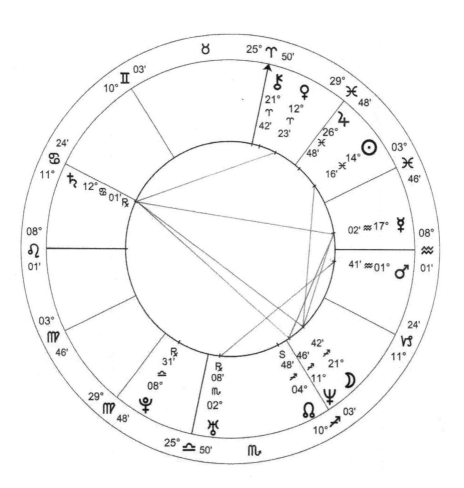

Symptom Picture

Case L has retained physical trauma from a car accident at nineteen (over twenty-five years ago), since when she has experienced back pain, which can be between the shoulders or in the lower spine, and tension in her neck. She has to take care of her back, which feels inflexible. Her acupuncturist says she has a place like a turtle shell on her upper back that is like a shield; physically, the place between the neck and her heart centre feels locked. Sometimes there is stabbing pain on the right side of her back beneath the shoulder blade. She also experiences repetitive strain injury affecting her right shoulder and arm. This health picture prevented her from carrying her children as babies and nearly stopped her completing her PhD. There is emotional trauma in the background. Her experiences have encouraged Case L to receive and explore many healing therapies and learn a great deal about the processing of physical and emotional trauma – to the extent that she practises professionally in this field of healing.

Accident	Mars square Uranus
Spine	Leo Asc, 5th house
Shoulders/arms, RSI	Mercury (in yod with Moon–Neptune and Saturn)
Stabbing pain	Mars (Sun/Moon midpoint)
Neck tension	Venus square Saturn
Emotional trauma	Venus–Pluto, Moon–Neptune, 8th house Sun

Purpose – the Path of the Sun

The Sun in Pisces in the eighth house shows she is developing awareness through emotional and sexual relating, intensity and transformation. She is opening to depth awareness in this lifetime, exploring 'what lies beneath' appearances, the mysteries and the symbolic or archetypal level of experience. Through this awareness, she is to be of service through healing and mentoring.

Undertow – the Pull of the Past

Saturn in Cancer in the twelfth house, Moon in Sagittarius in the fifth. The pull of the past is produced by lifetimes of service and servitude creating conditioning around what a woman may reasonably expect, which is ... more of the same. Unconscious patterns are of being cloistered and expected to look after others, or of being held in a state of dependency. There is a fear of being overwhelmed by duty, service and stifling femininity. The emotional default position is to cultivate individuality and acquire the attention of other people, perhaps as a guide or mentor. There is a performative element to this plus a great love of freedom and the desire not only to develop her sense of selfhood but also her awareness of the big wide world. Conditioning tells her there is a binary choice to be made: selfishness or self-sacrifice. She needs to discover the many modes of being between these poles.

Analysis

It is interesting that the impacts of ill-health on Case L affected her ability to carry her children and impeded her studies, for both of these things are represented by the Moon (mothering) in Sagittarius (tertiary education) in the fifth (children). This might already be a good clue to the nature of the problem. Case L's Sun squares the Moon, at their midpoint is Mars in Aquarius in the sixth house of health. The Sun/Moon midpoint is about basic vitality. The soli-lunar relationship fundamentally expresses the authentic identity in this lifetime *in relation to* the default settings of emotional conditioning inherited from early-life/past-life experience: the pull of the past.

Mars at the midpoint suggests a combative response to challenge. Mars is the will to be and to do, attacking and defending against impediments to that will. The strife between the new order and the old implies that the soldier, Mars, does not know whose order to obey. The Sun is the legitimate master, but while the old emotional habit holds sway the contest will continue. As Mars rules acute conditions and pain, and its activity is consistent with 'stabbing', it may be that an issue of *will* (and some confusion between conditioned responses and authentic identity) underlies the stabbing pains. The Moon, as the weakest point in this energetic conundrum, would register the impact. It is in the fifth house, whose associated body part is the spine. Mars is in a very close square to Uranus (the astrological signature of *accidents*), which contributes a spasmodic effect, also consistent with stabbing. Uranus is the impulse to break out of conditioning into the fresh air of the current identity, which can be challenging! Accidents, although horribly unwelcome, give our habitual patterns a radical shake up; they allow for change when we have become very stuck.

Leo rules Case L's ascendant and the Moon is in the fifth house, sharing the Leo vibration; Leo and the fifth house pertain to the spine, representing that which upholds and lends us *organisation* – the body's own personal Sun. The Moon is conjunct Neptune (on the cusp of the fifth house) showing that Case L's experience of her mother and the whole issue of womanhood, mothering and nurture (the Moon) is infused with sacrifice (Neptune). This conjunction can signify the abandoned baby; it has the effect of eroding one's sense of a boundary at the most personal level, rendering one open to whatever influences are in the environment (emotionally, mentally, physically and psychically). Naturally this can manifest in circumstances that feel very unsafe for the infant. It also sensitises a person to subtle information and energies, to which Case L is extremely open: this is her gift, and the compensation for challenges in her early life. It should be noted that Neptune is the ruler of Case L's Sun in Pisces.

Saturn, with the Moon, represents past-life conditioning that needs to be overcome in the current lifetime in order to orient towards the authentic identity, which for Case L is to develop the emotional aspect of her being (the Sun is in a water sign and house: Pisces, eighth), while getting in control of a self-centred use of power (Moon in fire). This requires her to work consciously with emotional transformation (eighth house) in service (Pisces) to others and to life. Her Saturn in Cancer suggests emotional armouring and repression (reminding me of the protective carapace, the 'turtle shell', at the top of her thoracic spine). As Cancer is involved this feels like a response to the issue of women, mothering and the realm of feeling (Moon). The Moon in Sagittarius in the fifth house shows a habitual tendency to seek freedom and pleasure in a self-centred way. This focus on self, an attachment to having things her own way, needs to be opened up to include awareness of others and an appreciation of subconscious material and the deeper emotional aspects of human experience.

As the Moon is in Sagittarius, ruling the liver, I would suggest that Case L make sure that her backache is not caused by liver debility; if this were the case though I would expect there to be digestive symptoms. The Moon–Neptune conjunction is part of a yod formation, with Saturn at its apex. It is quincunx Moon–Neptune on one side, and Mercury on the other. The quincunx is *the* health aspect, introducing a chronic sense of strain: the one most readily brought into somatic expression. Saturn rules structure and can certainly contribute to inflexibility and restricted movement. This might be interpreted as difficulty overcoming identification with an obsolete mode of being. The focal planet of a yod is a point of transformation in the chart: its negative aspects need urgently to be cast out, to release its potential. Negative Saturn is authoritarianism, patriarchal attitudes, strictness and repression; its positive forces are commitment, capability, opportunity, responsibility and healthy expressions of authority. In Case L's chart, Saturn rules the sixth house of health. I think most of the health symptoms can be found in this yod.

The Moon and Mercury, the two fastest-moving bodies, are the points of impact for Saturn. The Moon seems to reflect the condition of the spine in this chart, Saturn imposing an unwelcome sense of external authority, the need to live up to expectations, to earn approval from the withholding father figure. The spine organises and aligns the body's subtle energy system; it is at the centre of the body's 'solar system' just as the Sun needs to be at the centre of one's conscious identity. The memory of a former identity is a resource, but it organises nothing of itself. Neptune's involvement lends some confusion to the symptom picture – it notoriously evades clear diagnosis. This is, in a sense, because Neptune urges us to move beyond the little scope of personality concerns in order to see the ways in which we belong to the unified field, the *whole*. Acknowledgement of this spiritual perspective can go a long way in mitigating bodily symptoms, and certainly sets them in a different context.

Mercury rules the heart centre and the shoulder/arm (the RSI); in the seventh house it represents the right side of Case L's body (where several symptoms arise).[179] There is strain, again, about fulfilling expectations in order to receive approval for cleverness and mental aptitude. As Mercury is in the seventh house it will especially be triggered by relationship dynamics, which may also be a factor in the RSI.

---

[179] Odd houses rule the left side of the male body, the right side of the female (and vice versa).

Mercury reflects cognitive function and communication. The arms express how we give and receive, which need to be in balance. The arms are the channel to the heart, and if the heart is defended, arm function may be impaired. Case L feels the strain of responsibility for the other; there may be a deep belief that to be a valid human being one needs a partner. Negative Saturn (super-ego, taskmaster) needs to be turned round, so that Case L is able to enter relationship, and to give and receive with an authority that is all her own, not the berating voices of the fatherline, criticising and undermining her judgements and choices.

The midpoint of Mercury–Saturn is occupied by Pluto, so important for her eighth-house Sun, indicating that there is a need to drill down beneath appearances to recover the symbolic or archetypal level of experience, in order to bring healing and meaning to mental processes. Finding some freedom from Saturn operating as the Inner Critic will improve relationships, as this voice gets projected on to partners and others in general, for whom she readily feels overly responsible, something that easily furnishes resentment, naturally enough.

Finally, turning to tension in the neck: the neck is the conduit between head and heart. It represents our points of view. When these become rigid, the neck reflects this rigidity. The head and the heart want to work in concert: they need each other. When one goes rogue and tries to operate without the other, the dilemma can be reflected in the neck (it seems to me that this also pertains to the 'turtle shell' symptom, shielding the heart). The voice emanates from this area and reflects the head/heart relationship, and whether it is able to express itself truthfully or not. The neck is signified by Taurus, Venus and the second house. In Case L's chart, Saturn is not only the focal planet of the yod, but also of a t-square involving Venus and Pluto (the square between Venus and Saturn is exact). Saturn restricts and Pluto intensifies, deepening the tension Venus is bearing. Pluto, the slowest moving planet of them all, holds the Kali-like power here, insisting that the deepest level of truth must not be compromised, that it must be spoken. It is enacted in relating and personal values (Venus) and in acquiring an authentic sense of authority (Saturn).

This is a very charismatic, creative chart, with its strong Leo vibration, but the creativity in this lifetime is to be contributed to others, in service: to facilitate healing, transformation and the clearing of trauma. The Leo vibration helps her win others' attention, upholding her in positive self-esteem, both of which are required if she is confidently and capably holding others through healing processes. It is one thing being individualistic, another thing entirely to know and to share one's unique gifts in service to life and to wholeness.

Afterword

The body is a mysterious and amazing mechanism that houses and lends coherence to all of our subtle, non-physical, 'bodies' of experience: thoughts, emotions, impulses of the will and our own personal shard of divinity, the soul. It is in and through the medium of the body that this subtle information is revealed and made known to consciousness. The body and its processes are under the rulership, and are expressions of, the greater cosmic forces of *the Body of Stars* – the vast field of zodiacal and planetary vibration in which we have our being: thus, microcosm and macrocosm reflect and reveal each other.

The body as the locus of consciousness is constantly showing us what is going on with us, how we are being affected by our choices, habits, experiences, thoughts and emotional reactions. It directs us to our working edge and to our waking edge, prompting new understandings and change. As the body filters our mental, emotional and spiritual experience, naturally it is marked by content that gets stuck and finds a lodging within us that we find challenging or wounding. Symptoms of illness can be seen as a summons towards healing and wholeness from the higher self, or soul; like breaches in the dam of our conditioning: opportunities to address unhealthy patterns of belief, thought and emotion, being made available to consciousness by arising in the body. Being ill is not a personal failing or an aberration, just as dying is not; illness is a valid and valuable part of human experience, an aspect of the way in which we are called to become present to the *whole* of ourselves – mind, heart and spirit *in* the body. Embodied self-awareness is invited to arise through symptoms of all kinds and it is this quality of *presence through embodiment* that brings us closer to our authentic selves, closer to wellbeing and closer to reality. It is a shame to go through the pain and suffering wrought by illness and not to gain anything from it in terms of personal development, 'to have the experience and miss the meaning', as T. S. Eliot has it.

The development of embodied awareness is the route to coming home to ourselves and to truth. Underneath all our fantastical projections, constructions and elaborations of mind and emotion, we may potentially discover the human creature, infused with numinous spirit life. Physical life – our creatureliness – is our bottom line.

The possibility extended by the astrological interpretation of symptoms of physical or mental illness is that it allows us to reconnect the mundane aspects of our experience with the symbolic or archetypal. This, in turn enables a reframing of the narrative of our challenges; we can assign explanations that offer guidance, calling us towards deeply meaningful messages for our lives, and thus bringing healing and purpose to our lives. It also beautifully illustrates the way in which our seemingly separate individual bodies and selves are woven, meaningfully, into the whole, as part of the being and becoming of the One Life.

References

Abelar, Taisha (1992) The Sorcerer's Crossing: A woman's journey, *London: Arkana.*

Aeppli, Willi (2003) *The Care and Development of the Human Senses* (3rd edn) Forest Row: Steiner Schools Fellowship Publications.

Anthony, Carol K. (1988) *A Guide to the I Ching* (3rd edn) Stow, MA: Anthony Publishing Co.

Arroyo, Stephen (1992) *Astrology, Karma and Transformation: The inner dimensions of the birth chart* (2nd edn) Sebastopol, CA: CRCS.

Bailey, Alice (1951) *Esoteric Astrology,* London: Lucis Trust.
— (1953) *Esoteric Healing,* London: Lucis Trust.

Baker, Douglas (1975) *The Seven Pillars of Ancient Wisdom, Volume IV: Esoteric astrology.*

Barasch, Marc Ian (1993) *The Healing Path: A soul approach to illness,* London: Arkana.

Blackstone, Judith (1991) *The Subtle Self: Personal growth and spiritual practice*, Berkeley, CA: North Atlantic Books.

Brennan, Barbara (1988) *Hands of Light: A guide to healing through the human energy field,* New York: Bantam Books.

Castaneda, Carlos (1968) *The Teachings of Don Juan,* Harmondsworth: Penguin.
— (1974) *Journey to Ixtlan,* Harmondsworth: Penguin.
— (1993) *The Art of Dreaming,* London: HarperCollins.
— (1998) *The Active Side of Infinity,* London: HarperCollins.

Cramer, Diane L. (1996) *How To Give An Astrological Health Reading,* Tempe, AZ: American Federation of Astrologers Inc.
— (2013) *Dictionary of Medical Astrology,* Tempe, AZ: American Federation of Astrologers Inc.

Dethlefsen, Thorwald and Rüdiger Dahlke (1990) *The Healing Power of Illness: The meaning of symptoms and how to interpret them* (1983; trans. Peter Lemesurier) Shaftesbury: Element.

Gibran, Kahlil (1980) *The Prophet* (1926) London: Pan Books.

Greene, Liz (1990) *Saturn: A new look at an old devil* (1976) Harmondsworth: Arkana.
— (1997) *The Astrology of Fate: Fate, freedom and your horoscope* (1984) London: Thorsons.

Greene, Liz and Howard Sasportas (1993) *The Inner Planets: Seminars in psychological astrology, Volume 4,* York Beach, ME: Weiser.

Hand, Robert (1981) *Horoscope Symbols,* Atglen, PA: Whitford Press.

Harper, Jennifer (1997) *Body Wisdom: Chinese and natural medicine for self-healing,* London: Thorsons.

Hay, Louise (1984) *You Can Heal Your Life,* Carson, CA: Hay House Inc.

Hilarion (1982) *Body Signs,* Queensville, Ontario: Marcus Books.

Hill, Sandra (1999) *Reclaiming the Wisdom of the Body: A personal guide to Chinese medicine* (1997) Secaucus, NJ: Citadel Press.

Hollis, James (1993) *The Middle Passage: From misery to meaning,* Toronto: Inner City Books.

Holtzapfel, Walter (2013) *The Human Organs, Their Function and Psychological Significance: Liver, lung, kidney, heart* (1990; trans. Roland Everett) Edinburgh: Floris.

Jacobs, Tom (2010) *The Soul's Journey I: Astrology, reincarnation, and karma with a medium and channel.*

Jung, C. G. (1961) *Modern Man In Search of a Soul* (1933; trans. Dell and Baynes) London: Routledge & Kegan Paul.
— (1983) *Memories, Dreams, Reflections* (1963; trans. Richard and Clara Winston) London: Fontana.

Myss, Caroline (1997) *Anatomy of the Spirit: The seven stages of power and healing,* London: Bantam.

Nahmad, Claire (1993) *Earth Magic,* Destiny Books.

Nauman, Eileen (1982) *The American Book of Nutrition and Medical Astrology,* San Diego, CA: Astro Computing Services Inc.

Page, Christine R. (1992) *Frontiers of Health: From healing to wholeness,* Saffron Walden: C. W. Daniel Co.

Perera, Sylvia Brinton (1981) *Descent to the Goddess: A way of initiation for women,* Toronto: Inner City Books.

Purce, Jill (1974) *The Mystic Spiral: Journey of the soul,* London: Thames and Hudson.

Reinhart, Melanie (1998) *Chiron and the Healing Journey: An astrological and psychological perspective,* London: Arkana.

Ridder-Patrick, Jane (1990) *A Handbook of Medical Astrology* (2nd edn) Edinburgh: CrabApple Press.

Rilke, Rainer Maria (1964) *Selected Poems* (trans. J. B. Leishman) London: Penguin.
— (1993) *Letters to a Young Poet* (trans. M.D. Hester Norton) London: Norton.

River, Lindsay and Sally Gillespie (1987) *The Knot of Time: Astrology and female experience,* London: Women's Press.

Rudhyar, Dane (1968) *An Astrological Triptych: The illumined road,* Santa Fe, NM: Aurora Press.
— (1975) *The Sun is Also a Star,* New York: E. P. Dutton & Co.
— (1991) *The Astrology of Personality: A reformulation of astrological concepts and ideals, in terms of contemporary psychology and philosophy* (1936) Santa Fe, NM: Aurora Press.

Rumi (1990) *Like This* (versions by Coleman Barks), Athens, GA: Maypop.
— (1998) *Lion of the Heart* (trans. Coleman Barks) London: Arkana.

Sanford, Matthew (2006) *Waking: A memoir of trauma and transcendence,* Rodale.

Sasportas, Howard (1989) *The Gods of Change: Pain, crisis and the transits of Uranus, Neptune and Pluto,* London: Arkana.

Howard Sasportas and Liz Greene (1993) *The Inner Planets: Seminars in psychological astrology, Volume 4,* York Beach, ME: Weiser.

Schneider, Meir (1994) *The Handbook of Self-Healing,* London: Arkana.

Shapiro, Deb (2006) *Your Body Speaks Your Mind: Decoding the emotional, psychological, and spiritual messages that underlie illness,* Boulder, CO: Sounds True Inc.

Starck, Marcia (1982) *Astrology: Key to holistic health,* Birmingham, MI: Seek-it Publications.
— (1997) *Healing With Astrology,* Freedom, CA: The Crossing Press.

Steiner, Rudolf (2004) *Study of Man* (1947; trans. D. Harwood and H. Fox, rev. A. C. Harwood) Forest Row: Rudolf Steiner Press.

Stryk, Lucien and Takashi Ikemoto (1981; trans. and eds) *The Penguin Book of Zen Poetry,* London: Penguin.

Szanto, Gregory (1985) *The Marriage of Heaven and Earth: The philosophy of astrology,* London: Arkana.

Three Initiates (2010) *The Kybalion,* Aziloth Books.

Tolle, Eckhart (2005) *A New Earth: Awakening to your life's purpose,* London: Penguin.

van der Kolk, Bessel (2015), *The Body Keeps the Score: Mind, brain and body in the transformation of trauma,* London: Penguin.

Walsh, Neale Donald (1997) *Conversations With God: Book 1* (1995), London: Hodder & Stoughton.

https://www.dkfoundation.co.uk   Website of Suzanne Rough. A large collection of astrological material, written from an esoteric perspective.

https://www.tdjacobs.com   Website of Tom Jacobs, evolutionary astrologer, offering astrological and meditation resources.

https://awenastrology.wordpress.com   Author's blog.

Printed in Great Britain
by Amazon